MELTDOWN UK
THERE IS ANOTHER WAY

STEPHEN HASELER

Also by Stephen Haseler

The Gaitskellites
The Death of British Democracy
Euro-Communism (Joint Author)
The Tragedy of Labour
Anti-Americanism
The Politics of Giving
The Battle for Britain: Thatcher and the New Liberals
The End of the House of Windsor
The English Tribe
The Super-Rich: The Unjust World of Global Capitalism
Super-State: The New Europe and its Challenge to America
Sidekick: British Global Strategy from Churchill to Blair
Meltdown: How The 'Masters of the Universe' Destroyed the
    West's Power and Prosperity

First published in 2010 by Forumpress

Forumpress
c/o The Global Policy Institute
London Metropolitan University
31 Jewry Street
London EC3N 2EY, UK

ISBN: 978-1-9071440-5-9

A catalogue record for this book is available from the British Library.

The publisher has used its best endeavours to ensure that the URLs for websites referred to in the book are correct and active at the time of going to press.

For further information on Forumpress, visit our website: www.forumpress.co.uk

Typeset by Ben Eldridge www.beneldridge.co.uk

Printed by Lightning Source www.lightningsource.com

MELTDOWN UK
THERE IS ANOTHER WAY

STEPHEN HASELER

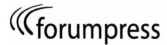
forumpress

Acknowledgements

I would like to thank colleagues at the Global Policy Institute and at the Federal Trust in London for helping to provide the stimulating environment which has helped me write this book (and its earlier companion volume *Meltdown*). But a special thanks to Jon Temple and Andrew Blick for invaluable research, to my wife Bay for her copy-editing and her patience, and also to Ben Eldridge for his usual splendid design work.

Contents

THERE IS AN ANOTHER WAY

On 22nd June 2010 the newly-elected coalition government in Britain announced its long-heralded drastic public expenditure cuts. The Prime Minister, David Cameron prophesied that these cuts were 'momentous decisions' that would 'affect our whole way of life' and 'stay with us for years, perhaps decades to come.' These cuts are a response to growing government deficits; yet these deficits are not, of themselves, the key problem – they are simply the result of a much bigger catastrophe: the spectacular private credit failure in the great banking crash of 2007-8, a crash that will change our world.

This bank crash set off the great global debt 'deleveraging' crisis which we are now living with. The recklessness of the banks, and the politicians who supported them, was breathtaking. The size of the credit bubble ran into multiples of trillions of dollars, and today's (2010) bank exposure in Europe is still well over $1,000 billion. Following the crash, governments were faced with a decision: either expand public spending, and the deficit, to bail out the banks and protect the people from recession (or worse), or let the whole financial system collapse. It is worth remembering amidst all the talk of government deficits that the private-sector bank crash of 2007-8 remains the great event of our generation – and that the public-sector deficits are but the response. Deficits remain a small thing in this big picture. And as of writing (June 2010) the big picture crisis seems to be deepening with a new round of potential bank failures, this time in Europe, on the horizon.

This book is primarily a work of analysis. In the early chapters it also outlines the story, as dramatic as it is frightening, of the implosion and failure of financial capitalism in Wall Street and the City of London. *Meltdown UK* looks at why it failed, and why financial capitalism can no longer properly and efficiently serve the needs of our western democracies. It looks at what I call modern capitalism's 'moral degeneration', certainly when compared to our earlier, more regulated, more responsible, and less financialised, capitalism. It also attempts to show how economic 'globalisation', and in particular, the global financial imbalances between Asia and the West (primarily the USA), has been a primary cause of the credit crisis, and of the shift of jobs and wealth away from the West (including Britain).

And in the interests of accountability, so important to maintain in a disastrous downturn like this, it allocates the blame – amongst the politicians, the financial corporates, and, because ideas have consequences, the intellectuals and opinion-formers.

I do not come to this subject as a conventional economist. My background is that of a contemporary historian cum political scientist cum politician, and I started thinking and researching this story when working on an earlier book in the 1990s – *The*

Super-Rich: The Unjust New World of Global Capitalism – about growing inequality, not normally a concern of contemporary economists. This book drew me into thinking about how the newly fully globalised capitalism of the post-communist era was creating huge unsustainable imbalances and was beginning to impoverish and destabilise western societies. It was a theme I carried forward, following the great crash, in my most recent book, *Meltdown: How The Masters of the Universe Destroyed The West's Power and Prosperity*. These books were bitterly critical of the economic and moral character of the whole 30-year-long neoliberal 'free-market' globalisation experiment which had started during the Thatcher/Reagan era, and was to end up with the great Wall Street crash of 2008. These books were written from a social democratic (and 'Keynesian') perspective – the political disposition I have always held, and still, hold today, and, like all good social democrats, I argued for reform.

Yet, following the crash, it soon became clear that the emergency changes to the financial system – including bailouts, part-nationalisations, initial stimulus packages – ushered in by 'Obama-Brown' in 2008, though necessary at the time, have not worked. Banks remain largely unreformed and recovery is unlikely; and the West stands on the brink of another, the 'double dip', recession. It seems to me that the 2008 measures have failed largely because they did not break sufficiently with the thinking of the governing market consensus.

BRITAIN

Britain, the focus of this book, is in a particularly difficult situation following the global financial crash. My own country is the most vulnerable of all the major western nations. She was in a very real sense the laboratory for the whole global neoliberal revolution – of markets, privatisation, and capital globalisation

– that got underway in the late 1980s. And for thirty years now its leading opinion formers have, along with American Wall Street conservatives, been the chief cheerleaders for this globalised and marketised world which came crashing down in 2008. Britain's financial and political elites have – as an act of policy – turned the British economy into the unbalanced, service-based, financialised, 'funny money', highly globalised, low-tax-haven, off-shore economy, that it is today.

Britain thus possesses a political/financial class that is ill prepared to deal with the crisis. This is perhaps hardly surprising. They did not see it coming, and now seem at a loss about what to do about it – except, that is, to follow the rules of the old, failed, market system and cut public expenditure. For them, cutting the country's deficit remains Rule Number One – and, as they continue to play by the old rules, understandably so. As they see it, what is at stake is nothing less than Britain's credit rating (which, under these old rules, are still issued by the same credit agencies that awarded sub-prime bonds in the US a triple A rating) and with it the stability of the British currency and economy.

Yet the fear must be that these cuts will so weaken the British economy as to tip it into severe recession. The great crash, and the great deleveraging that is now following it, will continue to ensure that the private sector remains stagnant, no longer the engine of growth, will mean low tax receipts and thus bigger deficits – which, under the perverse rules of globalised finance, would force the government to cut again, and again. As I show in the Postscript the country would enter a self-defeating, and self-lacerating, downward spiral with higher and higher unemployment, threadbare welfare services, dashed expectations and low morale, and possibly even social conflict.

But the mood of the time, as I write this, is to cut – cut services to keep the pound up, cut wages to compete in the 'global marketplace', and cut taxes to attract capital. The objective of all this cutting is to end up with a debt-free nation. Prime Minister David Cameron argued, whilst opposition leader, that the struggle up the mountain to a debt-free world would be difficult but 'the view from the summit' would be worth it. The only problem, in my opinion, is that this splendid view from the mountain top will be a vista of rubble. Yet, according to the financial elites still dominating governments in the aftermath of the crash: 'there is no alternative'.

NEW COURSE

In a book like this, analysis and criticism is never enough; indeed such criticism is always somewhat devalued if the critic and analyst offers nothing positive, no ideas of his own, ideas which in their turn can be criticised. So I have tried also to set out, in Chapter Seven and in the Postscript, an alternative to self-lacerating public sector budget cutting – with its continuing, and I believe endless, destruction of wealth, both public and private.

An alternative strategy would ensure that in order to protect against the ravages of global market competition Britain should now fundamentally reject the neoliberal market model, and re-embrace social democracy. Many social democrats have for some time argued for a shift away from the American-style 'free-market' model of capitalism towards the continental-style 'social-market' model. But so desperate are the times that even this social-model – as say operates in Germany – is also becoming dysfunctional. The central problem is that, particularly as it operates in Germany, it remains far too financially orthodox and tied into the global market and financial system. This continually puts pressure on the model to lower costs, cut incomes, cut deficits and generally deflate the economy.

We need a new model altogether, one that puts as its very first priority jobs, growth and the retention of wealth in the West. This new model will automatically involve accepting a stronger state, one large enough to balance off the markets and the rampant business interests which always seek after lower global costs; and one that can return us to what we used to call 'the mixed economy' with more public and mutual ownership (not just the national state but regional and municipal ownership as well). We also need a state capable of redistributing power within society and the basis of that power-income and wealth. We need to grapple with redistribution because inequalities, of life chances not just income and wealth, have grown so wide and, crucially, for the prudential reason that in our coming downturn the yawning gap between the middle classes and the super-rich is auditioning the country for social turmoil and conflict. I am aware that 'the state' is still, even after the bailout of the banks, a worrisome institution for many people; so I have spent many pages here attempting not only to re-establish the democratic state as central to a sustainable economy but also to the freedom and liberty agenda. However, I completely accept that, if the state is to play a larger role then the British state, uniquely so in the West, needs surgical and radical democratic reform, from top (the Monarchy and Lords) to bottom (local government) and all points in between.

Secondly, of course, Britain is small beer in the general scheme of things, and we need to realise that our future economic life is not wholly in our own hands. This global crisis will only be solved in a bigger context than that of the UK. Thankfully, though, we are a member of the EU – which, in the absence of international agreement, is big enough to engineer change on its own. So Britain, in its national interest, needs to stay open to deeper European co-ordination. As of writing, what *Financial Times* columnist Wolfgang Munchau calls 'small country thinking' prevails in Europe, as each country competes to be more austere than the others by competitive budget cutting. What we need, and what I believe we will eventually get, is some 'big country thinking' that puts growth and jobs first.[1]

But even should, as I expect, opinions change and a growth policy based upon a general European expansion take hold, Europe as a whole will still need to address the underlying employment, investment and inequality problem now growing throughout the continent – the accelerating challenge from low-cost Asia. The disaster of economic and financial globalisation is beginning now to reveal itself, and the only way out now for Europe – and to succeed this has to be Europe-wide – is to adopt what the Asians themselves (particularly the Japanese) have long operated in practice – a strategic trade policy in place of 'free trade'. Of course, such ideas will be traduced by calling them 'protectionist', but the world, including the West is already moving away from so-called 'free trade' (what on earth, we might ask, were the great bank bailouts and the various stimulus measures than 'protectionist' measures?).

Such a radical strategy, however, will first need a revolution in thinking amongst the elites and career politicians who are still wedded to the old rules. And such change will be mind wrenching for many of them – for it involves the abandonment of the assumptions of a lifetime. But such a new strategy remains the only alternative to continuing and deepening job losses, continuing and deepening inequalities, and growing social instability – with all the potential implications not just for our present standard of living but for our standards of social civility too.

CAN BRITAIN ADJUST?

But adjusting set thinking is not something our British political and financial governing class, contrary to myth, is very good at. In the postwar period they found it difficult to adjust to the loss of empire and rested on their laurels – so much so that Britain became the sick man of Europe in the 70s when it faced a choice of extremisms. Having chosen market extremism they still found it difficult to adjust to the country's reduced status and completely misread the slight economic revival in the late 1980s and 1990s under Thatcherism (when they regularly lambasted France and Germany for being 'sclerotic'). And now they and their intellectual heirs are finding it terribly difficult to adjust to the collapse of the neoliberal globalised economy that they did so much to bring into being. Intriguingly, these market and deficit-obsessed elites are still, as I write, running the show, still believe that the world is run from Wall Street and the City, are still urging deep public sector cuts, still unaware of the massive moral and social defects of contemporary financial capitalism, and still oblivious to the failure of their market-led system and its implications for future social instability.

In these circumstances to still be lecturing the rest of us – about responsible finance of all things – and to still control the national economic agenda is a considerable feat. Even so, these elites that brought us the excesses of the City of London and then the great crash, having spectacularly failed, should now no longer stand in the way of a new course.

Stephen Haseler
West London, 2010

BRITAIN ON THE BRINK

BROKEN ECONOMY, FAILED ELITES

'President Roosevelt is magnificently right...to explore new paths...
and to achieve something better than the miserable confusion and
unutterable waste of opportunity in which an obstinate adherence
to ancient rules of thumb has engulfed us'

**John Maynard Keynes on Roosevelt's decision to defy the orthodoxy
and withdraw from the gold standard, 1933**

BRITAIN'S BROKEN ECONOMY

The month of August 2007 witnessed the start of what may
yet become one of the great events of our time, a climacteric as
important as the outbreak of World Wars One and Two or the
end of the Cold War. For it was during that fateful August that,
all of sudden, and without any warnings from our leaders and
commentators, western banks stopped lending to each other.
The great banking crisis had begun; a crisis that would lead to
nothing less than the collapse of global financial capitalism in

the City of London and Wall Street – and to its rescue by placing the whole system on a government life-support machine. Private sector banks, the lifeblood of the world economy, had either collapsed (like Lehman Bros in the US or Bradford and Bingley in Britain) or been merged and 'nationalised' like Lloyds/ HBOS or just 'nationalised' like The Royal Bank of Scotland. The underlying, and truly dramatic, story was of a great global deleveraging, a drying up of private sector credit that put the world economy at serious risk of sliding into a global depression.

The sheer scale of Britain's share of this global private sector indebtedness was frightening. It amounts to a national horror story – one that has now been told by none other than Andrew Haldane, executive director of the Bank of England, who has set out the facts about the outlandish overextension of Britain's banks, and through them, the City of London. Haldane's official statistics show that Britain's banks have assets – for the layman a fancy accounting term for 'exposure' and debt – which amount to a staggering *five times* national output. Evidently, since the mid 1950s these figures of banking exposure have been growing steadily, but since the late 1980s and the deregulation of markets, have doubled in size.[1] And the implications are dire. Banking failures set off a spiral. They place governments, particularly the overextended British, at great risk – as the bailouts can cause 'sovereign defaults' (or governments' defaulting on their debts). And these 'sovereign defaults', as Haldane also pointed out, have historically led to 'the downfall of banking systems' as they did with 'the founding Italian banks, including the Medici of Florence'.[2]

Some two years after the great Wall Street crash (at the time of writing) this credit disaster is very far from over. The global debt mountain is alarming, and unprecedented in history. Sums vary – and one estimate in 2009 had 'more than $60,000 billion in outstanding CDS trades sitting in the market as a whole'. Yet what was certain was that, as the respected commentator Gillian Tett argued, since 2007 the global economy has been witnessing the biggest contraction of credit in the lifetime of everyone on the planet.[3]

Britain's own debt mountain, though difficult to quantify properly, is at the extreme end of the spectrum of larger western economies. The country's domestic credit – mortgages, loans and credit cards – got completely out of control; but, more important still, Britain's banks and credit machinery, recklessly hardwired into the global credit boom, left the people of Britain hugely exposed around the world. And the extent of this exposure, although a banking problem, was only made possible by the support and encouragement of the country's political and financial elites – successive governments during and since the Thatcher era. It is the central contention of this book that Britain's economic crisis is a result of the obsession of Britain's elites with a 'global role'. When this obsession is allied to market extremism it becomes a pathology – and that is exactly what has happened ever since the Thatcher revolution took hold.

As this disaster unfolded there was surprisingly little dispute about its causes. Most British commentators blamed an irresponsible global boom and bubble that got completely out of hand (spectacularly so in the American housing sector), a bubble caused by banks operating in deregulated 'free markets' which, instead of self-correcting, simply failed. There was less unanimity, however, about the extent to which 'globalisation' – that is, capital globalisation – had led to the crisis creating in the West, as I argue in the book, unbalanced economies, growing real unemployment, and an Asian fuelled low cost, low interest rate environment which allowed Wall Street and the City of London to run an uncontrollable credit boom.

Yet, intriguingly and worryingly, there has been little idea in mainstream British commentary about how to deal with the disaster. After the crash the main concern was the banks. Supporters of the market remained true believers, wanted the banks to go bust, attacked the bailouts, and believed the market would rectify itself at a lower level – believing that the social cost, in unemployment and misery, was worth it in the long-run. On the other hand the West's mainstream politicians, including the then new British Prime Minister, Gordon Brown, saw state intervention as essential – and acted in emergency mode placing the whole financial sector in the West, and through it the world economy, on a life-support system provided by the state. The British government, like all the western governments, simply tried to patch up the system. Gordon Brown, his ministers, and opposition leaders David Cameron and Nick Clegg, truly believed that the state's life-support machine should at some point be turned off and, as in a natural return to normality, the private sector (and private credit) would revive, growth would return, and we could go back to the old ways – suitably chastised and with a more regulated approach.

There were no calls at all for thoroughgoing Keynesian solutions. Keynes himself had argued for more state intervention than Roosevelt achieved, but had doubted whether 'democracy would ever have the courage to make the grand experiment necessary to prove my case outside the conditions of war'. In the event, though, real Keynesianism was introduced, for during the Second World War government spending reached 70 per cent of national income and the national debt rose above 200 per cent. It fell to the biographer of Keynes himself, Professor Robert Skidelsky, to become the one serious commentator to argue (in *The New Statesman* in May 2010) that such a wartime response might yet be necessary.[4]

Such a revolution in thinking was not, though, to be found amongst Britain's financialised political and media elites. Steeped in the rules and values of the highly successful, but now defeated, economic system they inherited, they were (and are) unable to fully accept the failure of their world – and their worldview, and too ready to believe that a patching-up operation is all that is needed.

So, at the time of writing (early in 2010) the consensus idea in Britain was still to try to refloat the old financial system on yet another asset boom – this time in the developing world, primarily in China. But the western debt deleveraging was still raging, and in May 2010 another banking crisis was looming, this time centred on the public finances of the European governments (including Britain). The danger was that should a 'sovereign' government fail (that is, default on its debts) then German, French and British banks would again be in trouble. It was clear that some sixteen months after the Lehman collapse, the patching-up operation of the mild Keynesians was not working.

A CRISIS MADE IN BRITAIN

There is little doubt that Britain's leadership class – its politicians, business leaders, and commentators – share a real, and special, responsibility for this crisis. Reagan/Clinton and Wall Street may have led the march to the abyss, but Britain was close behind. During the 1980s and to date the country provided some of the most prominent and influential creators and supporters of the financialised 'free-market' system: it was in Britain that the first European 'free market' political breakthrough occurred with the Thatcher revolution; it was the City of London (and its supportive politicians) who, post-communism, played a major role in extending 'markets' and corporate business methods around the world through 'globalisation'. In a sense, of course, Britain, or rather England, was made for this revolution, indeed had been auditioning for it. For decades past, England's elites, educated at expensive private schools, had seen a career in the city, rather than industry, as a normal progression and had populated the City's growing finance-based global networks. Searching for quick profits in a low cost world, rather than investing in the British economy (with its expensive indigenous labour) was hardwired into the thinking of these elites.

It all started sometime in the mid-1980s. With the Thatcher revolution secured at home – following the defeat of the Miners Union and victory in two general elections – Britain's new Thatcherite political class took a bold decision. They decided that the country's future lay in a complete break with postwar social democracy. Rejecting the postwar consensus they turned away from Europe and followed the lead of the Reagan-era ascendant American corporate right. Britain's increasingly Thatcherite opinion formers, in business and journalism, became entranced by the American economic model of corporate power and Wall Street finance-led business. And as, during the Thatcher and Major years, business gained power (at the expense of labour and the public sector), a pro-market sentiment became embedded throughout the upper reaches of British life.

Britain and 'Globalisation'

During the 1990s Britain's newly powerful business leaders, like those in the US, saw in front of them a once-in-a-lifetime opportunity. Following the fall of communism a great new global vista of cheap costs, particularly cheap Asian labour, opened up. Footloose capital-free from the regulations and high tax rates of governments and from the restrictions of domestic trade unions – had the world at its feet. This great new world of cheap labour was to underpin the new gilded age of mammoth profits, and the cheap money it also unleashed was to become the foundation of the great credit boom. The appeal of 'globalisation' – as capital globalism was called – swept all before it, not least in the mainstream political parties. The Conservatives and the Liberal Democrats both embraced it – Prime Minister Tony Blair (1997-2007) became a devotee – and an active campaigner for it. Earlier, Margaret Thatcher's administration saw one of the globalisers' key ideas – 'competitiveness' – begin to dominate the economic debate, and thus began a three-decade-long restructuring of the British economy away from heavy industry (deemed 'uncompetitive') and much of manufacturing (deemed 'uncompetitive'), towards services, the creative industries, and, of course, financial services in the City of London.

In the name of 'competitiveness' this 'restructuring' ultimately led to two simultaneous slow motion disasters for the British. First, as I outline in Chapter Two, there was the disaster of hollowing out. Jobs were lost that would likely never be replaced. And, although many new jobs were created, these were (and are) extremely vulnerable. The globalisers promised that jobs in the service sector would have a secure future – because, in the globalisers' mantra, we in the West would specialise in services whilst Asia, concentrating on manufacturing, would provide a growing market for our services, in Britain's case for banking and other finance. There was only one problem with this: as it turned out, Asia, and particularly China, simply did not live up to the role assigned to it by hubristic westerners. Like any prudent new superpower – for instance, the US in the late nineteenth-century – China, in its emergent years, was thinking strategically and was protecting its domestic market. To the surprise of the City, China was a protectionist power, and would (and will) only let western commerce penetrate up to a point – often where it can copy technology and intellectual property. It will, in sum, develop its own service sector. In a clear example of the British elite's enduring 'imperial illusion' (a theme of this book) many in the City and in Westminster truly believed that 'Chinamen could not do banking'. Instead of equipping itself to be a European player, the City remained global, seeking its future in a fantasy 'global' market.

And as British and western jobs and wealth were lost to Asia, a second disaster struck. Lowcost Asia created a global low-inflationary and low-interest environment which in turn allowed western governments (particularly the American and the British) to encourage a spectacular and reckless rise in credit. Britain desperately needed a credit boom for one simple reason: the economy had become dependent on consumer-led growth and, with incomes relatively stagnant (although profits were booming), more and more credit was needed to fuel such growth.

In sum, the great 'global market' experiment – the City-led, service-dominated, off-shore, low domestic investment, relatively low-tax, economy, was, once global markets started crashing, turning into a horror show. It had left the British economy overextended, unbalanced and highly vulnerable. It also produced a society marked by much greater inequality – as the capital-rich super-rich, moving their capital around the world, lived extremely well whilst the majority, in vulnerable jobs, became more and more insecure.

The Thatcher/Blair Era: Hollowing Out the Country

By 2008, the year of the City crash, Britain had already been through a long period of slowly increasing weakness and vulnerability. It had for, over three decades, wasted the revenues from North Sea oil. The country did not have the economic resilience to bail out the banks without creating severe effects on its government debt. The British faced a future decade or so of unwinding personal debt, rising taxes and restricted public services.

Yet, even in this dire situation, the new Conservative-Liberal Democrat coalition government elected in 2010, seemingly offered little that was, in fact, new. Career politicians will always be affected by events (and in May 2010 when Cameron-Clegg entered Downing Street very big ones indeed were facing them); the initial joint programme of the coalition, however, seemed set to continue the broad lines of economic policy and strategy developed by its Labour predecessor. It will be, no doubt, buffeted by events, shocks that could alter its shape, or tear it asunder but at its outset there was no hint of any new strategic economic direction – only 'Thatcherite' warnings of cuts to come. The new Cameron-Clegg coalition seemed on track to become the fourth administration of the old Thatcher/Blair era.

The truth is that Britain faces a future in which average living standards will fall, perhaps dramatically, and real unemployment levels will grow. And as governments start to unplug the state's life-support system for the economy by cutting public expenditure – as all parties were promising in the 2010 general election – then the resultant fall in public sector jobs and private sector state contracts will reduce living standards even more by further lowering demand. As we can no longer expect growth from the debt-ridden and deleveraging private sector, and as the country's political class will probably fail to launch the needed super-Keynesian boost, serious consumer-driven economic growth will become a thing of the past.

Falling living standards and widespread economic insecurity will be new features of modern British life. Previously, during the great depression of the 1930s the UK was still semi-democratic with lowish expectations and high levels of deference to authority. It seems strange by today's standards, but during the 1931 crisis many working class Britons sent pennies to the Chancellor Philip Snowden and to the King to help out with the nation's finances. In today's UK however the high material expectations engendered over the last thirty years by a burgeoning consumer society have developed an aspirational society completely shorn of deference – a society in which both material and democratic expectations are extremely high. It all presages a perfect storm – a near term future collision between the needs and expectations of 'the people' on the one side and the strategy of the cuts-induced lowering living standards on the other. The irony is, of course, that the very politicians who now call for cuts and lower living standards are the very same politicians who encouraged rising expectations.

In this environment both social peace and civility will inevitably become increasingly fragile. The new British co-Prime Minister David Cameron argued before the election of 2010 that British society was 'broken'. In fact, in the immediate aftermath of the global crash Britain was able to avoid 'breaking' society; yet the social stability which we have taken for granted may well fray, producing fertile ground for the rise of political extremism. It is a potential scenario in which the very hallmarks of Britain's advanced society, the rule of law, constitutional freedom and democracy itself, will be called into question. It is in this sense that the credit and financial collapse of 2007-8 can reasonably be described as a threat to our western civilisation. It is certainly a greater threat than Al Qaeda.

Our Failed Elite: The Great 'Non-Debate'

By 2010, two years after the crash, the British debate – much of it conducted during the general election – offered little in the way of a reassessment of financial capitalism. What there was was not very systematic. Any 'new thinking' was all about patching up the system, ensuring its 'recovery', and changing it only at the margins by more and better regulation. In the mainstream public policy debate there was little or no thinking about the fundamentals – about the structure of the firm, about ownership, about redistribution, and, determinedly, not about new values.

The reason for this apology of a debate was obvious: it soon became clear that it was the same people, with the same economic mindset and values, who had 'brought you' the crisis who were now 'bringing you' the recovery. In the general election the choice was between Prime Minister Gordon Brown, who had helped construct the failed global system, and the two new coalition Prime Ministers (David Cameron and Nick Clegg), both of whom were even more fervent supporters of global financialised capitalism. David Cameron, like his party, supported markets, both global and local, and the freed-up Thatcherite City of London, and, whilst in opposition made a big issue of the need for a smaller state (through his 'big society'); Nick Clegg was one of the original backers of the remarkable 'orange book' (a pro-market, neo-Thatcherite analysis of the economic system). Following the great crash all Britain's party leaders sought a 'recovery' in which the old system would simply be refloated with its essentials retained. The only dispute was about how and when to withdraw the lifejacket and whether to cut public spending earlier or later when growth restarted. (The collective assumption was that real economic growth could not be public sector led: and that only the private sector could seriously add to the wealth of the nation.)

Britain's non-debate meant that 'the guilty men' – the supporters and advocates of market forces, light touch regulation and City and Wall Street excess – stayed in power following the country's 2010 general election. In this sense Britain reacted somewhat differently to the crisis than did the US. In Britain power passed rightwards – to those who had supported the economic system even more enthusiastically than Blair and Brown. In the US, on the other hand, power passed leftwards. In Britain there was to be no transformational figure to equal President Barack Obama, who could at least give some semblance and hope of real new direction and change. And, just as important, former Fed Chairman Alan Greenspan and former Clinton Treasury Secretary Robert Rubin accepted a degree of blame and were publicly discredited; whereas in Britain, their equivalent leaders of the financial capitalist system – in the Bank of England, in the Treasury, and in the political parties – were still in the driving seat, listened to respectfully and still helping to set an agenda. The British scene was eloquent testimony not just to the seeming hopelessness of the situation, but to the sheer strength of the previous consensus.

Popular opinion, though, was more radical. The British public seemed to want heads to roll, and were fixing blame on the governing elites – or, at least some part of them. There was agreement that it was 'the bankers' who were to blame; and the public was so angry with the top bankers that Fred Goodwin, 'retired' CEO of the Royal Bank of Scotland, felt the need to stay abroad for a time during the meltdown.

There was indeed a case that a 'guilty generation' of financiers and credit alchemists – in both the City of London and Wall Street – could be held responsible for the crisis. After all, these were not simply young men, and some few women, doing a well paid job. They were major players in constructing a whole new financial world – they had not only operated, but also, proselytised for the new unsustainable finance-driven globalised system. They had inordinate influence over politicians and decision-makers. Top bankers and financiers profited personally, taking home outlandish salaries and bonuses; worst of all, they had created a 'masters of the universe' culture with its sense of entitlement and of separateness from the broader political community.

Our Failed Elite: Intellectuals and Media

Yet, the identification of blame needs to take in a wider canvas. Bankers, like most people, try to maximise their rewards: bankers will always be 'greedy'. But it was ultimately the political and intellectual climate over three decades in which these bankers operated that allowed the 'masters of the universe' mentality free reign. The rabid global credit boom came in the backwash of globalisation after communism fell in the early 1990s, gathered pace during the Major and early Blair years and opened full throttle after the dot com bubble burst in 2000. But the intellectual zeitgeist – the way people, particularly opinion formers, think about the economy, changed after Mrs. Thatcher's revolution had put its stamp on the country during the late 1980s.

Ideas have consequences, and so do intellectuals. And the intellectuals surrounding Mrs. Thatcher in the late 1970s and early 1980s – and those surrounding President Reagan as well – had more than most. Their 'free market' ideas took on the might of the whole postwar left-of-centre consensus (the 'social democrat' or 'socialist' generation) and they won – probably beyond their wildest dreams.

British thinking was at the centre of it all. In the 1970s and early 80s British academics and public intellectuals, many of them devotees of the great 'free market' gurus like Milton Friedman (at the University of Chicago) and Frederich von

Hayek (at the LSE), began to develop a serious challenge to the prevailing social democratic orthodoxy. Think tank intellectuals like Ralph Harris and Arthur Seldon at the hugely influential Institute For Economic Affairs (The IEA) in Lord North Street, campaigned for a new world of free markets, and Madsen Pirie and Eamon Butler at the equally significant Adam Smith Institute, promoted, and designed, the wave of privatisations that were to be implemented in the 1990s. These British pioneers of 'neoliberalism' worked closely with think tanks in Washington D.C. like The Heritage Foundation, The American Enterprise Institute and the Cato Foundation. Indeed, American conservatives, using their links with these British 'free-marketeers', pointed to the Britain of the 1970s as a case study in social democratic failure. In 1997 the American publisher Doubleday issued an influential book, edited by American conservative R. Emmett Tyrrell, Jr., entitled *The Future That Doesn't Work: Social Democracy's Failures in Britain* in which several British thinkers set out the case for a new market-based economic system. Peregrine Worsthorne critiqued trade union power, Colin Welch took on the leftwing intellectual class, Samuel Brittan outlined the debilitating effects of 'postwar egalitarianism' and Peter Jay made the case for 'liberal economics' as a way of saving Britain from its hopeless social democratic stagnation, or worse. In the late 1970s it was a set of arguments that, in Britain and the USA, was to win all before it and to represent the wave of the future.

This denunciation of postwar British social democracy was soon to be followed by an 'amen chorus' amongst the journalists and the commentariat in many of the main media outlets, And this media support for the ideas of 'the market' turned what in the 1970s had been a mere cult into a dominating consensus – one which was to take coherent form in the mid 1980s, make its breakthrough in the early 1990s, reach its zenith in the late 1990s, and run right through to its sudden death in 2007. It was a consensus that was to be as successful as the social-democratic consensus that had preceded it. In Britain and America it was fuelled by the intellectual confidence of its proponents, and it gained adherents in Britain throughout the 1980s because of the perceived threat from the marxist left and the militancy of the trade unions – a threat which social-democracy (and the old party establishments represented by Prime Ministers Wilson and Callaghan) were deemed no longer able to handle.

Indeed, this ascendancy of the idea of a new way – a completely new economic philosophy – was greatly helped by the international and domestic convulsions of the latter 1970s. The serial Middle East oil crises (with unprecedented oil price hikes and embargoes) and the resultant inflation (in Britain inflation reached an annual rate of 23.4 per cent at its height in 1976) led to great instability and a central trade union leadership challenge to the British government and political system.[5] This in turn led to a questioning of the merits and validity of the postwar 'mixed economy' and 'the welfare state' (and in the US of President Johnson's 'big spending' 'Great Society' programmes). So turbulent a time was it that questions were even raised about the 'governability' of Britain.[6] Images of the 1979 public sector strikes, dubbed 'the winter of discontent', remained a powerful media image that was to colour political thinking for decades afterwards.

By the mid 1990s, in the aftermath of the defeat of the miners (in 1984-5) and following the fourth Labour election defeat in a row (in 1992), this erstwhile cult of the 'free market' had moved from the margins to become official policy, and 'official' ideology. Helped forward by politically committed media owners (many of them living outside the country), these ideas became the received wisdom, the new government of opinion – and they dominated the economics and finance pages of leading British newspapers. Particularly influential were Martin Wolf (chief economics commentator, columnist and thence editor of *The Financial Times* who was awarded a CBE in 2000 for 'services to financial journalism' and was twice winner of the Wincott Award for economic journalism, an award administered by the 'neoliberal' think tank the IEA), Anatole Kaletsky (of *The Economist*, *The Financial Times* and thence economics editor of *The Times*, and also a winner of the Wincott Award), and Hamish McRae (associate editor of *The Independent*, and Business and Finance Journalist of the Year, 2006, at the British Press Awards). (In a sign of the changing times both Wolf and Kaletsky have since the crash courageously revised their worldviews, Wolf wrote *Why Globalisation Works* in 2004 but then *Fixing Global Finance* in 2009, both published by Yale University Press.)

So powerful was the need for urgent change in the 1970s that within Britain's elites it was felt that nothing less than a new, and radical, political direction was necessary; during the 1980s it was engineered. The election of Margaret Thatcher,'s Conservative government in 1979, and that of President Ronald Reagan in the US in 1980, were watershed events. And during the 1980s Reagan and Thatcher began to dismantle key aspects of 'The Great Society' in the US and the 'mixed economy' in Britain. These two leaders succeeded not only in changing the economic zeitgeist of their nations, but also altered the underlying power relations between state and market, business and unions, and the rich and the middle classes.

Yet during Thatcher's premiership the writ of markets – and marketisation – was still constrained. In her early years in office the Tory Prime Minister had opposition in her cabinet from a formidable array of 'wets' and over her whole premiership she could secure, at her height, only 42 per cent support of the British electorate. Although she had improved her political position by winning the 1983 general election, it was only after the breaking of the miners' strike in 1985 that the issue of trade union power was fully resolved – in management's favour. In 1986 Thatcher was able to engineer the deregulatory 'big bang' reforms in the City of London; and after her victory in the 1987 general election, some eight years into her premiership, she was able to get into her stride – and she started serious privatisations.

By the end of the Thatcher premiership in 1990 the revolution was still unfinished. The domestic political and labour opposition may have been roundly beaten, but, for the Thatcherites, Europe – and the potential for a social-democratic future engineered through European institutions and laws – still hung over the future like a dark cloud. She famously said, referring to the European Commission President, Jacques Delors, that for Britain to join the single currency would be 'entering a federal Europe by the Back Delors'.[7]

Heady Stuff

It was only after Mrs. Thatcher had left Downing Street that her revolution was made secure. For it was during the follow-on Major and Blair premierships, from the early 1990s through to 2007, that the market fundamentalists, and the big corporate business community, finally won their battle with the state. And the fall of communism, and the dramatic extension of the global market – in Eastern Europe and China – was the key. As the ascendant new right saw it, markets could finally work properly as footloose capital could now escape from all the constraints previously imposed by nation-states, politics, democracy and trade unions, and could pursue – in this 'wild west' world of the unregulated global economy – lower and lower costs and previously unimagined profits.

It became a triumphalist, 'no-limits' world. Freed from the spectre of communism, economic visionaries in New York and London saw a future global world order – with ascendant markets and weakened states. One of the leading proponents of the new world order, the American Philip Bobbitt, believed that in this new marketised world the nation-state 'with its mass free public education, universal franchise, and social security policies, promised to guarantee the welfare of the nation' was over; and a new form, 'the market-state', had arrived, which was set 'to maximise the opportunity of the people and thus tend to privatise many state activities and to make voting and representative government less influential and more responsive to the market.'[8] Political visionaries, like Francis Fukuyama (and later the neoconservatives in the Republican party), saw a world with the United States as the undisputed leader – and according to our own 'neoconservatives', primarily Tony Blair – with Britain as her premier ally. Britain's opposition Conservatives, dominated by 'euro-sceptics' and 'euro-phobics', supported Blair's worldview: determined to weaken Britain's position in the EU and strong supporters of the 'American economic model', these Conservatives began developing ideas about an American-British – Antipodean 'Anglo-sphere' where 'free-markets' and globalised finance would rule. The most articulate amongst them, the MP John Redwood even saw a potential for Britain to become the 51st state of the American union – something which, he argued, 'Churchill had in mind'.[9]

Overdrive with Blair and Clinton

It is one of the great ironies of this global capitalist revolution that, although it was constructed on the right, it went into overdrive during two so-called left-of-centre governments – that is during the presidency of Bill Clinton and the premiership of Tony Blair. Both these 'left-of-centre' leaders made their separate Faustian pacts with globe-trotting big capital. In Britain New Labour was created especially to accept this new globalised economic system – and in the run up to the 1997 election Blair sent his emissaries to the City of London, on the 'prawn cocktail circuit' to assure the City leaders that New Labour would be finance friendly. But Tony Blair went further: he became a convert to global financial capitalism, Anglo-Saxon style, regularly lecturing, and irritating, many of his continental European colleagues on its virtues. In the US, Bill Clinton was an equally zealous supporter of the whole financial globalisation project and a very good friend to the leaders of corporate America. Just as Blair listened attentively to the City's needs, Clinton listened to Wall Street in the form of his two top Treasury advisors, Robert Rubin and his successor, Larry Summers, and he re-appointed as Chairman of The Federal Reserve Board, the godfather of the whole system, Alan Greenspan.

The involvement of Clinton, a Democrat, and Blair, New Labour in the construction and working of the global financial system has created confusion in the political discourse about causes and responsibilities. And this is why I have felt it right to stress over and over again that the financial collapse – about to be responsible for the greatest destruction of living standards to be seen in a lifetime with all the dangers it engenders – was not caused by 'big government' or trade unions, or planning or 'socialism'. It was a collapse made by private global finance, all on its own.

OUT OF THE RUBBLE: A NEW KIND OF SOCIALISM?

Yet, no matter the locus of blame for the 2008 crash, some few years later a new economic and global system is already emerging. Out of the fog of the defeat of the global system, and as the state life-support system operates at full power, one thing is certain: with so much debt still left to eliminate there can be no return, even if we should want it, to the old neoliberal order. And in its place the contours of a whole new economic system may slowly be becoming discernible.

It remains very difficult to properly label this developing economic system. Some will, no doubt, use labels from the past – like 'social democracy' or 'democratic socialism'. Others, looking at its geopolitical or geoeconomic features, will call it 'protectionism' or even 'mercantilism'. But whatever its label, it already possesses one central reality: the return, this time as saviour, of the state. For, to invert Ronald Reagan's famous dictum, in this great global crisis the state has turned out to be 'the solution, not the problem'.

The Return of The State

It is still well worth reminding ourselves about the importance and scale of the British state's rescue of the private sector in 2008. There was little doubt that the stability of Britain's social fabric was on the line – for had the Brown administration allowed the banking system to crash by allowing a Lehman-like plus-size default in Britain, then a meltdown of the wider economy, with unemployment, food, energy and distribution problems, would have followed within a week. Former US Treasury Secretary, Hank Paulson, the organiser of the US state's rescue, and no feverish alarmist, has outlined the Armageddon dimensions of the potential American crisis, and there is no reason to believe that it would have been any less frightening in the UK.[10]

The extent of the bailout was impressive. The IMF has calculated that the cost to the British taxpayer has been anywhere between the upfront costs of £289 billion and, depending upon how the calculation is made, a staggering total of £1,183 billion. The IMF guesstimates that the British bailout probably amounted to about £550 billion, equal to £10,000 for every person resident in the UK, or about £35,000 for every family.[11] No wonder one European bank executive is quoted as saying 'we are moving into a world of socialist banking'.[12]

By 2009 state money and credit had become the very lifeblood of the British economy. For the financial capitalist system, and through it the wider corporate world, had become hugely dependent upon public sector spending. This life-support machine was (is) comprised of two key components – first, fiscal support based upon massive budgetary outlays (leading to deficit, debt and currency crises); and secondly, the unprecedented, and hitherto taboo, procedure of monetary 'quantitative easing' by the Bank of England, which includes purchases of Treasury bonds and direct money to businesses.

Yet Britain's opinion formers in the privately-owned media continued (and continue) to think that Britain is, in essence, a market economy – and that the rules of the market economy still operate (or 'should' operate). But this is damaging old-think. The reality is very different: for the fact is that the state, the public sector, is all-pervasive in today's British economy. There is a notional idea that 'the state' in its various forms employs about a third of Britain's workforce and the private sector two thirds. Not so: for any survey of employment in the private sector will reveal how large swathes of private sector employment are, in fact, dependent upon various forms of state contracts and state aid. Many firms may well be 'private' in the sense that their ownership is private – either single proprietors, partnerships or companies with shareholders and so on – but for all intents and purposes the company is dependent upon public sector contracts. Examples include: Britain's defence companies that contract with the Ministry of Defence, companies dependent upon the NHS, companies that contract with the education authorities, companies that act as 'consultants' for departments and agencies of the state, and companies that run state pensions schemes (like the firm Capita that runs The Teachers Pension Scheme). For an example of how interconnected some of these private sector companies are with the government the Qinetiq scandal tells the story.[13] And so does the mammoth Private Finance Initiative (PFI) programme of the British government – where private sector firms invest in public sector assets and in return receive interest from taxpayers paid over many years.

The British public sector was sizeable long before the 2007-8 banking crisis – around the mid-40s as a percent of GDP during the New Labour years. Since the collapse of the private credit sector, it is (2010) significantly higher – heading up to the 55 per cent level.

And as a result Britain's government indebtedness has also risen dramatically. In 2009 it rose to levels where questions about the country's ability to borrow were being raised.

No Going Back

However, even though there is, post-crisis, a widespread, though grudging, recognition of the centrality (and virtue) of the state (and the inherent fragility and danger posed by an unregulated private financial sector), this great bailout, this 'return of the state', has, so far, been seen by many as an emergency measure only. Two years after the collapse, the conventional wisdom still had it that the bailout was but a temporary infusion of taxpayers' money – enlisted simply to revive the old ways, so that the big company private sector, including the banks, can return to normal operations as though nothing had happened.

There is nothing temporary about it. In Britain, as elsewhere, private investment remained (remains) extremely sluggish, and the great global deleveraging process, which was the heart and soul of the economic crisis, meant that private investment would remain relatively low for many, many years.

So, in reality, there is now no going back. The raw truth is that any attempt to remove the state's life-support system too quickly will not lead to a private sector renaissance. And globally, any attempt to revive the idea of the old corporate-led global neoliberal system (with its minimal state) will only stoke up – yet again – the same old problem, the same old weaknesses, the same old bubble – that will burst with devastating consequences, this time more devastating than the last. As of writing, Nouriel Roubini, the academic who warned the world about the 2007 bubble, was now warning the world about the new bubble – the so-called 'echo bubble' in Asia (into which the rescued banks of the West are lending and making huge profits).[14]

A Sustainable Britain?

Yet, if we are to avoid another collapse of financial institutions, this time with real hardship, we need now to construct – hopefully before it is constructed for us, by events – a more *sustainable* economic system. Indeed, 'sustainability' – a term until recently associated solely with the environmental debate – is now becoming a watchword in the economic debate. And as the undergirding of a strengthened state allows a transition between the old unstable system and a new more sustainable one, what might some of the features of any new system look like?

As I have already argued, a stronger state will be essential to secure what it did during the earlier social-democratic era – that is to regulate capital, to balance off private ownership, to provide services for the public, and to sustain an enabling, opportunity, welfare state. But I would argue that today, in the light of the collapse, the government should go further. It needs to be able to enter the credit game itself, creating public credit alongside the private credit of private banks. (And, incidentally, as public credit – issued by governments – is not dependent upon the fragile nature of market 'confidence', it is arguably a far more sustainable blood flow for our economic system.)

However the idea of a 'strong state' is still widely, and understandably, feared. The power elites of the old system – primarily the internationalised super-rich and their supporters – fear it largely because of its tax implications, for they rightly see it as inherently redistributive. Others though see a strong state in less self-regarding terms – as an incipient threat to freedom, indeed to pluralism. These fears are real, which is why, as I argue in Chapter Seven, any increase in the power and authority of the state needs to balanced off by real political reform which will weaken the aggregations of centralised power politically and constitutionally.

The return of the state to a stronger position vis a vis the private sector will radically change the 'capitalist system' as we know it. Indeed the economy that is now evolving may well be unrecognisable as 'capitalism'. This development will be shocking to many. For 'capitalism' – whether old-style capitalism or new-style financialised, global, capitalism – has been widely believed to be a success story, and is widely associated with delivering huge benefits to the mass of people. Yet the fact is that, at least in its globalised, deregulated, form, it has now failed spectacularly. And, as I argue in Chapter Six, it has for some time past no longer been producing the outcomes expected of it. Quite simply it has degenerated both in terms of material success and in the values it entrenches.

In Chapter Six I show as well how modern global capitalism was becoming an economic disaster for the British (and western) middle class. Quite simply, the British middle class (income 'middle class' that is) was fragmenting, both upwards but, mostly, downwards while social mobility was at a postwar all-time low. I also argue that modern capitalism is no longer a progressive and meritocratic force – breaking down feudal barriers and hierarchies, nineteenth-century class barriers, promoting science and innovation – but has degenerated. Today's capitalism entrenches privilege and is creating a new inheriting aristocracy. Indeed, inheritance is now big business, perhaps the leading highway to private accumulation. And speculation rather than real long term investment, entrepreneurs laying off risk. Work and innovation are less well rewarded than birth and managing money. I also set out how global capital has eroded our democracies, the great gift and very definition of our western societies. In modern Britain global capitalism has been particularly devastating. It has created a huge, overextended banking and financial system which has unbalanced our economy and placed an unmanageable burden on the millions of British taxpayers.

Protecting People, Not Finance

This crisis of financial capitalism, though uncomfortable and even at times painful for people who had no hand in its creation, may yet be the kind of wake up call we need – an awakening that can reconnect us with some of the basic truths that the reckless and exciting fantasy of the global market adventure has obscured. It may yet help us re-learn the old 'social-democratic' verity that politics and society should determine economics, and not the other way round. And that the political community, that is 'the people' – with its own values and priorities – should come first, and the economy and finance be constructed as best as we can to meet these needs. At the moment this simple injunction is still ignored. Finance still dictates that deficits should be cut, with services and jobs lost and the economy pushed into a further downturn, leading to increased deficits, and thus further cuts. In other words a downward spiral.

'Putting people first' would mean taking a wholly different course. It would place employment as the overriding objective – for mass unemployment, whilst certainly an assault upon the dignity of the citizens affected, is also a waste of resources and a further trigger for depression. Putting employment first, genuinely so, would automatically lead to a whole new strategic direction – for in a recession or depression, with little or no private investment, high public spending would be the only way to create jobs and industrial policy and protectionism – against unfair, undercutting foreign trade – the only way to protect jobs.

A 'non-financial' approach would obviously place social objectives far higher up the list of priorities. And the greatest social objective of all in a civilised society is social peace and tranquillity. And this is where the argument for greater equality comes in. The British during the great boom may well have been, in Peter Mandelson's phrase, 'supremely relaxed' about rich people, even super-rich people. But the huge inequalities created during the 1990s, with its 'in your face' super riches existing alongside growing middle class insecurity and biting anxiety, and underclass poverty, may easily in recessions and depressions lead to social disturbances, violence and political extremism. Already, in the very early years of the downturn, inequality had become a driving political issue. By the time of the 2010 general election public opinion in Britain (as well as in the US) had turned decisively against the big incomes of top people – the left against egregious corporate executive salaries and bonuses in the City, and the right against big public sector salaries and pensions. People were asking: how much more do top executives need? For the first time in a generation people were questioning the ratio of pay between top and average employees. It was a mood that could easily turn nasty.

Indeed, reconciling today's assertive and aspirational democratic society to lower material levels of living may well be the greatest single challenge facing the next generation of politicians. You can operate an unequal wealth and incomes in a deferential, feudal society or under a military dictatorship but a modern democratic society will demand, more so in a downturn, a large degree of equality of opportunity and equality of outcomes.

This is the essence of today's case for social democracy – and a pretty far-reaching social democracy at that – that I try to set out in Chapter Seven. It remains the only possible way to reconcile modern democratic and civilised society with the tough times ahead. The British-born public intellectual Tony Judt has put the case for social democracy in highly realistic, and less than heroic or optimistic, terms. He argues that 'among the options available to us in the present, it is better than anything else.' It is, in sum, the only way in the coming social turbulence to preserve the bases of our civilised lives. He also argues that in the coming years simple raw fear – fear of unemployment, fear of poverty – will inevitably drive social democracy back to the centre of our thinking. As he put it in an arresting way, 'if social democracy has a future, it will be as a social democracy of fear', that is the fear of worse and, further, that such 'a social democracy of fear is something worth fighting for'. And he quotes his social-democratic hero George Orwell as saying much the same kind of thing while he battled against the extreme right and extreme left in revolutionary Barcelona during the Spanish Civil war: 'there was much in it that I didn't understand...but I recognised that it [social-democracy] was a state of affairs worth fighting for.'[15]

A PROTECTIONIST FUTURE
Structural Change: A Balanced Economy

Putting social objectives first, ahead of finance, would also demand a much more balanced economy than has been bequeathed us by the gilded age of out of control credit. Financiers, and the politicians who listened to them, have set their faces like flint against investing in the manufacturing sector in Britain, as such an investment was deemed as nothing less than a subsidy for uncompetitive industry. Thus finance dictated that capital move to lowcost Asia and that Britain concentrate upon its 'service sector' which – surprise, surprise – included as its major component the City of London. The theory was that of the old classical free traders: that Britain could afford to dump its manufacturing sector because its service sector would expand to supply burgeoning Asia (with the huge assumption that no indigenous Asian banking and service sector would be able to supply their own market and that the Asian and Chinese markets for services would remain open). The upshot of this finance-driven British policy is that Britain is now unique amongst the major industrialised economies in being seriously structurally unbalanced. (And, as testimony, OECD figures show that between 1995 and 2003 the UK's share of world exports of manufactured goods fell by 7.4 per cent, while its share of world services exports rose by 23.5 per cent.)

A balanced economy will demand a national effort behind re-manufacturing Britain. We will need to develop and improve those existing manufacturing sectors that have survived, and we will need to try to create new industries as well. It will also need a whole new approach to economic policy. In the neoliberal era, when business and markets ruled, particularist objectives and short term profit ruled out a long term strategic approach for the whole community. If we are to rebalance and restructure Britain's economy then it will need an industrial policy that allows us to restrict global market forces and to start thinking strategically instead of ideologically.

The Fall of Economic Globalisation

Thinking strategically becomes urgent now that the 'economic globalisation' process may be going into reverse. The governing idea of the 1990s was that global capital would rule the world. We would witness nothing less than an integrated global market with no global government – thus a minimal state. It was to be a future for western big finance and big business of 'onwards and upwards' with low costs, low interest rates and abundant, unending credit. But things were not to work out quite the way that the pro-globalising, pro-free trade, pro-debt, lobby had foreseen. The trade deficit with China was not to come down. Indeed it reached alarming proportions creating the huge 'global financial imbalances' that were a key cause of the 2007-8 credit crunch. Further, China did not open its markets in the manner expected in the earlier agreement to admit her to the WTO. She had placed severe restrictions on western penetration of many of her service sector markets, and had helped create an Asian market for her products, thus heralding the arrival of a powerful Asian internal market bloc with China at its hub.

Indeed, by the time of the great banking and credit crisis of 2007-8 it was slowly becoming a distinct possibility that the western leadership class may have got the whole China process wrong. Westerners glibly, and patronisingly, talked about 'managing' China's rise, as though the West was still in charge of events. The truth was looking rather different, indeed the other way round – for as the writer Mark Leonard has suggested some Chinese intellectuals were now talking about how China was now in charge of the process, seeing it as *their* duty to 'manage' change – in particular the decline of the West.[16] Supporters of globalisation were reviewing their commitment. Even the dedicated globalist Will Hutton was a convert, and argued that 'for years, we [sic] had assumed that trade and globalisation are an inevitable part of the landscape. They are not.'[17] And opinion in Britain was further influenced by the Nobel prize-winning economist, Paul Krugman, who by 2010 had changed his views and effectively thrown his weight behind a more protectionist US stance while blaming China for not playing fair in the free trade game.[18]

So, no matter the exact future power position of China and Asia, in the aftermath of the great bank crash it was becoming clear that the British economy was going to be profoundly affected by the fall of economic globalisation and the end of a world system led by the USA and Wall Street.

The Future of The City of London

The demise of economic globalisation has big implications for the City of London. London's financial district did supremely well during the gilded era, and Britain benefited too – both from tax revenues and from trade effect (in 2003 for instance Britain's trade surplus in financial services was reported to be more than double that of any other country).[19] It was unsurprising therefore that in the neoliberal era big finance became the dominant player in British politics – courted and deregulated by both the Conservatives and New Labour.

However, in a 2009 report, independent analysts from the University of Manchester have argued that the City is not as socially beneficial to Britain as may often be thought. They report that in the five years to 2006-7 the financial sector paid and collected £203 billion in taxes, but suggest that the bailout could end up costing us £1,183 billion; they also report that Britain's finance sector 'still accounts for no more than 6.5 per cent of the UK workforce'.[20]

There was always a severe downside to the expansion and deregulation of the City of London. And it was all about size. Quite simply, the years of hubris and greed led to a massively globally overextended banking system – more so than any other major advanced economy. Indeed so overextended did it become that the Bank of England warned in an alarming December 2009 *Financial Stability Report* that 'medium term reform [of the banking system] must remove the expectation that "too important to fail" firms will receive public support and that unsecured wholesale creditors will not share losses'.[21] In other words, the UK had reached a point where its central bank was in effect talking about the possibility of defaulting – including on foreign creditors. To avoid such a nightmare the British Treasury paid up – leading directly to a rumbling crisis in Britain's currency. It raised frightening questions of a British government default. Could Britain continue to borrow whilst Treasury bonds would have to be repaid in a shaky currency?

It all raised fundamental questions for Britain's political-financial elites. How could they have created a financial system which left the country with both an overextended banking system and, *at the same time*, wilfully weakened Britain's long-term ability to borrow and thus support the banks should they fail? For, for Britain to borrow on the necessary scale foreigners needed to know that they would be repaid in a hard currency? It was a case of decades of Euroscepticism – of free-wheeling London financiers disdaining the eurozone – coming home to roost!

In constructing a future for London's financial services industry Britain's politicians have a choice. The City can remain offshore, attempting to become a financial 'tiger' – a kind of super hedge-fund operating globally, outside of the regulatory umbrella of the EU. Or, alternatively, they can take a longer term, more strategic, view and seek to develop London's future within the EU single market and its regulatory regime. The City starts off with big advantages over Frankfurt and Paris. And it should build upon them.

'Fortress Europe': The Coming Age of Protectionism

Following the crash, the British economy is already operating in a very different world. The era of dynamic 'globalisation' has come to an end. The reality now is that following the meltdown of global finance and the potential collapse of the broader economic system, most nationstates have moved to protect their people. They have done so not out of a deep conviction about the need for 'protectionism', but because the global financial markets, having failed, have left their citizens in a vulnerable position.

It is a real irony, though, that even whilst 'protectionism' remains a dirty word, governments are practising more and more of it. Indeed, for many western nations 'protectionism' is an idea whose time has come – or is about to come. 'Protectionism' is normally associated with limiting trade (normally by tariffs and quotas); but it is no longer simply about trade (although trade protection is also on the rise). Rather, 'protectionism' is increasingly simply about the state, that is 'the people', the democratic community, moving into the economy when the private sector breaks down in order to 'protect' their citizens – primarily their jobs and their welfare. What else than a major act of protectionism is the bailout of banks and financial institutions? And what else is a national stimulus package? And what else are new regulatory rules designed to increase domestic lending at the expense of cross-border lending? And, crucially, what else is the great 2008-9 bailout of the Detroit car industry than a major act of protection? Of course, now that the big western banks and car companies have sought protection (through state aid) from their governments, protectionism is no longer such a dirty word.

Britain though is a trading nation. And it will be hit hard by the growth of protectionism around the world. There is little doubt that as protectionism grows everywhere the high levels of trade flourishing under a single *global* economic system in a single relatively integrated *global* market will diminish, perhaps dramatically. Trade will not cease, but will be determined less by 'the global market' and more by governments, with flows and market access increasingly negotiated between the new multipolar government centres.

However, competition remains supremely important for business, indeed for all economic units. And although proper, fair, competition was never possible with low cost Asia, it can still exist on the relatively level playing field of the huge single European market. Indeed in the coming world, trade, competition and exports will largely flourish within the trading blocs, not between them. Indeed, making the European single market work, and pursuing Britain's interests within it, will be the single most important strategy that a British government can pursue. It remains a lifeline for our struggling economy. So, we need to re-orient towards a trading policy with Europe and away from trade with job-destroying lowcost Asia.

Fortress Europe: Britain Alone Is Too Small

The raw fact is that the British state may simply be too small to protect the country properly and to see it through the present crisis. Britain's taxpayers can hardly be expected for long to bail out our banks, support the rebalancing of the economy, protect nascent industries (and withstand counter-protection from aggrieved foreigners) and also provide the necessary welfare to see us through without violence. We need to face the fact that in the modern dangerous post-crash world the UK state is simply not big enough or wealthy enough. This remains the gravamen of the case for Britain in Europe – that in this world Britain's prosperity and stability can only be properly secured by becoming part of a larger economic and political union. Dreams of 'sovereignty', most of them anyway simply imperialistic hangovers, need to be set aside in order to secure this future.

Any New Thinking? (About Spending and Cutting)

The British debate on the eve of the 2010 general election was all about fixing the public finances – those same public finances which had been thrown into turmoil mainly by the finance-led recession and by bailing out the banks. It was surreal – as though governments, and not banks and finance houses operating in the 'free', global, market, had caused the crash. It was (is) a mindset that should surprise no one as Britain's elites are – even two years after the fateful crash – still mired in the old-think of the previous, failed era. In the 2010 general election the Conservatives were arguing for an emergency budget and severe cuts in public expenditure, while Labour and the Liberal Democrats were pledged to cut the government debt levels dramatically but wanted to phase the cuts over a longer period. (No party, in the midst of this great private sector deleveraging crisis, was talking about the continuing and mammoth private sector debt levels, the debts on the credit cards, on mortgages and outstanding loans to banks.) All agreed that public sector cuts are needed to pay for the public money spent on banks. All were assuming, and betting the bank on, that there would be a recovery – which the private sector would sooner or later lead. It was a fanciful set of illusions.

But what will happen should a recovery neither materialise nor be robust enough to lift Britain's public finances? On this scenario the British government – mired in debt and deficit – will be faced with a run on the currency and, in response, will cut the public sector leading to a fall in demand and further loss of tax revenue, leading to further deficits, further runs on the currency, and further cuts – and so on into a downward spiral. Thus, the upshot of the banking spree and failure (and the state's attempt to fix it) will have been the pulverising of the British economy and the living standards of the people.

As the economic journalist Ambrose Evans-Pritchard argued, such a fiscal squeeze is 'demented and destructive' and, indeed, amounted to 'a Hooveresque strategy that will tip these countries [that do it] into a debt spiral, along the lines described by Irving Fisher in *Debt Deflation Causes of Great Depressions* (Economica, 1933). It [fiscal tightening] will prove self-defeating, starting with Greece [referring to the EU crisis in 2010]. It will rebound on the European banking system ultimately drawing us back into a deflationary swamp'.[22]

There Is An Alternative
By 2010, some three decades after Margaret Thatcher set Britain on a new economic course, Britain was, again, facing what she called a 'TINA' – 'There Is No Alternative' – moment: the economy was so dire that there was no alternative to a British economic policy overhaul, indeed a revolution in thinking.

As I try and argue in the concluding chapter, ultimately we need a total restructuring of the failed market model – and of the thinking and values that went with it. We could start by overcoming the obsession with fiscal deficits. As Peter Orszag, the Budget Director in the White House, has pointed out, the fiscal deficit is only one of the two important deficits. There is another deficit – the GDP deficit: that is the difference between what the economy can produce and what it does produce. In other words there is a huge amount of spare capacity caused by massive unemployment of labour and resources.

In this environment keeping employment up and unemployment down – by public spending if need be – becomes priority number one. After all, all that the post-crash growth in public expenditure is doing is filling in the credit vacuum created by the lack of private credit. This filling of the vacuum is, though, only a problem for those who possess an innate hostility to public spending – who see private spending and credit as qualitatively different (somehow 'good') and public sector spending and credit as innately 'bad'.

Just as deficits are worsened by public expenditure cuts, so they are reduced by higher tax takes – much of which can be secured from the banks and finance industry.[23] And the coming 'socialist' era will also likely see higher levels of tax on both salaries and retirement income – perhaps even 1960s levels of 99 per cent over a certain income. And why not, as in the 1960s, set an upper limit – say £150,000 per annum – on what any one person can earn? For the very highest earners this upper limit on income will certainly cause difficulties (in meeting school fees and so on), but it would also have real progressive side effects – such as greater upper income support for state schooling.

To the extent that the country will need new borrowing then nothing would make Britain more reliable as a borrower than joining the euro. For Britain could then promise to pay back its creditors in a hard, rather than potential basketcase, currency. In the British debate – as it stood in 2010 – the vast majority of commentators rejected euro membership thus, in the event of a borrowing crisis, supporting a policy of allowing sterling to sink – even though this would cause large price rises and – potentially – rationing in imported food and energy.

Regulation and, Yes, Public Ownership

Britain, like all western economies, will inevitably become more regulated as a result of the excesses and failures of the private sector, particularly the financial private sector. But, who should do the regulating? This issue will, once again, bring us right up against the European issue – for the country is part of the largest single market in the world (the EU) and trade within this market is our most important economic lifeline. But the single market has a regulatory regime – which both co-ordinates and on occasions can override our domestic regime. Unless Britain wants to leave the single market this regime is one we will have to live with. The sharpest problems for London will occur in the financial sector where the European Commission's de Larosiere proposals seek an overall regulatory regime for Europe's financial sector, including the City of London.[24] The City, having come off its binge, needs a sustainable future – and that must lie in its future as Europe's main financial centre, a role it can obviously only play if it accepts the European system.

We also need to look at new patterns of ownership. During this crisis a theme has developed which argues that shareholder power needs to be asserted over runaway management, particularly in banks. Yet in many cases it was the shareholders – as they placed the search for short term profitability ahead of any commitment to the long term health of their companies – who gave managers inordinate power during the boom times. As long, that is, as they were providing the profits.

Modern corporations are great political power centres in their own right. Even in the early 1950s the chairman of the editorial board of Fortune magazine was arguing that corporations had become so powerful that the president of the United States had a dependence on them that was, 'not unlike that of King John on the landed barons at Runnymede, where [the] Magna Carta was born'.[25] And by the 1990s *Financial Times* columnist Joe Rogaly could tell us to 'forget governments – companies rule, OK', and spoke for a growing number of opinion formers when he argued that the corporations now 'matter more than ever' and 'are heading for dominance over the lives of most advanced countries'.[26] For a time the role of the corporations became so controversial that a serious body of opinion in the West flirted with ideas of restructuring corporate governance – with more influence from an array of 'stakeholders' and less from managers and shareholders. *The Guardian* journalist Will Hutton pioneered this idea in Britain in his 1995 book *The State We're In* and his idea was apparently taken seriously by new Prime Minister Tony Blair whilst he was in opposition (but soon dropped when he entered Downing Street).[27]

There is no reason why a British government cannot at least start rethinking issues of governance and ownership – both within and without the EU context. A pluralistic system in which differing ownership systems – including mutuals and co-operatives – are encouraged could hardly hurt. And in the financial sector, once the situation is stabilised, why not establish a state bank? Why stick with one type of ownership – shareholding – only? Indeed, over the longer term, why not adopt a radical new approach and break up Britain's behemoth banks and operate the domestic retail banking sector through local and regional government owned (and run) banks?

Such new thinking about ownership could inform the privatisation (and any future de-privatisation) debate. Many of the numerous privatisations of the neoliberal era, particularly in utilities – gas, electricity and water – and transport services – railways and even airlines – have been less than resounding success stories. But any future programme to deprivatise some of these concerns, could, rather than return them old-fashioned state control (with national boards), take the opportunity to look at new types of 'stakeholding' ownership.

CAN BRITAIN SURVIVE?

The crisis, and the needed revolution in thinking to deal with it, will make the coming few years a real historic watershed. In looking at the British problem and the possible solutions, we should never forget that we are in this desperate position because, and only because, the previous world we inhabited has now collapsed under the weight of its own contradictions. Nor should we forget that it was we British (or, rather our elites) who, more than any other nation in Europe, bought into this great neoliberal 'free-market' globalised experiment (and into the fantasy money it unleashed). As a result our establishment has left us – a country of only 60 million people outside a hard currency zone – with an overextended banking system and a huge public spending crisis.

It is a measure of the difficulty we face that so many of our leading politicians and journalists, complicit in their support of the old world, are still unable to grasp the new thinking necessary for survival in the new. The sooner we move on the better.

CHAPTER ONE

THE CITY UNBOUND

SEEDS OF DISASTER

THATCHERISM: SOWING THE SEEDS

Margaret Thatcher, and the neoconservative ideology she stood for, made its first breakthrough in 1984 when, after its titanic struggle with government, the National Union of Mineworkers laid down its arms. In Britain the road was clear for Thatcher and her supporters to push forward her remarkable economic 'revolution'.

This great victory over socialism at home was further reinforced by the events of 1989 when the Berlin Wall cracked open, and the iron curtain parted ending the forty-years-long Cold War. It was another political triumph for 'the iron lady' and although she was ejected from office in 1990, she was to become – for a generation of Tories and for many Americans – an iconic free-market, anti-socialist leader who changed the very direction of her country. Indeed, unlike many premiers, she was to give her name to an 'ism'.

This 'Thatcher revolution', though bitterly opposed at the time, was later to turn into a new British consensus – encompassing most mainstream politicians, large sections of the media (and opinion-forming journalists and academics) as well as the increasingly influential business people. Between 1991 and 1997 John Major's Tory government continued the broad strands of Thatcherite economic strategy (marketisation, privatisation, demanufacturing, City-friendly taxation and a semi-detached European policy); and from 1997 onward, right up until the crash of 2007-8, so did, with a few tweaks, the New Labour government led by Tony Blair and Gordon Brown. So complete was this new consensus that by 2007 Britain had effectively become an American-style neoconservative country. Unlike its major European allies it had joined the US in invading Iraq. And, also unlike its European allies, it had allowed Wall Street-style global finance in the City to determine its economic policy.

What made this Thatcherite consensus so complete was the growing sense that it represented the wave of the future. The geopolitical defeat of communism was crucial here: for as the 1990s unfolded great new markets (principally China and Eastern Europe) were opening up, and the way seemed clear for a new unfettered form of western capitalism – global market capitalism – to emerge.

Global capitalism without global government meant one thing above all others – that Thatcherite market capitalism could be pushed to extremes – nothing could stop it, the sky was the limit. In these completely 'free' global markets ('free' that is from regulation) business could rule. Governments, with their welfare concerns, taxation and regulations, were fatally weakened as corporations could play one off against another. It was all a huge godsend for business, particularly financial business in the City of London. The City had been restructured to allow for a 'wild west' boom in the 'big bang' in 1998 – and it came, with a vengeance, as globalisation got underway during the 1990s.

BIG FINANCE

It was this new heady freedom for big finance, essentially for banks and hedge funds that was the direct cause of the great debt boom that collapsed in 2007.

The dimensions of the early twenty-first century private debt boom are staggering. The pressure for the debt inflation was released through of a range of very lightly regulated new vehicles – with acronyms like CDOs, MBSs, SIVs, and in the corporate sector CDSs. The US Bureau of Economic Analysis tells the incredible story. The ratio of private debt to GDP stayed at a steady 1.2 during the 1950s, 60s and 70s; in the early 1980s it started to rise significantly and did not stop rising, until at its height, it reached well over 3.1; that is, 200 per cent higher than in 1979. One analyst has suggested that 'something big happened in the early 1980s' to cause the ratio to rise.[1]

Truly staggering amounts of money were involved. These could hardly be calculated. Yet the *Daily Telegraph*'s Ambrose Evans-Pritchard, whose reporting on the unfolding debt crisis was amongst the most prescient and alarming, set out some of the dimensions in a series of powerfully argued articles in 2007 and 2008. When the US investment bank, Bear Stearns, collapsed in March 2008 and was bought in a firesale by JP Morgan, it was revealed that its 'total position' amounted to $13.4 trillion – greater than the US national income and equivalent to a quarter of the world's GDP. And all of it built on an asset-base of only $80 billion. Warren Buffet famously described these derivatives as 'weapons of financial mass destruction'. The credit default swap market (CDSs) amounted to $45 trillion![2]

One of the world's leading authorities on this debt bubble, the late Professor Susan Strange, has argued that this bubble was the product of the structure of modern capitalism – what she termed 'casino capitalism'. It had two main features. The first was the extreme 'financialisation' of the system – a term meaning more credit, more banks, more lending to new types of institutions like hedge funds, private equity funds and the like, and lending through an array of new and exotic types of financial instruments. In turn, this 'financialisation' was made possible by a systematic political programme of deregulation of financial markets – a deregulation which itself was made effective by the global nature of these markets.

It was this deregulation of capitalism (and particularly finance) that was obviously 'the something big' that had occurred in the early 1980s as part of the Reagan and Thatcher revolutions. And it was hardly surprising that the 1980s also saw the first serious rise in the ratio of debt to GDP, a ratio that has risen consistently ever since.

Even in the early 1980s, this 'pro-market'-inspired deregulation of western capitalism was not without its critics in the West's politico-economic establishment. Reagan's approach was famously called 'voodoo economics' by then Vice-President, George Bush, who was highly critical of 'supply side' economic deregulation and the tax policies that led to huge government debts; 'Reaganite' White House insider David Stockman was another who opposed the 'new economics' that was producing high forward trajectories for government deficits and debt; in the academic world Professor Strange who, in decrying what she came to call 'mad money', argued that 'it was, and is, wildly foolish to let the financial markets run so far ahead, so far beyond the control of state and international authorities.'[3] There were other voices too, but they remained in a decided minority – and, as the debt party got into full swing, they were drowned out, treated as curmudgeons and 'wet blankets'.

The fact is that successive British governments, the administrations of Thatcher, Major and Blair all encouraged this financial services explosion through their continuing support of deregulation. The Bank of England was also a major supporter of the deregulation and a 'light touch' regulatory system, a 'light touch' that allowed all manner of financial 'funny money' instruments. The American economist Nouriel Roubini – the leading seer of the debt crash of 2007 – has described the major debt instrument used in the debt-boom – the SIVs – of being 'off-sheet scams' and argues they should have been regulated.[4]

Following Thatcher and Reagan, the presidencies of Bill Clinton and George W. Bush and the premiership of Tony Blair all successfully resisted tougher regulation – surrounded as they were in Wall Street and the City of London by 'casino capitalists' and market fundamentalists. Their era of deregulation allowed what amounted to a shadow banking industry to build up – and become a primary purveyor of the 'funny money' of the 'casino'. These investment banks, hedge funds and private equity funds were, alongside the more regulated big banks, the engine drivers of this massive debt bubble. And these investment banks were allowed to take all the risk they wanted with their balance sheets without the government stepping in. Even as the banking crisis developed some supporters of the deregulation of the 1990s, like investment banker-turned Treasury Secretary Hank Paulson, were fighting a rearguard action as he tried to mitigate and water down the inevitable Congressional regulatory backlash.

A NEW UNTOUCHABLE CLASS: THE SUPER-RICH

This new age of capital also saw the emergence of a new political and social force in Britain, a new interest in the land – a super-wealthy elite. This new class consisted of traditional money (released to make even bigger fortunes), new money, and a new race of very top city professionals – the lawyers, the accountants – who serviced them. Add to this the big money attracted from abroad – from traditional centres like Arabia, and from new capitalist centres like Russia – and by the early 2000s Britain had became an offshore paradise for the super-rich.

By the early years of the new century London was hosting a new gilded age, and this new class was commanding wealth beyond imagining. It became potentially wealthier than any super-rich class in history (including the famed 'robber barons', those 'malefactors of great wealth' criticised by Teddy Roosevelt, and the nineteenth century capitalists who inspired the opposition of Marxists for a century). It also assumed the proportions of overlordship, of an overclass – as powerful, majestic and antidemocratic as the imperial governing classes at the height of the European empires. Indeed, so powerful did they become that they were able to seduce, dominate and bully the politicians of Westminster to an extent new in modern times.

The Conservatives were always ready to see merit in super-rich folk keeping and increasing their money (many banking and city families). But so powerful, and important to the economy, had the new class become that New Labour was also enlisted. By 1997 and the general election, New Labour had changed. It had become 'City friendly'. The New Labour project saw big finance as part of its new 'knowledge and service economy' strategy, and, in a kind of Faustian pact, regarded a successful City as a good source of tax revenue. As a result New Labour leaders increasingly refused to attack the rich and even the super-rich. On one famous occasion Prime Minister Blair refused during repeated questioning to say that it was 'unacceptable' for 'the gap between rich and poor to get wider' and argued 'it's not a burning ambition for me to make sure that David Beckham [a very highly paid soccer player] earns less money.'[5]

This 'Faustian pact' between New Labour, the City and the new super-rich may well have helped the government raise revenue for its spending plans. It has been estimated that 'in the five years to 2006-7 the finance sector paid and collected £203 billion in taxes'; but this favourable outcome may well have been wholly offset, or worse, by the costs of the UK bailout of the banks which has been estimated as amounting to £289 billion, and even potentially rising to £1,183 billion.[6]

But 'the pact' had one other outcome, perhaps the most damaging of all – the emergence of finance, and its institutions, as a political player which could dominate Westminster and set an agenda. The City began to rival the role played by the trade unions in the 1970s when the political agenda was set by an earlier 'Faustian pact' between government and union leaders (an agreement that created 'the social contract'). This time, some twenty years later, it was the sheer power of banks and financial institutions in Whitehall and Westminister that was creating a political climate – this time in favour of more and more 'free market' policies, including more and more deregulation. This time the banks and big capital were the 'overmighty subjects'.

A troublesome aspect of today's super-rich capitalists – one which separates them sharply from earlier super-rich – is that they owe little or no loyalty to community or nation. In previous eras the wealthy used to be grounded and bound within their nations and societies – a constraint that kept aggregations of wealth within reason and the rich relatively socially responsible. Now, though, the rich are free: free to move their money and their assets around the world. In the new global economy super-rich wealth (capital) is now freer than ever before to seek out the most productive – that is, high profit, low cost – haven; and with the entry into the global economy of China, India and Eastern Europe – these opportunities have multiplied. The super-rich are also free to move themselves. Although still less mobile than their money, they too are becoming less rooted, moving easily between many different locations. And all this freedom means one thing: an increase in the power of wealth over that of democratic politics – to the point now where wealth can buy, and is owning, politics.

MILLIONAIRES, MULTI-MILLIONAIRES, BILLIONAIRES

This essential mobility of the rich and their capital separates them from the rest of us – who remain rooted to the locale where we live and work. Indeed, it is the ability to escape from the world of work (and its rootedness) which effectively defines the modern super-rich. Ordinary dollar millionaires are by no means lavishly well off, particularly if they are in three- or four-people families or households. However they are able to be financially independent – as one commentary put it, they can 'maintain their lifestyle for years and years without earning even one month's pay'.[7] It has been estimated that in 1996 there were as many as 6 million-dollar millionaires in the world, up from 2 million at the end of the Cold War. By 2006 the number had risen to 9.5 million. Intriguingly they were spread relatively evenly across continents – with 3.2 million in North America, 2.9 million in Europe and 2.6 million in Asia-Pacific. The European breakdown includes: Germany with 798,000 and the UK with 485,000. This World Wealth Report uses the term

'High Net Worth Individual' instead of super-rich, and it defines net worth as including the values of private equity holdings, publicly quoted equities, bonds, funds and cash. It excludes primary residences and collectibles.

These ordinary dollar millionaires, however, found themselves at the *very* lower reaches of the world of the super-rich. They often work – if not for a living, then for extras – and their lifestyles are often not particularly extravagant or sumptuous. They are, in fact, poor cousins in comparison with the more seriously rich families and individuals who had been emerging in the global economy, people whose net worth would produce an *unearned* annual income of say $750,000. And in 2007 The World Wealth Report issued annually by Capgemini/ Merrill Lynch reported that the number of 'Ultra-High Net Worth Individuals', that is people with $30 million or more, amounted to 94,970 worldwide (roughly 39,000 in the USA, 21,000 in Europe and 19,000 in Asia-Pacific).[8]

These households are the truly super-rich, whose net worth, much of it inherited, is the source of considerable economic power and produces an income (mainly unlinked to work) that allows, even by affluent western standards, extraordinarily sumptuous lifestyles. Although huge amounts of the money of these multimillionaires are held outside the United States, in Europe, Asia and Latin America, this tells us nothing about the nationality of the holders. In a sense these super-rich multimillionaires are the world's true global citizens – owing loyalty to themselves, their families and their money, rather than to communities and territorial boundaries. Their money is highly mobile, and so are they themselves as they move between their various homes around the world – in London, Paris and New York; in large houses in the Hamptons in the United States, in the English and French countryside, and in gated communities in sunbelt America, particularly Florida, southern California and Arizona – as well as on yachts traveling between tropical paradises not scarred by local poverty.

'THE 950 BILLIONAIRES'

Amongst these multimillionaires there is a distinction to be made between those at the lower end – say the £10 million net worth households – and those at the higher end – say the $200 million plus households. During this recent gilded age in the UK the distinction was one of power, not lifestyle. From most perspectives the income from £10 million can, at least on the face of it, produce the same kind of lifestyle as income from the net worth of the more serious multimillionaires (for there is arguably a limit to the number of homes, yachts and cars that can be enjoyed and consumed in a lifetime). Wealth of £10 million in net worth, however, simply cannot command as much economic power – over employment, over small businesses – as do the resources of the really big time multimillionaires, much of whose money is normally tied up in big transnational corporations.

At the very top of this mega-rich world are the dollar billionaires, those who command over $1,000 million in net worth, a fortune that can secure an *unearned* annual income, depending on inflation and interest rates, of $50 million a year before tax – staggeringly well over 1,000 times more than the average *earned* US income. In 1997 estimates of the number of these mega-rich individuals varied from 358 to 447 worldwide. By 2007 the *Forbes* 'Wealth List' estimated the number of billionaires to be 946, with 178 'newcomers' (from the previous year). 415 of these billionaires were from the USA and, intriguingly, 20 were from China (a number that had grown dramatically during the year to reach 66, with some estimates suggesting 106!)[9] In 2007, the last year of the recent gilded age, *The Sunday Times* estimated that Britain had about 65 billionaires, up from 54 the previous year – although many of these were foreigners living in the UK.[10]

WHO ARE THESE BILLIONAIRES?

These 950 or so billionaires in the world are a varied lot. In one sense they are like the rest of us (and like those who will read this book). They are overwhelmingly western, primarily American or European, and male, but they represent no single ethnic group, no single social background, and certainly possess no single business acumen or financial secret which can explain the acquiring of these awesome fortunes.

Many, indeed most, of these billionaires, though, would not be in the mega-rich category without the aid of a substantial inheritance – for 'inheriting' remains the well-trodden route to great multimillion dollar wealth. The crucially central role of inheritance in wealth building is often underplayed by the super-wealthy and their supporters. It is also downplayed by supporters of the 'entrepreneurial society' and the 'free-market' who need to argue that money and success comes through hard work, creativity and intelligence rather than unearned privilege. In Britain in 2007 it was claimed that as many as 78 per cent of those on *The Sunday Times*' 'Rich List' had 'made their money themselves through business'. Yet the true origin of the wealth of today's super and mega-rich families normally involves the help of inheritance. For instance, in the late 1990s a survey claimed that of the top 400 wealthiest people in the United States, 39 made the list through inheritance *alone* – and many of the others had some inheritance to help get them started.[11] The British Queen, Elizabeth Windsor, is perhaps the most famous example of such massive unearned wealth. In 1997 Phillip Beresford (in *The Sunday Times*' 'Rich List',

Sunday Times, 6th April 1997) put her net worth at a staggering $10.4 thousand million in 1992 (double the 1997 figure for top-listed Joseph Lewis). However, after she took a rival 'rich list' to the Press Complaints Commission over its valuation of her assets, *The Sunday Times*' Wealth Register excluded from its calculations the royal art collection, which, had it been included, would have given her a $16 billion figure, making her the world's wealthiest woman and the second wealthiest person in the world, with half the net worth of the Sultan of Brunei but more than the Walton family.'[12]

In contrast to the inheritors, there are some 'self-made' men (very few women) in the billionaire class. Yet even these men of merit have not necessarily made their inordinate fortunes through extraordinary amounts of work and talent – certainly not its continuous application. Many of the self-made mega-rich are certainly talented and creative (and often ruthless), but many of them have achieved great wealth through one-off bursts of insight or risk or luck.

The American William (Bill) Gates is seen as 'self-made', very much the American entrepreneurial hero. His vast resources – *Newsweek* calls him 'the Croesus of our age' – have been built upon the meritorious image of having run a successful company which provides a real service, a real addition to human understanding and communication. In 2007 his huge net worth was listed as $56 billion by *Forbes* magazine (up from $36.4 billion in the 1997 listing) – and is based upon the value of his shares in his company Microsoft. It was Gates' original burst of imagination that created his fortune – the initial stock offering in 1986 of 100 Microsoft shares cost $2100 but by the first trading day in August 1997 this had risen to 3600 shares at $138.50 each! Gates' personal share of the company rose from $234 million to $37.8 billion in the same period.'[13] Certainly

Gates has managed the company and taken many crucial decisions. Yet as Microsoft grew he needed the more 'routine' skills exhibited by thousands of major company directors – such as managerial aptitude and the ability to stave off competition. As with all established businesses, less and less risk and less and less creativity was needed (a junior hospital doctor probably put in more hours).

Paul Raymond is a different type of self-made billionaire. Described by academic John Hills as Britain's richest man – in 1995 he placed him ahead of Joseph Lewis – Raymond's fortune in the mid-1990s was thought to be well over £1.65 billion. Having founded Raymond's Revue Bar in the Soho district of London, with topless dancers, he made his money by investing in soft pornography and property.[14] Like Gates he had the talent to spot a coming market – albeit one that was less elevating and educational. And also like Gates, and the other mega-rich, once the original burst of inventiveness (perhaps amounting to his one great insight) was over, the rest of his working life has consisted of simply managing his empire and watching his money grow – as long that is as the great boom worked its will.

Intriguingly, very few whose talent has been put to continuous use throughout his or her career or vocation – such people as writers, sportsmen and women, professionals such as accountants, architects, professors, teachers, engineers, even distinguished physicians and pop stars – makes it to the higher reaches of the mega-rich. Even the pop star Paul McCartney of the Beatles, with a mere £400 million, is only the thirty-seventh richest Briton.

The truth remains that the key to entering today's world of the mega-rich, and certainly the billionaire class, is not work or talent or risk-taking (millions of people have those attributes in abundance). Rather it is access to capital. For capital, once attained, can both grow and be lost very quickly – neither outcomes needing much work, flair or intelligence. For the mega-rich it was the capital start that was all-important; for in the last three decades – of seemingly endless finance-led growth – *keeping* capital, and *growing* capital, is nothing special. It needs none of the skills, character and hard work associated with building and running an old-style business.

Perhaps the most perfect exemplar of modern capitalism – finance capitalism – is Joseph Lewis. By 1997 he had arguably become Britain's richest person, overtaking both the Queen and the Sainsbury family, and he was approaching the foothills of America's 'top twenty' mega-rich. His lifestyle conformed to the popular image of the global capitalist, virtually a parody of the genre. He lived in a Bahamas villa and owned a 62-metre yacht four storeys high. He played the exchange markets in front of a bank of computer screens. Whereas fellow finance capitalist Jimmy Goldsmith built an estate in South America, Lewis bought a whole village. He has invested in British football and in the auctioneers Christies (which, along with fellow auctioneers Sotheby's probably own the most impressive intelligence records on the world's high-net-worth individuals).

Born in the East End of London, Joseph Lewis made his fortune in foreign exchange dealings. Starting out as a London caterer laying on medieval banquets for rich tourists (with a sideline in cashmere shops) Lewis only made real money when he went into foreign exchange dealing. He, as well as other mega-rich dealers such as George Soros and the Barclay brothers, use relatively small amounts of money to move markets, and profit from the changes. This is often condemned as 'speculation' or worse (the prime minister of Malaysia once called Soros 'a devil').

Yet 'speculation' conjures up the idea of considerable risk. The reality, however, is very different. It normally takes rather small amounts of money – particularly if the big players cooperate – to start the ball rolling (that is, create a selling spree in a marginal market) in an overvalued currency. In this 'Canute Play' the super-rich currency players find a central bank that is 'playing Canute' – trying against all the odds to bolster an ailing currency – and then target its home economy. When the process gets going, devaluation becomes inevitable; and in such an environment it takes very little intelligence (or risk), though considerable capital, to make huge profits. And in these 'Canute Plays' the capital often comes not from the individual himself but from huge lines of credit made available by foreign currency trading banks. (One estimate has it that at one point credit lines of up to £6 billion were available for Joseph Lewis's currency operations.) Britain fell to a 'Canute Play' in 1992 when the British government handed £5 billion to 'the market' in an attempt to shore up the unshoreable.

Lewis's fortune was certainly the result of talent. For all self-made, mega-rich people, capital needs to be earned, and often their own work and talent (together with considerable luck) help to create the precious capital in the first place. However, once an initial amount of capital has been acquired, life suddenly becomes much easier. Moving further up the line from super-rich to mega-rich to billionaire – hardly requires extraordinary talent, hard work or even risk (certainly no more talent, hard work or risk than that offered and encountered by millions of the non-wealthy). As a fortune builds it can often assume a dynamic all of its own, with the owner of the original wealth simply being carried along as the fortune grows and grows. In a relatively stable economy it is very difficult to lose a fortune. In a bust, though, even the super-rich can lose big money (Lewis himself lost a portion of his fortune in the Bear Stearns collapse in 2008); but what is left at the bottom of the cycle is often more than enough to 'make' another fortune in the up-swing.

THE SHEER MAGNITUDE OF SUPER-RICH WEALTH

This group of early twenty-first century billionaires are, by any standards, outlandishly rich. They not only dwarf their 'ordinary' super-rich contemporaries but also the earlier race of mega-rich 'robber barons' who were so identified with the burgeoning capitalism of the early twentieth century. In terms of resources at their personal command, in 1997 William Gates was three times richer than John D. Rockefeller (Standard Oil) was in 1918, Warren Buffet was over ten times richer than Andrew Carnegie (Steel) was in 1918, and the wealth of the British Queen would also be well inside this 'robber baron' category.

The resources at the disposal of these billionaires, and the broader swathe of super-rich families, represents a huge pool of the globe's wealth and is beyond the wildest imaginings of most people. In 1996 the high net worth individuals (HNWIs, as they are depicted by the financial services sector that serves them) accounted for almost $17 trillion in assets in 1996. By 2007 they accounted for a staggering $37.2 trillion.[15]

These mammoth sums are not just a measure of wealth, they are also a measure of power. And this power derives from the command over resources that wealth brings. Measuring this egregious concentration of power now enjoyed by the world's super-rich is difficult, but it can be given some meaning by making comparisons. For instance, even though it is not exactly comparing like with like, there exists an astounding statistic: it shows that in 2006 the combined wealth of the world's dollar millionaires ($37.2 trillion) is almost three times the entire gross national product of the United States ($13.2 trillion) and also much higher than the combined GNP of the 'Group of Seven' countries – the US, Japan, Germany, France, Britain, Italy and Canada. What's more, figures show that this gap – between the super-rich and the USA is growing – for in

1996 the super-rich had only twice the gross domestic product of the USA.[16]

By comparison with the broad super-rich, the mountain of wealth owned by the 950 billionaires assumes Himalayan proportions when comparisons are made. For instance, the world's richest 500 billionaires together have an income greater than the world's poorest 420 million people. Also, the 950 billionaires have combined wealth a third bigger than the gross domestic product of the whole continent of Africa and three times the size of South America's MERCOSUR (whose members include Argentina, Brazil, Paraguay, Uruguay and Venezuala). Nearer to home, the combined wealth of the 950 billionaires amounts to a third more than the total US federal budget and two thirds more than the US government's combined Social Security, Medicare and Education budget.

Individual wealth comparisons are even more invidious. In 1998, a good decade into the 'globalisation' process, it was calculated that 84 of the world's richest people had a combined worth greater than that of China, so that the wealth of *just one of these super-rich individuals is equal to that of about 12.5 million of his fellow humans.*[17] And since then the figures have become even starker. For instance, in 2007 it was claimed that Lakshmi Mittal – the Indian-born steel magnate and the 'the world's fifth richest person' – has a personal net worth larger than 30 countries listed in the World Bank's GDP table, and that Bill Gates's $56 billion of personal wealth gives him greater resources than 50 countries.[18]

On some counts the world's richest individual (at the turn of the century) was not Bill Gates, but rather the Sultan of Brunei who, it has been estimated, commands more resources than the combined GNP of 40 nation-states. To give his wealth some form of reality, it was also estimated to be larger than the GNP of the Czech Republic (population 10.3 million); and Gates was believed to command more resources than the GNP of Africa's oil-rich giant, Nigeria (with a population of 111.3 million), the Walton family more than the GNP of Vietnam (population 73.5 million), Paul Sacher and the Hoffmann family more than the GNP of Bulgaria (population 8.4 million), Karl and Theo Albrecht more than the GNP of Panama (with its 2.6 million inhabitants); and Joseph Lewis more control over resources than his country of residence, the Bahamas.[19]

Get the world's top 3 mega-rich (dollar billionaire) people into one room at the turn of the century and you would have assembled command over more resources than the GNP of Israel; the top 4 and you would tie with Poland, the top 10 and you would beat Norway and South Africa. Europe's 20 richest families command around $113 billion, a little more than the whole Polish economy; America's richest 10 and Britain's richest 1000 families together command more resources than the GNP of the entire Russian Federation.[20] And if the top 200 or so billionaires could ever be assembled together, then the command over assets, in that one room, would outrank the GNP of each of Australia, the Netherlands, Belgium, possibly even Brazil; and with 400 or so billionaires the one gathering would outrank Britain and almost overtake France!

Another way of looking at concentrations of wealth is through the proportions of national wealth held by each nation's own passport-holding super-rich. Super-rich concentration in Britain – the world's most globally-oriented large economy – is also striking, as is its growth. In Britain in 1998 its 'top 50' owned $69 billion – but by 2007 the same amount was owned by the 'top 10'.[21] (In 2004 the top 1 per cent of American households owned 34.4 per cent of the US. More striking still, the top ½ per cent of households (500,000 households) owned well over a quarter of the US.)

A particular feature of the British super-rich scene is the concentration in very few hands of land ownership. Britain – or rather the land area known as the United Kingdom – is, quite literally, owned by a very small caste; as is the capital city, London. It remains a poignant commentary on wealth concentration that large tracts of London are owned by just a few individuals. The Duke of Westminster, through the Grosvenor Estate, owns around 200 acres of Belgravia and 100 acres of Mayfair – a dynastic inheritance created by the seventeenth century marriage of Cheshire baronet Thomas Grosvenor to Mary Davies, the '12 year old heiress to a London manor that at the time included 200 acres of Pimlico'. Viscount Portman owns 110 acres north of Oxford Street. Lord Howard de Walden's four daughters, through a holding company, own 90 acres of Marylebone. Elizabeth Windsor, the Queen, remains the 'official' owner of 150 acres of 'crown estates' in central London, as the eight crown estates commissioners address their annual report to her. Andrew Lycett has argued that although 'millions of pounds are exchanged every week in leasehold property deals…London still has no sizeable new landowners' with the exception of the Sultan of Brunei and Paul Raymond.[22]

It is these kinds of statistics that bring into sharp focus the economic power of the global super-wealthy compared to that of politicians, presidents and prime ministers – who have to share their economic power with cabinets and parliaments. Later in this Chapter I look at how the super-rich can, in essence, buy political power in a democracy. But there are many ways of influencing policy – both indirectly and directly. One such was on display when the super wealth of the Murdoch empire used its money to influence general elections. Another can be seen in the way the super wealth of Lord Ashcroft has been directed to influencing the outcomes in specific marginal constituencies in the 2010 general election. It is a measure of Britain's anaemic democratic culture, and the fact that all parties benefit from it, that there is so little outrage at this blatant politics-buying big money. (American media billionaire Ted Turner decided to donate at the stroke of a pen $1 billion to the United Nations and 'to put on notice...every rich person in the world...that they're going to be hearing from me about giving money'.[23] For a western politician to similarly move a billion dollars in the direction of the UN would have involved months and months of negotiating and a bruising campaign.)

RICHER STILL, YET RICHER

And the super-rich continue to get richer. Alan Blinder, a former vice chairman of the US Federal Reserve Board, said in 1997 – only a few years into the Wall Street globalisation era – that 'I think when historians look back at the last quarter of the twentieth century the shift from labour to capital, the almost unprecedented shift of money and power up the income pyramid, is going to be their number one focus.'[24] It was a prophetic analysis. The figures are indeed dramatic – showing not just the success of the rich, but also the squeezing of the middle classes. Using a very modest definition of 'rich', then in the US in 1979 – at the beginning of the Thatcher-Reagan age – the incomes of the richest 10 per cent (90th percentile) were 110 per cent greater than the middle 10 per cent (50th percentile); but by 2004 they had become 147 per cent greater. A more accurate definition of rich – say the top 1 per cent or the top ½ percent – would have shown much greater rises by the rich over those of the middle class.[25]

Another way of looking at the 'richer and richer' story is to note the continuous growth in the sheer number of the world's super-rich. In 1996 – when the era of the super-rich was just getting underway – HNWIs numbered 4.5 million and their wealth amounted to $16.6 trillion. By 2001 the rich had grown to 7.1 million and their wealth to 26.2 trillion. By 2006 they had risen to 9.5 million persons and their wealth to $37.2 trillion.[26]

The global distribution of these rich folk is changing – away from America and Europe and towards Asia. Intriguingly the 1996 super-rich 'market' grew more rapidly in Latin America than anywhere else – perhaps a function of the ease with which millionaires can be created where a traditionally stratified social structure is melded with global capitalism. Yet it is in Asia where the most consistent growth in the new millionaire super-rich has taken place – an incredible 15 per cent annual growth rate in the HNWI market over a decade up to the Asian market collapse in early 1998. In the 2007 World Wealth Report 'Singapore, India, Indonesia and Russia witnessed the highest growth in HNWI populations' and China recorded a huge growth of billionaires (from 20 to 66 during the one year of 2006-7).[27]

AND GREEDIER?

As well as larger and richer, the new super-rich class, at least before the great downturn, were becoming even greedier. Whereas 'old capital', bounded and constrained by nation and social responsibility, tended to seek preservation of capital and long-term goals, 'new wealth' – particularly that generated in the post-cold war era – seems concerned with immediate investment performance. In an era of low inflation (where there are small returns from deposit markets) the performance-driven super-rich seek out securities, futures and options. In the Chinese-led low inflationary environment they are more able to take risks than their forebears, they diversify more easily, and buy and sell more readily.

Above all – in the post-communist environment – they are driven by profit, and it is this insistent search for return and profit that makes them global – and 'offshore' – in their reach and interests. And this new need for performance (mainly of profits) was a major cause of the growing private banking market – Goldman Sachs, Credit Suisse, UBS, JP Morgan, Merrill Lynch – as it catered to the new millionaire class by diversifying their investments across both asset classes and the globe.

GOOD AS WELL AS RICH? ANYONE FOR NOBLESSE OBLIGE?

Yet when the investment has been a success, and the profits are made, can we expect our new global wealthy to develop the sense of social obligation that infused the more traditional upper classes and helped to create the social cohesion and welfare states of modern continental Europe?

It is unlikely. Traditional western capitalism's essential individualism and cultural egalitarianism always placed great limits on the feudal instinct of *noblesse oblige*, but the new global capitalism can be expected to expunge it altogether. Not only is modern global capital less rooted in a social or moral sensibility, but increasingly it also has fewer and fewer roots in the community or the nation – or indeed, the civilization. Robber barons with a social conscience giving back to their nation have become a newsworthy curiosity. And as capital moves easily from nation to nation and from west to east in search of profits, local identities and obligations fade away.

No doubt generous and compassionate feelings exist within many a super-rich breast. But the growth of so-called 'giving' has become less a true sign of moral sense or old-fashioned compassion and more a strategic business operation – primarily a good way to improve one's public relations. The Prince of Wales – as a part of his campaign to become King – has mastered this art of 'giving', and organising other people's giving, as a form of public relations.[28] As has Bill Gates. Indeed, 'giving', particularly 'mega-giving' (none of which actually hurts or even limits the lifestyle of the 'giver') serves the continuing human need to be 'good', or to be seen to be 'good', as well as rich and powerful. It certainly used to be more difficult for 'the rich man to get into heaven than for a camel to enter the eye of a needle', but 'giving' can perhaps make it a little easier.

Yet, at root, this kind of high profile 'mega-giving' remains yet another instrument of power. In a sense the super-rich have it both ways – not only the power of the possessor of egregious accumulations of wealth but also the power derived from 'giving it away' to charities of their choice, thus further imposing their tastes and values on the wider public; and, in the case of political 'giving' and influence, helping to determine the politics of nations.

WHERE IS THE MONEY?

What the new global super-rich actually do with their money is no idle speculation. For in the new global economy decisions about how to deploy these gargantuan portfolios can move economic mountains, change governments, even regimes. By a stroke of a pen, as mighty as that wielded by any politician, the super-rich can touch and change real lives of real people the world over – whether it be creating or destroying jobs, building or guiding charities, supporting culture or investing or disinvesting in sport.

Intriguingly, the super-rich hold their wealth in very different ways from average middle-income households. The mass of middle class Americans have a large proportion of their net worth in their principal residences and in cars – and of course their debt liabilities, through mortgages and non-mortgage consumer debt, is alarmingly high and unsustainable. By comparison, only a small per cent of the net worth of the global super-rich is in principal residences, and a miniscule amount in cars themselves. As for debt – the bane of the middle classes in America and Britain – the global super-rich do not like it and do not need to have it.

The super-rich are conspicuous for their love of the stock market – and during the great post-communist Wall Street bonanza many fortunes have been made in equities. In 2006 the global super-rich invested 31 per cent of their financial assets in equities, 24 per cent in real estate (including commercial real estate – a market that collapsed on them in late 2007, 21 per cent in fixed income investments, 14 per cent in cash, and, intriguingly, only 10 per cent in the 'alternative investment world' of hedge funds, private equity and derivatives (down by 100 per cent over 2005).[29]

There is also a growing amount of super-rich money going into luxuries and collectibles (and the annual *Forbes* Wealth Report has produced a tasteless 'Cost of Living Extremely Well Index' – the CLEWI – to monitor the rising cost of super-rich living. These luxury investments – dubbed 'investments of passion' by analysts – include 'cars, boats and planes' (accounting for 26 per cent of super-rich 'passion' spending), art (20 per cent), jewelry (18 per cent), and a new entrant – investments in sports, including football teams (6 per cent). A recent development in Britain has been the investment by foreign billionaires – such as Roman Abramovich (in Chelsea, in London) and the Mittal family (in QPR, also in London) – in football teams.[30]

RICH FAMILIES AND THE CORPORATIONS

It is not surprising that super-rich individuals and families hold a considerable part of their wealth in, and through, corporations. Some sociologists, though, point to a subtle, though crucial, difference in shareholding between the mega-rich and the super-rich. At the very top of the globe's social pyramid the mega-rich – probably amounting to no more than a few hundred families – own sizeable interests in large enterprises, and can often have an influence in decision-making.

However, because of the growth and dispersal of shareholdings – held by pension funds, banks, even universities – even the mega-rich do not tend to have outright control of large corporations. One expert has suggested that 'it is doubtful whether family holdings of less than five per cent can signify "control", and there are few examples of such concentration.'[31] Alongside these large enterprise stockholders there are a group of investors – many of them just as mega-rich – who come nowhere near to controlling companies because they diversify their portfolios into a variety of enterprises. The number of these 'rentier shareholders' (essentially big time coupon clippers) has grown dramatically with the rise in values of stock exchanges and the ability to spread financial risk around the world. These 'rentiers' were described by Edward Luttwak – in terms that can apply to Britain as much as the US – as those who:

> live off dividends, bond interest...and real-estate rentals, rather than the active conduct of a business or profession. When seen on the golf courses and boat docks of the fenced in and carefully guarded residential enclaves they so greatly favor...[they] resemble businesspeople or professionals on vacation. But their vacation never ends.[32]

A further strand of the globe's mega-rich – some of them bordering on being only super-rich, some of them even believing themselves to be 'middle class' – are the salaried executives or directors of some of the large corporations. To these super executives need to be added the new race of those who hold multiple part-time directorships and non-executive positions in a variety of enterprises (what the Marxists call 'finance capitalists'). The salaries of these executives are so huge that they themselves can build up considerable shareholdings or pension funds, receiving the kind of income almost akin to the big-time owners of capital.

And, of course, some of these mega-rich people can have multiple identities. 'A rentier capitalist may also be a finance capitalist...the daughter of a rentier capitalist may marry an entrepreneurial capitalist, and an executive capitalist may regularly play golf with a finance capitalist.'[33] And what have been called 'kinecon groups' build up over the generations. These are sets of 'interrelated kin who control the corporation through their combined ownership interests and strategic representation in management'.[34]

Below these mega-rich individuals and families the majority of the ordinary super-rich – the top 1 per cent of wealthy Brits or Americans – also hold a large proportion of their wealth in businesses, but normally in small and medium-sized businesses, often their own (many of which, though, are dependent for their future upon the large corporations and the mega-rich).

THE RICH PRIVATISE THE CORPORATIONS

During the global financial bonanza of the 1990s the corporations began to give way in the affections of the super-rich to a new kind of capitalism – private equity. New folks began to appear on super-rich lists (whilst, of course, many of the old super-rich got even richer) – and what in 2004 *The Economist* described as 'the new kings of capitalism' were crowned.[35] Private equity served two purposes for the super-rich: first it purchased major corporations from shareholders, thus releasing the new owners from legal obligations such as disclosure and, secondly, it 'leveraged' the acquired companies. Stewart Lansley in his extremely well-researched 2006 book on the super-rich revolution in Britain described Philip Green as a 'classic example' of one of these new 'kings of capitalism'. He reported that 'Green has built his fortune by buying up underperforming companies, often on the cheap, pumping them full of debt, stripping them down, refinancing them and making a pretty tidy profit in the process.'[36] By 2005 private equity had become so controversial in Europe that when the Chairman of Germany's SPD described private equity as 'locusts' his remarks were greeted with general approval. He said 'they remain anonymous, they have no face and descend like a swarm of locusts on a company, devour it and then fly on'. And even the British held a parliamentary investigation in which some of the major figures in the City of London's private equity world – such as Damon Buffini of Permira and Mike Smith of CVC – had to answer their critics in public.

The Carlyle Group has perfected the art of global private equity investment for the super-rich. With offices around the world from New York to Tokyo and Barcelona this US-based firm describes themselves unabashedly as having a 'mission to be the premier global private equity firm leveraging the insight of Carlyle's team of investment professionals to generate extraordinary returns.' It reports that it has $75 billion of equity capital under management – more, that is, than the fortune of Bill Gates. With investment money coming from the super-rich of the US (65 per cent) and Europe (25 per cent) Carlyle invests across the world in a range of industries, including aerospace and defence, energy and power, and telecommunications and transportation.

Carlyle specialises in political influence – indeed it remains a text book example of how the mega-rich can influence the world of politics which in turn can influence business and profits. Present and one-time members of the board include a glittering array of the globally powerful – including two US presidents (George H.W. Bush and George W. Bush), a former British Prime Minister (John Major), a former US Secretary of State (James Baker III), a former US Secretary of Defense (Frank Carlucci), a former Premier of Alberta and a former president of the Philippines. Carlyle's political acumen was on display when it engineered a remarkable – indeed, on its own terms, admirable – raid by its super-rich investors on the public assets of the British government. In 2002 an agency of Her Majesty's Government was privatised and turned into a company called Qinetiq. The Carlyle Group moved swiftly to invest £42 million at auction in the new company. By February 2006 its share value was worth £351 million and Carlyle sold half its shares at a profit of over 800 per cent. As it had bought its shares through a series of 'special purpose vehicles' based in the offshore tax haven Guernsey these profits were tax exempt. A former Defence Procurement Minister, John Gilbert, described Carlyle as having taken 'The Ministry of Defence…like a lamb to the slaughter'. He considered that 'all the value [in Qinetiq] was built up by public servants using public money' and that the whole operation was 'a complete outrage, a scandal'.[37] In the Qinetiq affair Carlyle had certainly lived up to one of its objectives in its mission statement: that of 'generating extraordinary returns' for its investors. Yet, maybe it had fallen short in another: that of maintaining 'our good name and the good name of our investors'.

INHERITANCE AND THE RICH

This perfectly legal financial play by the Carlyle Group in the Qinetiq affair is simply one amongst a myriad of techniques used to make the super-rich even richer. The post-cold war world of finance (together with governments that provide light touch regulation) have allowed big money to make bigger money – quite easily as it happens. Yet, an even more fundamental question needs asking. Where do those who have the money 'to play' – and therefore to grow – get it from in the first place?

The myth has it that today's super-rich fortunes are largely the product of the merit and enterprise of the 'self-made' as they work in the market. Thus periodically when inequality becomes an issue, the western media tend to highlight not the amount of private capital but rather 'excessive' top salaries and remuneration. Corporate pay is easy to grasp, and outlandish corporate remuneration is a real feature of modern capitalism. The heads of America's 500 biggest companies took home an aggregate pay raise in 2004 of 54 per cent, and *Forbes* reported that the compensation of these 500 amounted to $5.1 billion (up from $3.3 billion in 2003). Intriguingly, the bulk of the compensation of CEOs now takes the form of stock gains – thus allowing the CEOs to build up a large capital sum which transports them from well-paid salaried officers into the realm of capitalist 'movers and shakers'. Two examples of the huge amounts involved in 2004 were Terry S. Semel, CEO of Yahoo, who received total 5-year compensation of $230 million made up of salary, bonus and stock (which amounted to $229 million); and Edwin M. Crawford, CEO of Caremark Rx, who received 5-year compensation of over $77 million (of which over $69 million was in stock gains.[38] Other examples include: Stephen Hubert's $39.6 million from Conseco Inc., Lawrence Coss's $28.9 million from the Green Tree Financial Corporation and James Donald's $25.2 million from the DSC Corporation. Some spectacular examples of those also feeling no pain were Andrew Grove of Intel, paid a salary of $3,003,000 and $94,587,000 in long-term compensation in 1996, Edward

Pfeiffer of Compaq Computers, paid a salary of $4,250,000 and $23,546,000 in long-term compensation in the same year, and, a mere twentieth in one rich-list in 1996, Drew Lewis of Union Pacific, paid a salary of $3,131,000 and $18,320,000 in long-term compensation.[39]

So 'excessive' were corporate compensations becoming during the 1990s that even the market-oriented British Labour Party campaigned against 'exorbitant' top corporate salaries in the run-up to the British general election of 1997. Gas chief Cedric Brown's salary – then at £475,000 – and perks sparked off a national controversy, and the CBI set up a Commission to look into 'top people's pay'. Since then, and during the time of the corporate-friendly Blair government there has been no noticeable lowering of top company remuneration. And time only will tell whether the banking crisis and reforms of 2008-10 will have any long-term effect on the generality of corporate pay and remuneration.

The often outlandish remuneration of corporate executives clearly creates pockets of wealth that can often lead to significant capital accumulation. Yet, this route to riches is at least linked to some form of effort, skill and intelligence – and the sums involved are miniscule compared to those that are inherited or essentially derived from inheritance. The fact is that the new global rich are a mixture of 'new' and 'old' money, of 'earned income' and inheritance – but with inheritance playing by far the larger part. The old adage that 'it takes money to make money' holds true – more so now than ever – as does the other rueful popular belief that 'to him that hath…'

'Old money' is still very prominent in New Labour, free-market Britain; and the traditional aristocracy remains a highly privileged group. Tom Nicholas has suggested that 'becoming a business leader in Britain is still largely determined by the interconnected characteristics of a wealthy family and a privileged education...there has been no democratisation of British business over the last century and a half.'[40] For all the rhetoric of 'the need to reward enterprise and skill', 'old money' has done extremely well out of the Thatcher-Reagan revolution and the global market economics that it spawned. Like all capital, 'old capital' was bound to survive and prosper in a low-tax, deregulated economy. And 'new inheritance' – that is the wealth of the sons and daughters of the self-made of the postwar years – has now joined 'old inheritance' in an economy (and culture) dominated by inherited wealth.

The amounts are staggering. The economist Robert Avery of Cornell University argued at the beginning of the 1990s that 'we [in the US] will soon be seeing the largest transfer of income in the history of the world' as the older generation leave wealth to the baby boomers.[41] Some guesstimates place inheritance at 6 per cent of US GDP each year![42] Apart from straight gifts during the lifetime of the giver, there is also the mammoth transfer of unearned wealth – including whole businesses – upon the death (or retirement) of the super-rich giver.

And this inheritance culture will continue to grow. Two dynamics will see to that. First, the global economy has made the present generation of super-rich wealthier than any before. Second, this burst of super-wealth coincides (or, is the cause of) the increasing financial pressures on the young. Hence, leading political scientist Kevin Phillips has argued,

> for young Americans, those under thirty or thirty-five, two decades of polarization had brought a special, though widely unappreciated, irony: not only were they (and those younger) in danger of being the first generation of Americans to suffer a lower standard of living than their parents, but they would be the first generation to receive

– or not receive – much of their economic opportunity from family inheritance, not personal achievement.[43]

A troublesome feature of this new economy and culture of inheritance is the growth in the number of recipients of unearned cash income – the use of inherited money to consume and live on. There are a considerable number of people within super-rich families whose unearned annual income is not derived from their own net worth, but rather from their parents' or grandparents'. One estimate suggested that in the 1980s 46 per cent of the US 'affluent' gave at least $15,000 a year to their adult children or grandchildren.[44] But partly because it is often shrouded in mystery some of the egregious sums involved are, unlike huge salaries, rarely exposed to public view.

The sting is often taken out of the censure of super-rich inheritance because in the modern economy many middle class families and individuals now inherit money themselves (albeit fairly small amounts). And this inheritance – normally the family house – is a very welcome addition to the stretched household economies of millions. The great housing and debt boom of the early twenty-first century priced many younger middle class people out of housing altogether, and, as a result, passing housing down the generations was the least the older generation could do for their offspring. The middle class housing crisis creates a considerable constituency of approval for inheritance, from which the super-rich inheriting classes benefit. So, politicians in the West (particularly in the housing boom and bust lands of America and Britain) either accept inheritance as untouchable – except at the margins – or even support it ideologically as creating 'islands of independence' from the state.

Neoliberals and 'free-marketeers' – who philosophically may remain meritocrats – nevertheless often support the idea of wealth as 'cascading down the generations' as a bulwark against socialism. Yet, ironically, what has now begun to emerge is a capitalist version of the much-derided state welfare 'dependency culture'. For too many, dependency upon the family inheritance has been substituted for dependency on the state.

A GLOBAL RULING CLASS?

These super-rich families and individuals possess huge personal wealth and command considerable influence over resources. They have control of, or influence over, the great corporations, and they hand their extraordinary wealth down through the generations. But, do they amount to a new ruling class?

Certainly the new class regime of global capitalism is very different from the old class model. Today's mega-rich are not like the 'old style capitalists' who owned great businesses outright and could – and did – personally direct huge resources and thousands of workers. These traditional 'mogul' capitalists (the popular image derived from nineteenth century capitalism) still exist, but are now called 'entrepreneurial capitalists' and run their own shows (in Britain people such as the late James Goldsmith, Alan Sugar, the founder of Amstrad, and the late Anita Roddick of Bodyshop are good examples). Yet the wealth of the world's richest people is no longer held in this way – rather it is held 'impersonally', primarily in the form of stocks and bonds.

The nineteenth century Marxian notion of 'a class' of capitalists – based upon highly concentrated capitalism – is also now redundant. A modern socialist analysis now argues that the control of corporations is still highly concentrated in 'knots of financial power' by small numbers of financial capitalists operating interlocking directorships and cross-shareholding – in other words, concentrated shareholder power. However in today's huge and diverse global economy, such traditional concentration simply does not exist. The emergence of the modern globalised corporate economy has dispersed shareholdings and separated ownership from control.[45]

So, given the size and variety of today's global super-rich, is it fair to describe them as a class at all, let alone a ruling class? Historically, capitalist societies, such as the first one – imperial Britain – have produced what amounts to a class: a cohesive, self-conscious, self-confident, socially exclusive, super-rich upper class possessed of a community of feeling. Yet, today's global super-rich are too numerous, too fragmented nationally, ethnically and geographically, and too divided into different types to be an old-fashioned class in the Victorian sense. And as for a 'ruling' class, modern global capitalism – too individualistic, too lacking in team spirit – is rather bad at rulership. However, there is some evidence to suggest that a US 'business establishment' did exist in the early decades of post-World-War-Two America. Then many amongst the American super-rich held multiple directorships and many 'key positions in the intercorporate network' tended to be drawn from a more integrated social background – exclusive boarding schools, a listing in the Social Register ('the crucial indicator of social exclusivity') and membership of exclusive big city clubs.[46] And of course in Britain (with cohesion amongst the super-rich secured by public schooling and the shared experience of land ownership), in France, and amongst the Japanese zaibatsu, the sense of class or caste was always pronounced, and this was reflected in their postwar business culture as well.

However in the US in the 1970s and onwards, with the rise of Dallas, Chicago, San Francisco and Los Angeles, the American business establishment, historically grouped along the eastern seaboard, became less cohesive – certainly in geographical terms. And with new generations coming on stream, capital inheritance can often mean dispersal. As well as disputes over money – which may sour fellow 'class feeling' – the average size of individual holdings within the inheriting family group falls, and dynasties dissipate into a number of rentier families.

In one of the most systematic and sophisticated analyses of postwar capitalism, John Scott argues that this more dispersed shareholding has led to 'a consequent reduction in, though not a disappearance of, family control and influence'. He suggests that those with less than 5 per cent of the shares of a company have little purchase on decision-making, and those with 5-10 per cent have only a 'potential for control'. Very few super-rich have such a concentration of shares – in fact they usually disperse their shareholdings among a variety of enterprises – thus lowering risk but diluting the sense of ownership.

Of course the dispersal of the character of share ownership developed apace with the huge growth of pension funds during the 1970s, 1980s and 1990s. In reality, modern global corporations are now controlled by 'constellations of interests' – families, banks, pension funds.[47]

So the big question remains: who drives these great corporations? For if corporations run the world and shape our lives – certainly more than other institutions – then those who run the corporations are truly a new ruling class. For a time a new 'managerialist' theory emerged which argued that shareholders no longer controlled corporations; rather there was a separation of ownership and control, and the decisions of these great corporate behemoths were now taken by a new managerial class – 'captains of industry' such as Britain's Sir Peter Waiters or John Browne of BP, and Iain Vallance of BT. Such managers or 'executive capitalists' can virtually write their own huge incomes, but can only enter the ranks of the super-rich by accruing, through their remuneration packages, large amounts of shares and bonds. These executives are in capitalist situations that give them power as well as high personal reward.

In 1941 James Burnham, in his famous book *The Managerial Revolution*, argued that this growth of managerialism was bringing family capitalism to an end. And in 1963 A. A. Berle argued that 'the transformation of property from an active role to passive wealth has so operated that the wealthy stratum no longer has power'.[48] However, the new global capitalist order has rendered this debate somewhat redundant. Whether the power to direct the affairs of the corporation resides amongst the 'capitalists' or the 'managers' hardly matters anymore. For it is the logic of the market – and increasingly the global market – which dictates. And both capitalists and managers have to dance to this new tune. The great decisions of the corporations are informed and determined by short term market profitability – 'performance' in the lingo – and not by the particular preferences, tastes or style of individuals or families or managers! There used to be room for these preferences – many of them of them reflecting a social or moral concern. In the modern Wall Street regime those days are now over.

A GLOBAL OVERCLASS (WITHOUT A COUNTRY)

If the new global super-rich do not amount to an old-style ruling class, they are certainly becoming an overclass: the mirror image of the better known urban underclass. In a very real sense the new super-rich are becoming transcendent – removed from their societies, separated from the rest of us. This is happening physically. The higher levels of the super-rich have always lived apart: within their walled estates or in wealthy ghettos in the centre of Manhattan, London and other cities. They have always owned possessions that have singled them out. Today, of course, mere diamonds, helicopters and expensive cars no longer signify the apex of great wealth. Now it is the luxury yacht (normally personally designed by John Banneman), the personal aeroplane – the Sultan of Brunei has a Boeing 747 – (normally supplied by Grumman), and one or two of the highest value paintings that signify someone has reached the top.

Although the ordinary super-rich – including simple dollar millionaires – cannot afford this mega-rich lifestyle, they too are increasingly becoming separated, removing into wealth enclaves. Some estimates suggest that by 1997 there were 30,000 gated communities and that in parts of the US a third of all new homes were being built behind walls. These gated communities are home to over eight million Americans, and thus have become a normal aspect of the lifestyle of the vast majority of the top 10 per cent of US wealth holders and their families.[49] Gated communities have their own security forces, amenity centres and codes of acceptability – ranging from the colour of doors and the planting of shrubs to rules against political posters – which residents accept as part of the local social contract. It amounts to an embryonic privatised local government, an epochal development that will inevitably lead those inside the communities to demand deep cuts in local taxes and services. Schooling still exists outside the gated communities, although the demand for private schooling within the walls can be expected to grow. Such a separated existence found its extreme form in Yeltsin's capitalist Russia, where the new super-rich mafia were not only separated by money but were also essentially above the law.

The American journalist and writer Thomas Friedman has written that we should 'never trust a country where the rich live behind high walls and tinted windows. That is a place that is not prospering as one country', and that such 'fragmentation undermines the very concept of civitas – of organised community life…which is the notion behind the US.'[50] Yet such separatism is increasingly the reality. And if the perceptible growth of inequality within western societies continues, then for the super-rich the world outside the ghettos of the wealthy will become even more unattractive – and hostile.

'ONLY THE LITTLE PEOPLE PAY TAXES'

Of course one test of loyalty to a society is a willingness to pay taxes, particularly if they are not onerous. Yet increasingly the super-rich are dodging the taxes of their countries of origin. The late Leona Helmsley, the billionaire New Yorker, famously made her name when she bragged that 'we [the super-rich] don't pay taxes. Only the little people pay taxes'.

In 1997 the *New York Times* reported that:

> nearly 2,400 of the Americans with the highest incomes paid no federal taxes in 1993, up from just 85 individuals and couples in 1977. While the number of Americans who make $200,000 or more grew more than 15 fold from 1977 to 1993, the number of people in that category who paid no income taxes grew 28 fold or nearly twice as fast, according to a quarterly statistical bulletin issued by the IRS.[51]

So difficult was it for the US authorities to collect taxes from the super-rich that Congress introduced a new tax altogether – the Alternative Minimum Tax – to catch them. With the American 'middle classes' – the middle income groups – paying a larger percentage of their earnings in taxes (including sales taxes, property taxes and social security payroll taxes), super-rich tax evasion and avoidance is becoming a growing cause of economic inequality and social fracture. And during the George W. Bush administration, tax cuts made the super-rich even richer. And some Republicans wish to benefit the wealthy still further. The Republican politician John McCain, by no means a low-tax extremist, argued during the 2008 presidential campaign that 'entrepreneurs should not be taxed into submission...John McCain will make the Bush income and business tax cuts permanent' and 'will fight the Democratic plan for a crippling tax increase in 2011'. As the economist Paul Krugman commented, this 'crippling' plan was the proposal to let the Bush tax cuts for people making over $250,000 a year expire.[52] Also, the abolition of the income tax – proposed by the Republican politician, libertarian and champion of the super-rich, Steve Forbes – may help a range of people but, should it ever be enacted, would be a triumph for the wealthy.

In Britain the super-rich also escape paying their fair tax share. The British Queen – who until 1994 was allowed by her government to pay no taxes at all, and since then has only had to pay some of them – is literally above the law as far as tax is concerned and remains a role model for tax dodging as does her son, the heir to the British throne. Charles Windsor has also been placed above the law by British governments as he is specifically exempt from paying corporation tax, capital gains tax and death duties. The Duchy of Cornwall, owned by Charles and run as a company, has not been liable for tax since 1921.

Other British super-rich, who unlike the royals are not 'above the laws' of taxation, nonetheless manage to avoid their share of taxes. Lloyd's 'names' are a striking example. 'According to Robson Rhodes, the accountants, the most striking advantage is that Names are treated like businesses...so losses incurred in the market can be offset against other earnings...they enjoy business property relief for inheritance tax purposes on their deposits and funds which support their underwriting.'[53] Dodging taxes – even in global capital's highly friendly tax environment – is final proof, should it be needed, of the lack of even a residual loyalty to nation and home society on the part of many super-rich families.

During the Blair government in the late 1990s London became a haven for a species of super and mega-rich called 'non-doms' – shorthand for rich people who had domiciles elsewhere. These 'non-doms' paid no tax at all to the British government – who refused to tax them, unlike other countries including the US, on their worldwide income. And whilst the 'little people' were compelled to pay their taxes, in Britain, under the Labour government elected in 1997, private equity partners paid tax on income at 10 per cent and 'entrepreneurs', who turn their income into capital gains, also got taxed at 10 per cent of their income. As the economist and commentator Martin Wolf argued this super-rich tax haven had become so egregious that it was 'subversive of any enduring political compact amongst citizens' leading to a situation in which the 'political community will collapse'.[54]

Companies – huge, large and medium-sized – are also well into the tax dodging game. One scam, made possible by global economics, is 'transfer pricing', which allows companies to pay tax where they want to, which naturally is the country or haven with the lowest tax regime. They can engineer this by doing much of their spending in the high-tax countries, thus cutting their tax obligations, and making most of their profits – using subsidiaries with little more than a front office with a few staff – in low-tax countries.

For super-rich tax dodgers a helpful dynamic often sets in. Home governments, make strenuous attempts to keep money at home by lowering even further the tax burden on rich people. The idea, not always fanciful, grew that more tax money could be attracted by taxing less. In Britain the top rate of tax was reduced from 98 per cent to 40 per cent during the country's move to market capitalism, and in the US, even after a decade and a half of falling taxes for the upper income groups, by the late 1990s the authorities were still struggling manfully to lower the 'burden' further by even lower capital gains taxes.

This timidity of national governments in their relations with the super-rich takes many forms. For instance capital flight is conducted primarily via computers – cash in suitcases smuggled on board aircraft bound for exotic places are now fantasies from the past – and national governments can therefore, if they really want to, get at records stored on hard-disks in headquarters in New York, London, Paris and Frankfurt. But the threat by banks and financial institutions to relocate in the event of such an oppressive intrusion into their 'secrecy' prevents individual governments from doing anything more than the occasional slap on the wrist.

In this environment it is hardly surprising that the amount of 'offshore' money is growing rapidly. The IMF reported that a staggering $2000 billion is located beyond the reach of the countries in which the money was made – in the growing number of safe-haven tax shelters, ranging from the Cayman Islands, through the Channel Islands and Lichtenstein to Singapore. In the late 1990s German commentators estimated that 100,000 tax-evading rich people had transferred many of their assets to a new favourite safe haven: the rock of Gibraltar.[55] 'Trickle down' – the 1980s public relations term for the idea that wealth trickles down to the masses from those who make and own large chunks of it – has now been replaced by 'gush up and out'.

Another sign of the detachment of the super-rich from their domestic societies is their decreasing involvement in those societies. Potential economic and social changes in their countries of origin and residence used to be of great concern to the wealthy. They saw their destinies as linked to their countries of birth, and they spent considerable amounts of money (and acquiesced to relatively high tax regimes) in order to stabilise and ameliorate social changes that might otherwise threaten their interests. This strategy enabled the progressive, centrist politics of the western world in the twentieth century to develop.

Now, though, domestic – that is, national – social and economic changes are no longer of such urgent concern. Should a local environment turn hostile to them – not just because of a government's economic policy, but also, say, because of its law and order or policing strategy – then they can simply up sticks and leave, both financially and in person. And often the mere threat, or assumption of a threat, to withdraw their assets and patronage is enough to persuade the domestic politicians to secure a friendly environment. Such threats are now regularly made, either implicitly by corporations (who take jobs with them) or explicitly by high-profile, super-rich individuals, as was the case before the 1997 British general election with the musical entrepreneur Andrew Lloyd Webber, the actor Michael Caine and the boxer Frank Bruno.

Of course emotional ties to the land of their birth may remain; and there will doubtless be a certain discomfort in being forever on the lookout or potentially always on the run – not, like the Jews, because of persecution, but because of the possibility of advantage and gain. However the arrival of global communications – particularly satellite television for entertainment and the internet for financial transactions – and the increasing number of locations that welcome the rich, has made mobility, even expatriation, much easier to handle.

This twenty-first century overclass is being built upon a fundamental divergence of interest between the global super-rich – both members and aspirants – and the rest of us. Simply, there will be those whose interests are tied to the performance of the global economy and those, the majority of people in the West, rooted in their own communities and dependent upon local jobs and welfare, who will continue to depend upon the success or failure of their own countries, regions or cities. George Orwell's aphorism that 'the poor are the only true patriots' may take on real meaning, but will need to be amended to include, as well as the poor, large sections of the western middle class.

While 'the locals' will need skills in order to be employed and avoid the minimal (or worse) welfare systems, the new global overclass, not needing to work, will need financial advice, and will be catered to by professionals, some of whom themselves will get rich and become part of the overclass.

And there is a further frightening twist. The dread prospect exists that for those who need jobs – those who have only their labour to fall back on – even this haven will be removed. Old-style capitalism, as Eric Hobsbawm and others from a Marxist perspective have argued, may have exploited the masses, but it also, crucially, included them. Now, though, new global capitalism in its search for 'performance' places cost-cutting and outsourcing above jobs. Thus, as China and India produce more and more, the demand – the need – for British workers may well be over. And in the market system, little or no demand for labour means low or no wages – and a pauperisation of whole sections of the middle class in an era when the pressure on the welfare systems of the West are already becoming acute.

CHAPTER TWO

HOLLOWING OUT THE UK

GLOBAL CAPITAL, 'FREE TRADE' AND THE UNBALANCED NATION

UP, UP AND AWAY: CAPITAL GOES GLOBAL

The new super-rich business class that has dominated the British economy and politics in the Thatcher/Blair era is, of course, the product of the early 1990s worldwide triumph of capitalism in the Cold War. It was this victory that allowed financial capital to go global. And going global was a godsend for London's financiers (and their neoconservative political supporters). They called it 'globalisation', which sounded highminded. But what this 'globalisation' gave western capital was unheard of profits – profits based upon mobility.

Whilst capital became mobile, those forces that previously constrained it – the state (governments) and the trade unions – remained local. Thus global capital won the battle with the state by allowing capital and the corporations to play one western government off against another; and it weakened the trade unions by undercutting western wages (through the new pool of labour now available in Asia and Eastern Europe).

The upshot was a new world – one in which western capital could lower its costs and raise its profits almost at will. This was the great trick that during the Thatcher/Blair/Clinton era built up unprecedented profitability for the western money men – as it ushered in a world of minimal regulation, massive capital flows and, with the addition to the global market of China, low inflation and gigantic debt. There was, consequently, unprecedented scope for leveraging. It was a world where profits would fall from the tree like overripe fruit.

That the new 'globalisation' was good for profits became clearer by the year. A good measure of profitability was the remorseless rise of share prices on the London Stock Exchange. The FTSE equivalent rose from just over 1,000 in mid-1984 to over 3,200 in mid-1995 to over 6,100 in mid-2000 to a high point of over 6,500 in early to mid-2007 – just before the 2008 crash. The New York Stock Exchange's Dow Jones Industrial Average also rose considerably during the globalising years. On 19th October 1987, after its largest one day fall, the average was 1,738. A decade later, by 19th October 1997, it had risen to 7,161. And a decade later still, by 9th October 2007, it had risen to 14,164. The era of globalisation had seen it rise by a gigantic factor of 14 – little wonder that Forbes's High Net Worth individuals in their search for profitability, have been very keen on stocks.[1]

Access to global capital movement – and to profits – is typically and primarily through shares and bonds which since the end of the Cold War have become the main conduit for capital mobility. By investing in shares – particularly those of multinational companies – western capital (including the money of the super-rich) stepped off the local platform onto the up escalator which lifted it to an altogether new level – the promised land of global profits and higher and higher returns.

The spectacular growth in the operations of the great stock markets of New York, London, Frankfurt, Paris and the leading markets in Asia show how millions upon millions were taking this shareholding route onto the up escalator. The percentage of net worth of both Americans and Britons held in stocks and bonds has risen considerably in the post-cold war years.[2] And millions of non-super-rich western individuals and families have placed, or have had placed for them by managers, at least a portion of their assets on the up escalator to this higher, global, level of economic return. Many 'ordinary' families, too, have had their pension money moved from the domestic economies to the global arena.

'Performance' or 'high return on profit' for these millions of shareholders was (and is) increasingly likely to be found in low cost areas in Asia where the wage levels are much lower than in the western societies from which the money originally came. Exact figures on Asia's lower wage levels and costs are difficult to unearth, but World Bank figures for 2006 show that, even after almost twenty years of 'globalisation' Chinese per capita income is a staggering twenty times lower than that of the US and eighteen times lower than Germany and France. A decade earlier China had been over fifty times lower – a dramatic catch-up but still leaving room for big cost savings by western capital.[3]

It was always obvious that producing goods with any sizeable labour content in low cost areas will provide much greater profits for the shareholders of the companies involved. James Goldsmith, a major global financial capitalist himself, put it this way in the early years of the 'global rush' – as early as 1994:

87

In most developed nations, the cost to an average manufacturing company of paying its workforce is an amount equal to between 25% and 30% of sales. If such a company decides to maintain in its home country only its head office and sales force, while transferring its production to a low cost area, it will save about 20% of sales volume. Thus a company with sales of $500 million will increase its pre-tax profits by up to $100 million every year.[4]

Lower social costs – the taxes on business and capital that governments force corporations to pay in order to finance various aspects of the welfare state – are a key gateway to profitability, and thus share performance. As long as countries can provide a secure political framework (democratic or undemocratic it hardly matters) and a pool of relatively skilled workers, then shareholders will increasingly demand investment in low-social-cost areas – Asia, Russia and Eastern Europe and those western locations where costs and taxes are still competitive by western standards. And within the West there have also been 'low cost' countries seeking to undercut each other. The Thatcher/Blair plan for Britain since the end of the Cold War has included a strategy of keeping social costs (primarily taxes) low as a way of competing with Britain's European neighbours without increasing real productivity. British social security costs as part of indirect labour costs are significantly lower than those of France, Sweden, Germany, the Netherlands and Portugal.[5]

THE 'GLOBALISATION' GAME

The frantic search during the 'global rush' years for lower and lower costs, and for lower and lower taxes, by the western super-rich is the engine which has driven the increasingly integrated global market for capital. The really big money is made by speculative capital – often borrowed or 'leveraged' – that dips in and out of countries making money either by exchange rate changes or by the 'carry trade' – borrowing on lower interest in one place, loaning on higher interest in another. This speculative finance is huge, and makes people very, very rich. And, like George Soros, famous too. The amounts involved, though, are difficult to measure. Much easier to measure is the less glamorous, though just as deadly, end of the capital market where jobs are immediately made and lost – and, from the western perspective, are shipped overseas. The figures for foreign direct investment (FDI) – that is, investment which takes a longish term, if not lasting, interest in foreign enterprises – are impressive. FDI, that is the inflow and outflow capital from locations in one country to locations in another, continues to grow. UNCTAD reported that foreign direct investment reached $1,306 billion in 2006, the third successive year in which it rose, almost equalling its record high in 2000.

During the 1990s the proportion of FDI going to low cost areas in non-western countries had risen to 27 per cent in 1991 and 40 per cent in 1993, and remained at or around this record level for some time (it was 35 per cent in 1995) And FDI inflows into all developing countries rose from $31.9 billion in 1995 to $38.5 billion in 1996, falling back marginally to $37.2 billion in 1997. But by 2005 South, East and South East Asia *alone* were receiving $165 billion in 2005 with East Asia accounting for three-quarters of the total Asian figure. South, East and South-East Asia are still the main magnets for these inflows into 'developing countries' with most of this increase going to a handful of countries – the bulk of total 'Third World' FDI investment ended up in China, Singapore, Malaysia, Thailand, India, Hong Kong, Taiwan, Mexico, Brazil, Argentina and Egypt. China – with $108 billion – was the single biggest player in this league.[6]

During the boom years of the 'global rush' the West also received significant inflows (with the UK at the top of the western list). And it may well be that – initially at least – these inflows to the West will reach much greater heights following the banking and credit crash as western banks – with the connivance of western governments – both seek and accept 'sovereign wealth funds' from Asia and the Middle East. As of writing Citigroup was putting the finishing touches to a big capital-raising exercise as it sought up to $14 billion from both China and Kuwait. As the news commentary in *The Financial Times* put it in what was the understatement of the year: 'The deal underscores the depth of the problems faced by banks that suffered heavy losses in the US sub-prime mortgage crisis.'[7] (One of the investors in this case, was called the China Development Bank, in reality the Chinese Communist Party, which as well as financing infrastructure products at home also funds Chinese companies as they develop abroad. This 'bank' has also taken a stake in the British-based bank, Barclays).

However, much of the capital inflow into the West still comes from other western countries, much of it based on intra-western mergers and acquisitions (M&As). In 2005 UNCTAD reported that cross-border M&As rose to $716 billion close to that of the merger boom year of 2000. Of course many of these mergers and acquisitions, and often privatisations too, may be intra-western, but they also serve to reduce costs (involving the laying off of domestic labour or the employment of new labour at lower rates).

FEAR AND BLACKMAIL. 'THE FAUSTIAN PACT'

Although the new globalised world was being built upon mobile capital, debates about its size are not the whole story. For the future of jobs and living standards are influenced not just by the amount of capital flight, but also by its *possibility* – indeed its increasing probability. For the tough fact is that in the 'global rush' mobile capital (and the corporations that wield it) can blackmail whole nations. The threat to any government is clear: if a corporation does not get its way – that is, if wages or the social costs to business (taxes) are too high, or if the tax-breaks or local skills are not appropriate – then capital can (and does) simply up sticks and move to more accommodating areas. This kind of blackmail – by corporations, by mega-rich individuals threatening to go into tax exile – is now routine, and is mostly conducted in secret. Sometimes it is public. And sometimes it is used to attempt to change general public policy. The Swedish government is a case in point. In the 1990s it was successfully and blatantly publicly intimidated by both Peter Wallenberg of Scania trucks, who threatened to move his headquarters unless the government brought down the budget deficit, and Bjorn Wollrath, of the insurance company Scandia, who threatened to boycott Swedish government bonds.[8]

More often, though, such threats are not articulated. They do not need to be as the effect is the same. As *Newsweek* magazine has argued, governments are induced into what it calls 'a Faustian pact': they can have access to global capital as long as they obey the imperatives of corporations, and the super-rich behind them, about the need to constantly provide capital with a low cost environment.[9] The shareholders are believed to demand it.

CORPORATIONS AND COMPANIES:
'ALIEN' STATIONS CIRCLING THE EARTH

This free movement of capital – out of the domestic economies and into the global system – is largely made possible by the great arteries of the system carrying the life-blood of big mobile money. These arteries are the corporations – what used to be called multinationals but are now more accurately termed transnationals.

The size of these transnationals is awesome.[10] And it was unsurprising that they were powerful enough to punch their way into a global future – powerful enough to override political resistance and forge the new world of global capital.[11] According to UNCTAD, in the 1990s, as the 'global rush' was getting well underway, about one third of all private productive assets in the world were under the 'common governance' of transnational corporations, and many, many more were linked to and reliant upon them. It has also been calculated that the sales of each of the top ten transnational corporations amounted to more than the GDP of 87 countries. General Motors, Ford and IBM almost outranked Britain in terms of GDP (and, of course, when calculating the GDP of Britain the productivity of British-based transnationals is counted in!).[12] Staggeringly, of the 100 largest economies in the world at the time, more than half were corporations, not countries. General Motors' sales figures were higher than the GNP of Denmark. Ford's were higher than the GNP of South Africa. Toyota's were higher than the GNP of Norway; and the top 200 firms' sales added up to more than a quarter of the world's economic activity – and have been growing ever since.[13]

These transnationals are no longer simply domestic commercial operations that increasingly operate abroad, as did many British corporations during the empire or the great American corporations during the period of the Cold War. In truth the modern transnationals should no longer be viewed-as they have been since the inception of capitalism-as commercial entities owing a loyalty to, and even deriving an identity from, their nations.

Robert Reich, as early as 1991 in his path-breaking book, *The Work of Nations*, saw clearly how, in the new corporate-run global order, corporations were unconstrained by national loyalties. To believe that the big transnationals are loyal to their countries of origin, he argued, is 'charming vestigial thinking'. He suggested that what he called 'the new organisational webs of high-value enterprise' were replacing the old core pyramids of 'high-volume enterprise' and they are reaching across the globe in such a manner that there will soon be no such organisation as an '"American" (or British or French or Japanese or West German) corporation, nor any finished good called an "American" product'.[14]

Some fifteen years later such 'charming vestigial thinking' is still prevalent. Much popular journalism still treats the big corporations as though they were national businesses. Even when it is clear that great icons of 'Britishness' or 'Englishness' are owned by foreigners (as of writing Rolls Royce (cars) is owned by BMW, HP Sauce and Lee and Perrins Worcestershire Sauce are owned by Heinz, Jaguar is owned by Tata Motors of India and Rowntree Chocolate is owned by Nestlé, and Cadburys, by Kraft) it takes time for the public to see the corporations in a new light. Can you get more 'American' than General Electric, Proctor and Gamble or IBM, all of which are now essentially stateless, with highly decentralised 'corporate webs' spreading around the globe with foreign profit centres and employees? As are the foreign-owned Doubleday, RCA, Giant Foods, Pillsbury or Goodyear? Can you get more 'British' than the ocean liner *Queen Elizabeth II* (in the 1990s owned by Norwegians) or *The Times* of London (owned by Rupert Murdoch, formerly an Australian but now a US citizen)?

Robert Reich has given life to all this by drawing a vivid picture of what – and from where – consumers are actually buying when they deal with one of the big cosmopolitan corporations:

> When an American buys a Pontiac Le Mans from General Motors... he or she engages unwittingly in an international transaction. Of the $10,000 paid to GM, about $3,000 goes to South Korea for routine

labour and assembly operations, $1,750 to Japan for advanced components (engines, electronics), $750 to West Germany for styling and design engineering, $400 to Taiwan, Singapore and Japan for small components, $250 to Britain for advertising and marketing services and about $50 to Ireland and Barbados for data processing. The rest – less than $4,000 – goes to strategists in Detroit, lawyers and bankers in New York, lobbyists in Washington...and General Motors shareholders – most of whom live in the United States, but an increasing number of whom are foreign nationals.[15]

This depiction, written at the beginning of the 1990s, is now, in the first decade of the new century, underdrawn. So diverse (and, in terms of nationality, often unknown) is their ownership that almost the only certain link between a transnational corporation and its supposed nationality is the city of its headquarters. Both in their ownership and their activities transnational corporations are now wholly independent world actors. Instead of being a part of a nation they are increasingly nations themselves – in competition with nations for resources. In their tactical operations they may live within the laws of nations, but strategically they operate on a global basis. They float above the domestic economies as majestically as alien spacecrafts circling the Earth.

They may need 'the people' below in the domestic economies – for skills, and as consumers of their services and products. But they are now autonomous beings, able to rise above their national base, bargain with their current 'host' nation as well as other nations, and shift resources from one to another.

THE BANKERS' REGIME

These transnationals produce goods, and are not, technically, financial institutions. Yet, in the 1970s and 1980s as they forged new global markets and created global networks – in what came to be called 'globalisation' – they were but a part of a deeper global conquest being established by the great American banks and finance institutions on Wall Street and their satellites in the City of London.

The great investment banks – Merrill Lynch, Morgan Stanley, Goldman Sachs, Lehman Bros., Bear Stearns, Credit Suisse – were the dynamo of the emerging global financial system, but the traditional banks – Citigroup, Bank of America, UBS, Deutsche Bank, Barclays, RBS – although depository institutions, were also adopting some of the features, the flexibility and 'innovation' of the investment houses.

Wall Street got its first big break during the Nixon presidency when in 1971 the link with gold was broken and the dollar was allowed to float against other currencies. This early example of US unilateralism ended the role of nation-states in managing currency exchanges, and meant that, as the US government controlled the one reserve currency, the dollar, US dominance over the dollar area was embedded. With the petro-dollar recycling of the mid-1970s as a kind of dry run, the 1980s, with Reagan in the White House and Paul Volcker at the Fed, brought the end of capital controls and the beginning of the era of huge flows of private finance around the non-communist world. And with the collapse of communism these flows spread wider and wider.

It was during this era that the British joined the party. As communism collapsed, and capital globalisation got seriously underway, the City of London was 'freed up' to take advantage of the new opening. Thatcher's 'big bang' of October 1986 deregulated London's financial district and paved the way for its financial success and excess; and London's newly-emboldened and enriched financiers went on to become nothing less than the most powerful interest group in the country as they established their dominance over both the Major and Blair administrations.

95

It was an era in which the City and Wall Street were getting large new amounts of money to play with. The political leaderships in London and Washington opened up new vistas for the City and Wall Street by opening up the wallets and savings of 'The High Street' and 'Main Street' to the banks. They also, through 'globalisation' allowed the City and Wall Street to start managing, and speculating in, large new pools of savings from around the world. They called it the 'liberalisation' of the global economy. Through a major change in tax law US private pension funds ballooned and created a huge new pool of money for Wall Street to use. By the turn of the century it amounted to around $2 trillion.[16]

It was the pension funds that gave the City and Wall Street huge amounts of capital to play with, yet these funds represented the savings of millions and millions of ordinary people, who indirectly (and unknowingly) take part in the stock markets. 'When the Cold War ended in 1989 there were less than one hundred million people in the world economy who owned shares through pensions. If present trends continue, then in twenty-five years time this number could expand to 2 billion'.[17] In Britain in 1957, pension funds owned 3.9 per cent of beneficial shares in British enterprises; by 1993 this had risen to 34.2 per cent.[18]

Pension funds were becoming truly enormous. In Switzerland, Denmark, Holland, the United States, Britain and other Anglophone countries private pension programmes have assets that equal 50-100 per cent of GDP. And pension funds are set to grow. Demographic changes already mean that two thirds of all people who have lived to the age of 65 are still alive today.

Pension funds were also in the vanguard of the internationalisation – and globalisation – of money. They are as mobile and footloose as other capital. And they – or rather pension fund managers – encourage corporations to promote a higher return on capital for their shareholders, a process that reinforces the search by corporations for low cost production centres. Pension money has considerable power in the stock markets of the world. Take the US mutual fund industry. One reason why it has grown from $1.1 trillion in 1990 to $14 trillion today is the growth of defined-contribution retirement savings programmes which now account for about one third of all mutual fund assets (for the giant Fidelity group, 65 per cent of its assets in 1997). As David Hale argues, 'Instead of the Japanese and Anglo-Saxon forms of capitalism encouraging different investment agendas, pension fund trustees will require managements everywhere to focus on maximising the return to corporate shareholders, not stakeholders such as corporate suppliers, main banks or employees.'[19]

Thus the desire for performance, for profits as the key economic need, can no longer simply be dismissed as the product of the greed of the super-rich; it is now emanating from those who act for the ordinary man and woman – the pensioner and future pensioner. Should pensioners ever be asked, they would obviously want – maybe even demand – that their fund manager invest their pennies in the most profitable manner, and therefore globally.

Yet in a very real sense this pension money was (is) a hostage. Although the City/Wall Street 'globalisation' regime – as this book argues – increases divisions in the West and, potentially at any rate, threatens the living standards of vast swathes of the West's population, responsible politicians (those who agree with this analysis) can do little to limit its effects. The living standards of pensioners and future pensioners – the very living standards that the political critics of financial globalisation tend to worry about most – would, paradoxically, be put at risk if the pension industry could no longer invest globally to secure the biggest immediate return. It creates a very hard choice.

Along with the pension money London's financiers and Wall Street's 'masters of the universe' were also hugely boosted by the 1980s and 1990s growth in the global bond market, which by 1997 was estimated to be $23 trillion, a large portion of which was in government bonds. Thus, the way things worked in the weird and wonderful world of global finance, as the US and UK deficits grew, so too did the market for bonds, and every loan by the banks improved the assets of the banks.

The banks now had big resources to make profits from. And the golden key to making money is 'arbitrage'. Just as the transnationals made money by exploiting differences in national conditions, so too, and on a huge scale, did (do) the financial capitalists of Wall Street. The late Professor Peter Gowan of the Global Policy Institute in London outlined how arbitrage works. The key was that there may have been a global order, but the world was not 'flat' – that is, not the same:

> The world remained broken up into radically different financial markets in radically different economic, regulatory and institutional configurations, as before; but now the big Wall Street institutions could enter and exit these markets at will and exploit differences between the conditions in each. In short, the new architecture provided enormous scope for arbitrage, exploiting the differences between these still segmented markets...Arbitrage of all kinds has thus become an enormous new field for profitable activity...'[20]

Arbitrage needs a world canvas – for it needs to be able to dip in and out of the nations of the world, making profits at each entry and exit. Above all it needs open borders and 'free trade'.

ONE 'FREE TRADE' WORLD

Preventing government – any government, national or global – from interfering with the world of trade is a major aim of the City/Wall Street order. Ever since the Bretton Woods agreement 'free trade' – including, crucially, the free movement of capital – has been a sacred cow, And any attempt to replace this 'free trade' market by thinking and acting strategically and politically about trade (usually dubbed 'protectionism') has been considered by supporters of the Wall Street global order as economically injurious, indeed one step away from war.

The formidable coalition supporting 'free trade' in the West was headed up by the leaders of the great US and European based corporations and their supporters in the political and journalistic class. Every single president since 1945 has supported the policy of free trade. As have all US trade representatives. As have all British Prime Ministers, some fervently so, like Margaret Thatcher and Tony Blair – Blair in particular saw free-trade and globalisation in almost messianic and religious terms. The George W. Bush administration's trade philosophy was standard fare – said its trade representative's office: 'free trade is good for American workers, because when American workers compete on the world stage, American workers win.'[21] Opposition to 'free trade' has not been absent in the US, but has been very much a minority sport – coming from the weakened labour movement and from marginalised political figures such as the 1992 independent presidential candidate, Ross Perot, and the conservative columnist and two-time presidential candidate, Pat Buchanan.

In postwar Europe 'free trade' has also been the orthodoxy – led by the powerful German export industry and by the global financial interests in the City of London. Although some

European political leaders – particularly in France – often flirted with a measured protectionism (latterly called 'economic nationalism') none would ever seriously and frontally challenge the idea of 'free trade'. There was a serious protectionist movement in Britain in the early decades of the twentieth-century (mainly gathered around the imperial preference concepts of Joseph Chamberlain and the Tory party) but since 1945 'free trade' has become a near-national dogma.

As 'free trade' critic Ravi Batra commented in the early 1990s 'the idea [of free trade] is now embraced as economic theology around the world'.[22] Its powerful grip on the minds of western intellectuals is reinforced by a particular view of history – principally the belief that interwar 'protectionism' was a cause of the 1929 financial crash, the interwar depression and then the war itself. The fact that the Smoot-Hawley Tariff Act – demonised in the West during the 1990s – followed, not preceded, the great Wall Street crash, and the fact that US unemployment rose from 3.2 per cent to 8.7 per cent long before the consequences of the tariffs were felt, has little effect upon this powerfully embedded received opinion.

The accepted wisdom about trade was that protected markets hinder economic growth. Much of this comes from the British experience in the nineteenth century when the flourishing protected imperial market system was mistaken for 'free trade'. So well propagated was the benign character of 'free trade' and the malign nature of 'protectionism', that the fact that the United States protected its home market for most of the period of its spectacular economic growth during the nineteenth century is often overlooked – as is the role of 'protectionism' in the postwar Japanese economic miracle, and the rise in the 1980s and 1990s of the newly industrialised 'tiger' economies of Asia, particularly Taiwan and South Korea.

During the global postwar boom years 'free traders' relied on the powerful theory of comparative advantage which dictated that two countries forming a trading partnership (that is a single market without trade restrictions) should specialise in the production of goods and services in which they have an absolute or comparative advantage, and that together they are more productive than they are separately. Yet this theory has always rested on the proposition that companies are part of a country's economy – that is, capital is essentially national, rooted in place. As John Gray noted 'in the classical theory of free trade capital is immobile', and he quoted David Ricardo as arguing that 'every man...has a disinclination to quit the country of his birth...[and this] checks the emigration of capital'.[23] But in the age of footloose, mobile capital, the world is very different. Gray himself is one of a number of theoreticians who believe that 'both in theory and practice the effect of global capital mobility is to nullify the Ricardian doctrine of comparative advantage', and according to Martin and Schuman, 'Ricardo's basic postulate [comparative cost advantage]...is now completely out of date.'[24]

THE HOLLOWING OUT OF THE WEST: THE LOSER POPULATIONS

Yet, theoretical disputes about 'free trade' aside, the overwhelming new characteristic of the financially-driven global trading order was the sheer scale of change – and its suddenness. Its size and speed had no historical precedent; and in comparison the previous bursts of globalism, of capital moving beyond the confines of its home in Northwest Europe (through western colonialism and the paced migration into North America), looked paltry. This time there was the 'China factor' and the 'India factor' – the 'six billion factor'. The emerging City/Wall Street world order, as seen from the early 1990s through the turn of the millennium, was of a world economy that virtually overnight embraced an additional 4-6.5 billion people, a quantum leap not seen before in economic history.

In the early 1990s the late magnate and British political activist James Goldsmith became a prescient and eloquent critic of this new world – and like other magnates he was often more incisive than the academics in the field. In a series of slim volumes he drew the attention of anyone who would listen to the fact that with the end of the Cold War four billion people had suddenly entered the world economy, and that these newcomers would 'offer their labour for a tiny fraction of the pay earned by workers in the developed world'. And in a none-too-veiled shaft at his fellow global super-rich he argued that 'it must surely be a mistake to adopt an economic policy which makes you rich if you eliminate your national workforce and transfer production abroad, and which bankrupts you if you continue to employ your own people.'[25] Goldsmith had sounded an early warning about what was later to become known as the 'hollowing out' of the West.

The writer, Edward Luttwak, was another early critic of the new global order and its 'free trade' fundamentalist assumptions. In his 1998 book *Turbo Capitalism*, Luttwak conceded that 'free trade' theory may be more efficient globally – producing the same goods by replacing expensive workers with cheap workers – but adds that 'in affluent countries…now increasingly afflicted with the return to poverty in the most vulnerable fraction of their population, it is not necessarily a good idea to enrich the kingdom by turning some of its subjects into paupers'. And he criticised the 'free trade' economists for 'leaving the scene' whenever compensation schemes for the unemployed and low-waged – which are 'never implemented' – are mentioned.[26]

These early critics of this 'hollowing out' process were reacting to the loss of manufacturing jobs. But the western political establishment could see off these critics because it was only the lower skilled sections of the populations of the West that were being affected – either by being replaced or by facing stagnant wages and fewer benefits.

It was also an article of faith that the West's losers would never outnumber the West's winners. And this hopeful prognosis was adhered to stubbornly as with each passing year the real job situation worsened throughout the West. In Britain real job losses were hidden by the growth of a low wage economy further reinforced by the invasion of massive growth in the numbers of cheap foreign labour. In Europe the losses showed up in higher unemployment numbers throughout the larger continental economies; in the United States the losses were hidden by the creation of less well-paying jobs without benefits, and by very odd survey methods of employment.[27]

And all the time the West's 'free traders' continued to serve up large doses of fatalism. They argued that western nation-states could do very little about the loss of jobs, and that the lost jobs would not be returning. (In 2008, John McCain, then Republican presidential candidate, made this clear as part of his 'straight speaking' campaign.) Some put the loss of jobs and growing inequality in the West down to technology, and not to global capital and trade. Robert Lawrence of Harvard University, in a scholarly defence of free trade, made the argument that 'technological changes and changes in management practices, rather than trade, are the source of growing inequality'.[28]

All that the politicians could do, they argued, was to try and relocate the loser populations in new jobs – in 'services', although where these jobs were coming from, and what kind of jobs they would be, was not normally spelt out in any detail.

The general policy of the 'free-market' governments was to prepare their populations for the tough new world of the global economy by encouraging new 'skills' – 'training and skills' – so that both the loser populations and the new generations could compete with the Asian competition. (Although the rhetoric remained, long gone were the old-fashioned, Victorian-utopian ideas of creating an 'educated population'.) This task of maintaining and enhancing the skills of local populations was conveniently not assigned to global capital itself, but rather to the western public sector. British Prime Minister Tony Blair once went so far as to argue that such 'skilling' and 'reskilling' was nothing less than the 'greatest single priority' of government in the global economy. (Global capital would of course play its part in this process – as a kind of umpire, picking and choosing between nation-states as to which ones have performed best, and rewarding the winners by investing, for a short period, in their local populations.)

Some market enthusiasts though disagreed with 'reskilling' being a proper function of the state. Pressures on public expenditure – and the need to maintain a low tax regime – would limit the amount of resources that could be expended. And in a sign of the tenor of the 'free market' times, the following suggestion was seriously made: 'market forces will do this automatically…for instance, if workers with low levels of education in OECD countries saw their wages fall to levels equal to those of workers in developing countries, they would have a tremendous incentive to invest [personally] in education'.[29]

BUT, WHAT ABOUT SERVICES?

But low-skilled manufacturing loss was to be only half of the story. As the new century got underway it was becoming clear that rising Asia was offering more than sectoral competition – it was making a general and strategic challenge to the West.

The complacent view that China and India could never be able to compete with the West in the service sector, particularly financial services, and in hi-tech, died hard. Consider this, from a study commissioned by the OECD: 'some processes and technologies can be moved internationally...the most significant sources of higher productivity in the developed countries – the superior levels of skills and the tacit knowledge of the workforce – cannot move abroad.'[30]

But this complacency slowly began to lose its hold as it became clear that Asians were quite capable of competing across the board. As Australian writer-diplomat Gregory Clark could argue, 'for East Asia the western myth of free trade is a good joke', and that 'today, in Asia at least, some [countries] are equal or superior to the West in work ethic and ability to absorb technological skills'.[31] And it was also becoming apparent that Chinese men and women might well be able to do banking! Over time, they could also do virtually anything else that westerners could do – and at a lower cost.

Yet, the pioneering geopolitical thinker Michael Lind was something of a lone voice when he argued, in 1995, in a passage which deserves quotation at length, that:

Within a generation, the burgeoning third world population will contain not only billions of unskilled workers, but hundreds of millions of scientists, engineers, architects, and other professionals willing and able to do world class work for a fraction of the payment their American counterparts expect. The free trade liberals hope that a high wage, high skilled America need fear nothing from a low wage, low skill Third World. They have no answer, however, to the prospect – indeed, the probability – of ever-increasing low wage, high skill competition from abroad. In these circumstances, neither better worker training nor investment in US infrastructure will suffice...It is difficult to resist the conclusion that civilised social market capitalism and unrestricted global free trade are inherently incompatible.[32]

By the turn of the century it was also becoming apparent that China in particular was not going to play the free-trade game – and fully open up its own market to the West's service sector; and that ultimately it would be able to, and seek to, serve its own growing market – and other markets – through its own financial service sector. There were lessons here for the financial services sectors of the City of London and Wall Street, as well as the hi-tech engineering industry of Germany and the computer industry of California.

THE WEST LOSES WEALTH

By the late 1990s the writing was more than etched upon the wall. It was carved into it. The world, in Der Speigel analyst Gabor Steingart's words had 'seen the integration of millions of Asians but the disintegration of millions more westerners'.[33] 'Globalisation' was not going away; indeed was only in its early stages. It was not a difficult call to predict that China was likely to retain a huge competitive advantage over the West as China's billions – its large pool of reserve labour – were still massing on the edges of the coastal areas waiting to enter the labour market. Nor was it difficult to see a real danger for the West in the fact that China's increasingly skilled urban population could easily begin to move into the service sectors.

Yet, western financial capital still had (still has) the prospect ahead of it of a deep, rich seam of cheap labour and cheap costs to mine. In sum, there were many more western jobs to lose and much more western wealth to be transferred. And as for the politics of it all, China remained an enigma. The predominant western view was that integration in the global economy meant integration into the West, including into its political and cultural system. It would take time, but China would be westernised. So, confronting the Chinese political, and geopolitical, question could best be left until later. And, anyway, after 2001, radical Islam was the greater problem.

By century's turn it was clear that the essentials of financial globalisation would continue on into the new century. As the prescient William Greider, after writing his long critique of the global system, could argue in the early 1990s: 'the [western] elites of media, business, academia and politics have already made up their mind on...the global economic system – and [about] defending it from occasional attacks from angry, injured citizens'.[34] Incredibly, almost two decades later, following the great crash, and with the damage of hollowing out all around them, most of these elites still had their minds made up, though less determinedly.

DEBT SAVES THE DAY

There was to be no popular rebellion in the West against 'globalisation' and global capital and the slow but remorseless hollowing out of the West – certainly not so in Britain. There were numerous violent protests on the streets outside some big global governance meetings, and these were played up by the media. But during the 1990s not one serious western political party ran on an anti-free trade platform. And there was to be no equivalent of the early twentieth century British Conservatives who adopted 'protectionism' as their platform and campaigned on the issue. Today's equivalent – a political party in a major country openly advocating economic protectionism as a way of maintaining jobs and living standards – has simply not yet appeared.

The fact was that during this early phase of the new global order the bulk of the American and European populations suffered no loss of living standards. By the late 1990s the West was in the middle of boom times. It was a phoney, unsustainable, boom and it was interrupted by a sharpish recession at the turn of the century, but the boom was to return with even greater intensity until it burst in 2007.

It was a party fuelled by cheap prices from Asia. These Asian-driven low costs were a godsend. For cheap Chinese men and cheap Chinese women – working away in low-standard sweatshops in greater Shanghai – provided a low inflationary global environment in which westerners could live well beyond their means. It was this Chinese-led global low inflationary environment that allowed the West's leaders to keep their peoples' living standards up temporarily by creating massive private – and public – debt. Western workers – middle class and blue collar – may have found their pay packets shrinking, but their credit cards came to the rescue. Low inflation meant low interest rates, and low interest rates meant low sub-prime mortgage rates and easy money to buy houses; and as the house prices rocketed in value 'globalisation's losers', now feeling the 'wealth effect', could run up their low interest credit cards and car loans.

For 'globalisation's losers' – those out of work, or those in low-paying work, or those in part-time work, or those in work but with few benefits, or those in work with two or three low-paying jobs – low inflation did them the dubious and dangerous favour of increasing their credit card and their mortgage debt. It was a 'favour' that was to be called in with a vengeance when in 2007 the housing boom, fuelled by low inflation and low interest rates, suddenly came to an end – with all the damage inflicted by repossessions and loss of confidence. And it did them another favour. It provided the growing legions of the working poor with the wonderful world of Wal-Mart: low prices for most everything for the house, low prices to suit low wage packets.

For the West's smaller number of winners this Asian-induced low inflationary world was also a real boon. Inflation has always been a deadly enemy of the super-rich – the global rentier class of wealth holders. As the columnist Bob Herbert saw it 'Alan Greenspan's purpose is to protect the assets of the very wealthy. The value of those assets erodes with every up-tick in the rate of inflation.'[35] The assets of the less wealthy are also devalued by inflation, and for the middle classes, and those on fixed incomes, inflation can also be deadly. Roger Bootle in *The Death of Inflation*, a pioneering book on the consequences of what he believes may be the coming age of zero inflation (or even deflation), has argued that a zero inflation economy – as long as it doesn't tip over into serious deflation – can be generally beneficial, but is specifically good news for shares, the engine room propelling the growing wealth of the rentier super-rich. He argues that zero inflation 'would imply a higher level of real equity prices at each stage even if the level of bond yields and the rating of equity risk were the same'.[36]

In any event the free market revolution of the 1980s and the City/Wall Street world order that followed it were built upon the foundations of low inflation – indeed upon an anti-inflationary zeal. During the decades of the social democratic (post-Second World War) era the West lived with inflation. Anyone born after the 1920s has known a world in which prices rise every year. Yet suddenly counter-inflation became a political if not a populist issue, gathering a degree of public support. Post-Second World War German opinion was always hostile to inflation, indeed obsessed by it, because of the Nazi experience in the 1930s. But a broader anti-inflation constituency throughout the West emerged following the oil price crisis of the 1970s when unusually high price rises led to serious social unrest and political instability (this was particularly marked in Europe, where radical political change, including the possibility of 'Euro-communist' governments, was only just averted).

As a reaction to this inflationary dislocation the anti-inflation campaign – led in the early 1980s by Federal Reserve chairman Paul Volcker and politicians Reagan and Thatcher – took hold. And since then the goal of low or zero inflation has become orthodoxy, and any policy that can be attacked as 'inflationary' stands little chance of a serious hearing. The arguments against an inflationary society remain strong, even for social democrats, but so too do the arguments against deflation.

Yet the Wall Street global capitalist orthodoxy still appears prepared to take risks for one course, but not the other. And so fixated on low or zero inflation have the western economies become that those who question the orthodoxy of low inflation are few and they tend to argue their corner rather tentatively. Yet they are beginning to emerge. The late 1990s centre-left political regimes in Germany and France tolerated somewhat higher levels of inflation than their predecessors. Even amongst economists some heads appeared above the parapet. James Tobin of Yale University argued that a small amount of inflation helps 'grease the wheels' of the economy.[37] The highly-experienced former British Treasury minister Joel Barnett suggested that 'it seems untenable to put inflation on a unique pedestal', and that it should be considered alongside other objectives such as 'growth and exchange-rate management'.[38]

The western consensus was, and still is, a long way from replacing anti-inflation as dogma with inflation as technique – as merely a mechanism to help secure economic prosperity and social and political goals. And we are still a very long way indeed from understanding that the large internal western markets (in the US and the European Union) can, partly because of their still relatively low exposure to trade, easily tolerate rather higher inflation levels than those which prevailed in the 1990s.

HOLLOWING OUT: 'SELLING THE ROPE'

So, before the great crash the new global system, with the London financiers at its heart, appeared to be working for almost everyone. The winners were making money; and the losers were saved by low prices and the credit boom.

In London, capital was boss, and the world its playground. And Asia remained the new frontier. Big western capital had gone global and was beginning to make prodigious profits and the prospect was of much more to come. The constraints on the City and Wall Street doing exactly what they wanted had been removed. Governments were weakened by 'globalisation'; the trade unions were dead men walking; rampant individualism reigned, and 'greed was good'.

What's more, although serious trade imbalances with China were beginning to show up, China was helping the West by recycling its huge surplus into US government securities – thus allowing the Americans and their British and other economic satellites in the West to party some more, and continue to live beyond their means.

And all the time the dark cloud on the horizon – the growing pauperisation of the loser populations in the West – could be ignored. The good news, at least for London's City and for western capital, was that the high costs of doing business – and the expensive western jobs and high taxes that caused these high costs – could now be jettisoned without any comeback from the impotent western governments and peoples. So began the historic hollowing out of the West. And in Britain this hollowing out was even more deadly, for it was more fulsome. The major EU economies at least kept some kind of balance between services and manufacturing, and between finance and industry.

In a previous era Vladimir Lenin could catch a sort of truth when he asserted that 'the capitalists will sell us the rope with which we will hang them'. Today's communists, the much more peaceable leaders of rising China, are, almost a century later, still being sold the rope.

CHAPTER THREE

FATAL ATTRACTION

BLAIR, THE CITY, AND GLOBAL AMERICANA

NEW LABOUR JOINS WALL STREET

1997 was an important year for the global super-rich and the economic system of free market neoliberalism. In May Tony Blair became British Prime Minister, and a few months earlier in January Bill Clinton had taken the oath of office, for a second term, as President of the United States. These two new world leaders – both of them left-of-centre politicians – had sought to draw a line under the Reagan/Thatcher revolution and had set out on a new course – which they called the 'third way'. And they had the wind at their backs. In 'Anglo-America' the 'free market' years were becoming controversial, increasingly seen as the 'decade of greed'; and pollsters were finding that publics were more willing to contemplate paying higher taxes for better services.

Yet, both Blair and Clinton were to turn out to be very good news for the big players in the City of London and on Wall

Street – and for the 'globalisation game' that was the financiers' ticket to unheard-of riches. The youthful public school radical from Islington and the dirt poor boy from Arkansas had come to power at a time when some of the structural economic changes – that would open the way to the full flow of 'global capital' – had already been secured. Yet they both had a clear opportunity to limit, and even reverse, the process. Yet, neither Blair nor Clinton showed even the remotest inclination to do so. Instead, with the super-rich riding off into the 'globalisation' gold rush, Blair and Clinton, and the western political class to which they gave leadership, decided to ride shotgun.

Clinton's opportunity came first. He was elected in 1992 during a sharp recession when a major milestone in globalisation, the North Atlantic Free Trade Association (NAFTA), was top of the American agenda. It was an election in which Ross Perot had achieved a record-breaking 20 per cent of the presidential vote as a third party candidate dedicated to ending the free-trade agreement. Perot built his whole campaign around the 'hollowing out' argument, famously, and presciently, declaring that once NAFTA was in being 'you will hear a giant sucking sound' as jobs are 'sucked out' of the US.

The anti-NAFTA campaign had many supporters in the Democratic party, and with presidential leadership, NAFTA could easily have been emasculated, if not completely abandoned.

But Clinton had made his bargain with corporate America and, as president, both introduced, and became a stalwart defender, of NAFTA and the next great burst of 'globalisation'. Also, Clinton's abandonment of any serious attempt to bring in a comprehensive health service to America – which would inevitably have created an incentive for corporations to pay taxes at home instead of investing abroad – meant that Clinton was even abandoning the attempt to 'shape globalisation' to

American needs. Rather, Americans would, in effect, be told to 'accept it', shape up and compete in the world.

The truth was that Clinton had, long before becoming president, embraced US big business and their linked agendas of market reform (deregulated markets and low taxes) and economic globalisation. His first term assured corporate America that their revolution was safe in his hands. And he made clear there would be no going back when in 1995, as president, he reappointed the intellectual godfather of the revolution, the extreme pro-market, Randian, economist Alan Greenspan, to yet another term at the Federal Reserve.

Tony Blair, who came into office some five years after Clinton, also had a window of opportunity through which to bring a halt to the rampant globalisation then already underway. Blair had taken over from Prime Minister John Major, and the big question was: Would his New Labour administration weaken the Thatcherite imperative of ever greater marketisation and privatisation, ever greater financialisation, ever greater integration into the minimal governance global economy, ever greater trade with low cost Asia – in other words, ever greater globalisation. Would the New Labour government, true to much of its left-of-centre general election rhetoric, usher in a true change of direction?

As it happens there was a new strategic direction, a new, more left-of-centre, route open to the new government should it have decided to take it during that post-election summer and autumn of 1997. It would have involved some serious adjustments, but it was open to New Labour to embark upon a full-hearted commitment to Europe and to the Europeanisation of Britain – with all that would have entailed for British economic policy, for household debt levels, for the state's relationship with the market and, importantly, for a future more modest and sustainable role for both the City of London, and indeed for British foreign policy. Such a course would have ended up with a country less dependent upon the global economy, less leveraged, less imbalanced than the Wall Street model which it was later destined to follow.

When Blair took over in Downing Street, the City of London was already the major player in British politics and was seeing its future in Thatcherite terms as inexorably global. Yet, at the same time, a majority of City opinion was in favour of the country joining the eurozone. It saw the City as being able to combine global influence with a future as the financial centre of the European hinterland (like Wall Street to the USA). And Blair's New Labour, ever sensitive to City opinion, had fought the election on a pro-euro platform. He had pledged a referendum, and would probably have won one – particularly if it had been held fairly soon into the new regime.

Yet Blair lost his nerve. Had he gone for it, and won the referendum, then Britain, melded into the European economic scene, would, inevitably, been set on a course in which British economic policy would become Europeanised. Blair himself was later, whilst still Prime Minister, to lament this grave error of judgement. Speaking in Ghent, only a few miles from Bruges (where Margaret Thatcher had famously opened her campaign against further British integration in the EU) he bluntly stated that 'Britain's hesitation over Europe was one of my country's greatest miscalculations of the postwar years…Britain's destiny is to be a leading partner in Europe'.[1]

Britain's 'Global Destiny'
From his earliest days as Leader of the Labour party Blair had, like Clinton, made his pact with Britain's corporate business community. Blair had proved his market credentials when, before

becoming Prime Minister, he formally scuppered socialism (and social democracy) by rewriting the Labour party constitution. He later went on to become a true disciple of 'free market' themes and big corporate business, and his attraction to the American economic model, the Wall Street model, weakened his desire to commit Britain to a European future. As British prime minister he would regularly lecture the 'sclerotic' social capitalists in Europe about the virtues of the American model.

Blair gave his considerable rhetorical gifts and public relations expertise to the cause of 'globalisation'. He argued to anyone who would listen that economic globalisation was 'inevitable', and could not, Canute-like, be turned back; rather, it needed to be 'accepted', and adapted to. Both Blair and Clinton tended to avoid making the case for globalisation solely by reference to economics, profits and cheap consumer goods. They sought instead to create domestic support for globalisation by stressing its positive moral content. Clinton saw it as a great progressive force unleashed to save humanity. For him it was 'world without walls' – 'the only sustainable world; and globalisation was 'an explosion of democracy and diversity within democracy'.[2] Blair regularly made the same kind of case – and even some months after leaving office he was setting globalisation in a slightly mystical, moralistic and religious, context during a speech entitled 'Faith and Globalisation'.[3]

By the mid-1990s 'globalisation' was the rage amongst western opinion formers – an army of academics, economists, journalists and pundits also saw 'globalisation' as a positive force in the world. A strong moral case was consistently proffered with many believing that 'one world', fuelled by the communications revolution, mass tourism, and growing trade, was finally in the making. The leading British academic of globalisation, the sociologist Anthony Giddens (who influenced much of Blair's thinking) saw globalisation in these terms – as a truly transformative agency. 'We have a chance' he said in 2001, 'to take over where the twentieth century failed, and a key project for us is to drag the history of the 21st century away from that of the 20th.'[4] Amongst western journalists *New York Times* columnist Thomas Friedman also took a lead in seeing globalisation as progress – with its 'inexorable integration of markets and nation-states'.

Economists and economic commentators tended to take a narrower, more precise, perspective – seeing globalisation through economic, rather than political and moral, eyes. Indeed, as Ralston Saul argued, they saw 'civilisation as a whole through an economic prism'.[5] And, for a time, there was a near unanimity of opinion amongst economists on the subject – in globalisation's favour.

There was also a very strong correlation between 'free market' supporters and advocates of 'the global market' and globalisation. Leading 'free-market' economists Martin Wolf and Jagdish Bhagwati saw globalisation as both inevitable and good for aggregate global living standards and good, too, for western prosperity (after suitable 'reforms' and adjustments, particularly in Europe). The overwhelming consensus was that the West needed to adjust to the new global reality and that the forces that opposed such adjustment, protectionists and pro-welfare politicians, would, by interfering in the workings of the global market, end up causing even lower living standards. Even Joseph Stiglitz, a trenchant and bitter critic of prevailing orthodoxies, only went as far as criticising how globalisation was managed – in part under his tenure as Chairman of President Clinton's Council of Economic Advisors. His primary criticism appeared to be that the US used globalisation to advance her own interests. Looking back in 2003 he suggested that 'we had no vision of the kind of globalised world we wanted, and we weren't sensitive enough about how what we wanted would be viewed by the rest of the world'.[6] Stiglitz developed a powerful critique of a world of economic globalisation without global economic governance – but with global governance still an impossible dream, his readers were left not quite knowing whether he believed that the whole post-cold war project of economic globalisation, and its free trade component, had been wrong in principle.

THE WASHINGTON CONSENSUS

In the real world of moneymaking, globalisation was much more than a nice theory – for it was the practical method of opening markets, deregulating commerce and finance, and raising profits worldwide. For Wall Street and the City (and Washington) it was heady stuff. The West's finance capitalists were setting rules and norms for the whole world – their own rules and norms.

These rules were to be set out in what became known, appropriately enough, as 'the Washington Consensus'. This 'consensus', unveiled in 1989, was a ten-point programme setting out what western bankers wanted from indebted Latin American countries. It amounted to a regime that would be imposed on countries which fell into debt, a regime that took advantage of distress in order to impose ideological market solutions.

A precursor to this 'Washington Consensus' was the Structural Adjustment Programs (SAPs) of the World Bank instituted following the oil crisis of 1973. These programmes ended the passive (and short-term) loan role of the international financial authorities, substituting a more direct and controlling approach which restructured the market of debtor countries to open them to foreign investment and to promote exports in order to repay the debt. In 2006, W. Easterly, a World Bank official and supporter of these SAPs, reflected that 'the over-ambitious reforms of shock therapy and structural adjustment were the flight of Icarus for the World Bank and the IMF. Aiming for the sun, they instead descended into a sea of failure'.[7]

Icarus regularly fell to earth in Africa where there is considerable evidence that these SAPs were major failures, for the fact was that those countries that implemented the most SAPs either had neutral or negative growth. The same was true for the countries of the former Soviet Union who agreed to SAPs. The World Bank funded a number of SAP projects as well that caused considerable environmental damage in Brazil and Indonesia.[8]

The bottom line was clear: the West, through international organisations, sought to draw the less-developed countries into an integrated market-based global economic system which it would lead and control and which would be run according to its economic precepts. These 'emerging' economies were forced to rise and fall with the West; and were not allowed to develop indigenous markets, the key to long-term economic growth and success. The idea was 'one world, one market' – but 'one world, one market' run from Wall Street.

John Williamson, who drew up the blue-print for the 'Washington Consensus', later argued that he never intended his plans to work out the way they did but they implied and then led to 'policies like capital account liberalization, monetarism, supply-side economics, or a minimal state…getting the state out of welfare provision and income distribution.' (And he added that, for his part, he now hoped, in 2002, that 'we can all enjoy its wake'.)[9]

The 'Washington Consensus' regime was to be tried out in a major way in the Asian crisis in the late 1990s. Malaysians, Thais and Indonesians were all to get the treatment – what one critic called 'redemption' through 'economic and social self-flagellation'. In other words, in return for being bailed out countries would need to introduce a full 'neoliberal' 'reform programme' based upon 'opening' markets and 'liberalising' economies. And in the process the way would be cleared for western economic and financial elites to do business and to make money. And to continue to make money – as through this global 'reform programme' the whole world would turn into one giant Main Street serviced by Wall Street.

As the Asian countries dutifully 'reformed', then western hedge-fund money swept in, and western hedge-fund money swept out; and left in its wake a devastated and debilitated terrain.

However, not all was plain sailing for western mobile capital. Malaysia rebelled. Its maverick and articulate leader Mahathir bin Mohamad broke ranks and re-established capital controls and trade protection. It was a rare act of defiance; and was treated in the West as an act bordering on sacrilege. His heresy unleashed 'a tidal wave of contemptuous condemnations' from around the world 'writing off Malaysia as a basket case and [Prime Minister] Mahathir as mentally unstable'.[10] Mahathir returned the fire with sarcasm. He declared the Malaysians to be 'stupid' but asked the market liberals to 'leave us to do the wrong things we want to do'.[11] Of course, the Malaysian leader did not believe that the rebellious course he had set was wrong, and soon Malaysia was doing well even by the economic indicators used by the western-dominated international organisations. George Soros could predict that 'if Malaysia looks good in comparison to its neighbours, the policy may easily find imitators.'[12]

Intriguingly, during the Asian crisis, China was not one of the countries that western market 'neoliberals' could dictate to – in part because the Asian giant's currency remained pegged. In the world of 'free trade' China was the proverbial 'elephant in the room'. For the Asian giant has been growing by doing all the things 'free traders' were telling them not to. It had a pegged currency, it has capital controls, and it has refused to 'liberalise' many key sectors of its economy. China, as it emerged, was going to work to its own, not the West's, rules and agenda.

Surviving The Challenges

Yet, the finance-led globalised order was to display considerable resilience. It ultimately survived the Asian crisis. And it also survived three other serious challenges – the 1998 bailout of the mammoth hedge fund LTCM, the Russian default crisis of 1998 and, most importantly, the 2000-1 bursting of the dot.com bubble.

On 10th March 2000 the dot.com's main index NASDAQ peaked at 5132, more than double its value of a year before. Its rise had been accompanied by extravagant claims about how the California-based technological 'new economy' was a wholly new phenomenon – a 'new paradigm' – that was going to rewrite the rules of economics and change the world. Yet, on 10th March the prick was administered and for the rest of the year and into 2001 the dot.com bubble burst. The IT revolution had run its course – an important new technology but not one that was going to sustain the global economy.

Yet Wall Street did recover. The Dow Jones bottomed out at 7,286.27 on 9th October 2002 and it was then onwards and upwards again. By the end of 2003 it had reached 10,000 (and by January 2006 it broke through the 11,000 barrier).

ANGLO-AMERICAN CAPITALISM RULES

In this climate the 'masters of the universe' in the City and Wall Street, and their supporters and enablers amongst the politicians in London and Washington, could be forgiven for believing that American financial genius when married to globalisation was an unstoppable combination. And they could be forgiven, too, for believing that the global economic order that had been fashioned in their image, had been tested and had survived, was now unstoppable.

Thus economic globalisation and Americanisation (of the Wall Street business variety) became one. And supporters of this Global-Americana were not bashful. It was good for the world as America stood for capitalism and democracy. It was a compelling vision. Robert Samuelson has described its outlines when he argued that 'after the Cold War, global capitalism offered a powerful vision of world – prosperity and, ultimately, democracy. Multinational companies and investors would pour technology and capital into poorer regions, creating a transnational mass market of middle class consumers who would drive Toyotas, watch CNN, eat Big Macs – and, incidentally, demand more freedom.'[13] This was Wall Street's economic counterpart to Francis Fukuyama's famous political and cultural vision of one world in which 'western liberal-democracy' reigned as 'the end-state of the historical process'. For both Fukuyama and the Wall Street visionaries, although they would not say so openly, something like America (or more like America than anywhere else) was what the 'end of history' would look like. (Although Fukuyama was, much later, to say that he had in mind the EU rather than the USA).

No wonder that in that spring of 2003 the British-born neoconservative Harvard historian Niall Ferguson – who, in a long line of British writers was making a name for himself on the American right – could be moved to declare that the United States had the world at its feet, and that the republic was not only an imperial power but was *good* as well. For many elite Britons US power was a vicarious experience, lending to the sons and grandsons of empire a glow of imperial nostalgia. 'The reality,' Ferguson argued, 'is that the United States has – whether it admits it or not – taken up some kind of global burden... And just like the British empire before it, the American empire unfailingly acts in the name of liberty, even when its own self-interest is manifestly uppermost.'[14]

AMERICAN-STYLE CAPITALISM AND THE MINIMAL STATE

'Liberty' was to be advanced by the market. Indeed the market was American global capitalism's great universalist idea. And this belief in the market developed a visceral quality, a militant conviction that a brave new world was being born. It amounted to a certainty of religious dimensions. Indeed, it became a secular religion. William Greider argued that 'the utopian vision of the marketplace offers...an enthralling religion. Many intelligent people have come to worship these market principles, like a spiritual code that will resolve all the larger questions for us, social and moral and otherwise'. And Edward Luttwak described the orthodox monetarism at the heart of the new capitalism as having 'like all religions a supreme god – hard money – and a devil, inflation'.[15]

This new religion was 'Gekko's world' view. It was the vision too of Ayn Rand and her student, Alan Greenspan, of Keith Joseph and his student, Margaret Thatcher, and of a host of academic economists who followed in their footsteps and were beginning to populate the think tanks. They called themselves 'neoliberals'. And it was this 'neoliberal' world which in the mid-1990s Bill Clinton and Tony Blair had signed on to renew.

This religion of the market made few conversions amongst the West's masses, but it did enthral and entrance many of the West's elites – and not just the opinion formers in the big corporate media outlets and at the annual World Economic Forum in Davos. For it even lit fires in the minds of the men in the staid world of officialdom and policymaking. True believers could be found not just in the White House and Downing Street, but also in the great international institutions like the IMF, the World Bank, the WTO, and even in key parts of the European Commission.

These true believers saw the market – the global market – as being nothing less than an expression of American freedom itself. 'Freedom' was what America stood for, and this 'freedom' could only be guaranteed by the 'free market' because, so the argument ran, entry to the market – unlike to the state – was essentially voluntary, and this ensured the liberty of the individual. Thus in the mind of the believer the ethical idea of the sovereign individual fighting a battle for liberty translates easily into a more prosaic and materialistic economic individualism.

In this way 'free markets' became one of the security and foreign policy goals of the West. For instance, NATO was no longer to continue as a defence pact but would instead become a military alliance dedicated to change, to remaking the world on western lines. It would, according to Colin Powell, testifying before the Senate Foreign Relations Committee in 2002, 'promote democracy, the rule of law, and promote free markets and peace throughout Eurasia.' For the first time NATO possessed a specifically economic agenda. In a big win for the market revolutionaries, 'free markets' were to be backed up by bayonets, another example of Wall Street's objectives signed on to by the Pentagon.

Thus the market developed a moral and political content, for it was not only by far the best way of allocating resources, it was also virtuous – both efficient and good. And the roots of its goodness lay in its protection of the individual – the sovereign individual. Thus, the market and individualism became one. The market was as American as apple pie.

And, for the true believers, if the market was an essential engine for individual freedom then, by contrast, 'the state' –

in all its guises, federal, state and local – was a serious threat. Thus was 'the state' demonised as 'un-American'.

A flavour of the near-religious fervour – indeed vehemence – behind much of this contemporary anti-state impulse is provided by this intriguing passage from a 1980s new right propagandist:

> The New Right must propagandise mercilessly against the state. It must stress unremittingly the enduring moral bankruptcy of government. It must constantly compare the burden borne by the taxpayer, to fill the government trough from which the interest groups are feeding with the benefits received by the swine at the trough…we must underscore relentlessly to our un-organised fellow taxpayers their direct interest in the unremitting attenuation of the state.[16]

Re-Writing the History of the State

A religion – even a secular one – needs a favourable history. And the winners, of course, write the history books. So global capitalism's victory over socialism – and the market's victory over the state – became the occasion for such a new history. In this new history the state took a veritable drubbing. The state came to be associated with limiting freedom, with oppression, even with persecution. Socially it induced sclerosis and politically it automatically centralised and bureaucratised. And most cutting of all, the state was an expropriator – of property and, worse still, of taxes. In such an environment the positive idea of the state as helping to forward pleasing images such as enabling, helping and opening up democracy and rights could not get house room in the government of western opinion.

The gravamen of the new globalist history was the view that raw capitalism – the Anglo-American model of free market, minimal government capitalism – is the world's great success story. This well-entrenched thesis was built around the extraordinary economic success of the western world, and in particular, in the twentieth century, of the United States. The received wisdom had it that the US (and to a lesser extent Britain), the two great examples of high, free-market Victorian capitalism, uniquely ushered in the industrialism (and later the commercialism) that made the West the predominant civilisation of the world; and that through the good graces of global capitalism this huge success story will be repeated worldwide.

This history of private and market triumph completely undervalues the role of the state – the public sector – in the success story. Britain in Victorian times was by no means the raw capitalist society of myth. Its great free-trade, free-enterprise, free-market system, it should never be forgotten, was built upon the back of a worldwide empire – an empire sustained by government and its agencies in the military and civil services.

Likewise, the history of the economic development of the US is hardly a story of undiluted capitalism. That great engine of American capitalism, the continent-wide internal market, was the result of government – the geopolitical expansion of the US 'feds' through military conquest. The British Royal Navy the military arm of a foreign state – but a state nonetheless – ensured the protection of the US capitalist economy during the formative decades of the nineteenth century. And American *state* craft helped defeat US capitalism's great enemy – the imperial protectionist system of the old European colonialists. And of course it was the state – the US state (with its *public sector* military, diplomatic and political arms) – that, by prevailing over the Soviet Union and its command economy, preserved western capitalism and gave global capitalism its lift-off. In the face of such overwhelming evidence it is impossible not to see the history of the US as the history of capital and state working together.

Of course, one of the primary reasons for US capitalism's great leap forward in the twentieth century had nothing at all to do with its economic system, and everything to do with politics and the international game of states. Unlike its competitors in Europe, the US was relatively unscathed by the two world wars – the great conflicts that destroyed the European empires and set back the European nations for over half a century. It was the wisdom of politicians, the leaders of the US state – primarily General George C. Marshall and President Harry Truman – who, by pouring public sector money into the regeneration of the European economies, provided an expanded market and represented the single greatest boon to US corporations in their history, and made them the global players they are today.

The clash of political ideologies and state interests that was the Cold War also helped US capital and capitalism to make their mark. The post-1945 bipolar global political framework, with the US as the leader of the West, helped US capital to penetrate global markets; and the military confrontation with Russia helped create a huge market for American business – the big business of defence procurement and the small businesses it generated.

State and capital worked together in another way too. The American success story in the twentieth century – 'the American century' – is too often attributed to the economic dynamism unleashed by bustling entrepreneurs, tough-minded robber barons and, later, the efficient management of global American corporations. Yet this is only half the story. For there was a political dimension too – a governmental genius was at work as well. To create, and then to bind together this geographically and socially diverse, continent-wide federation was no small achievement. It was a political document, the US constitution (liberal, flexible, adaptable) that helped keep a fractured nation together in a single economy. It was the political genius of President Abe Lincoln and his supporters, who, by keeping the union together, preserved a single internal market – perhaps the most important of all the reasons for the later blooming of the US free-market system.

Rewriting – that is, talking down – the history of the state, and of government itself, often involved depicting the state as simply a phase of history. In an echo of historical Marxist determinism, supporters of the market see 'stateless' global capitalism as the end-point of history. 'Prehistory' was the history of nation-states; these nation-states may have been progressive in their way (they did, after all, serve to organise democracy and introduce concepts such as rights and accountability), but they were riddled with contradictions, and were unstable. This instability has given way to a new, stable system of globalisation. Globalisation is historically inevitable and represents 'the end of history'.

Britain's Minimal State Visionaries

Global capitalism is a godsend to such anti-statists. By weakening the hold of the 'interfering' and 'expropriating' nation-states, state power is automatically marginalised. In the great clash between market and state, power thus swings decisively towards the market.

In an unusual alliance with libertarians, big corporate capital saw all too clearly the advantages of a weakened state: the unhindered mobility of capital (so those who invest can punish those states and societies that do not encourage sufficiently acceptable returns), low or zero inflation (in order to ensure low interest rates and thus boost the prices of shares and bonds), low taxation (so that the returns from capital remain high), and 'flexible labour markets' (in order to keep costs, particularly social costs, low and therefore raise profits and the return on shares).

Most serious proponents of the 'free market', however, did not waste their time arguing for the abolition of the state – the campaign objective was more limited: it was to shrink the state, to reduce it further and further until it became a 'minimum state'. Adam Smith's aphorism that governments should do only what cannot be done in the market – or what cannot be done by individuals – became the central idea; and that injunction is now interpreted as limiting government to a small number of 'absolutely necessary' functions, leaving the rest to the market. And in our own time the libertarian philosopher Robert Nozick in his famous 1974 work *Anarchy, State and Utopia* has argued that these 'necessary functions' are very few, including defending the country and enforcing contracts.[17]

In practical terms, minimalists want the state to withdraw not only from economic life through lower and lower levels of taxation, through privatisation and deregulation, but also from the four main welfare services: education, housing, medical care and insurance for income in retirement. As Arthur Seldon declared, 'the vision of capitalism is the prospect of minimal government. It excludes the state, or its agencies, from the production of goods and services...This vision thus requires the eventual withdrawal by government from most of its accumulated activities.'[18]

In Britain during the late 1960s and 1970s advocates of such a minimal state began to put policy flesh on these bones – with some very practical proposals. Clustered around the Institute for Economic Affairs in London, and led by Arthur Seldon, they pioneered many of the ideas that, in the 1980s, conservative politicians began to introduce to a wider public. B. G. West wrote *Education: A Framework for Choice* in 1967, F G. Pennance wrote

Choice in Housing in 1968 and Charles Hanson wrote *Welfare before the Welfare State* in 1972. Later, in 1981 Arthur Seldon wrote *Whither the Welfare State*, and in 1985 David Green wrote *Working Class Patients and the Medical Establishment*.[19]

Some extremist minimalisers even wanted the government to withdraw from law and order functions, even from controlling the currency. Another school of thought amongst them argued that although government should be largely withdrawn from economic life, it should nonetheless be used to liberate 'the poor' by a gift of money to enable them to acquire the means to exercise choice and to take responsibility for their health, education and old age provision. This was the plan behind Seldon's provocative 1977 pamphlet 'Charge' in which he advocated charging everybody for all kinds of erstwhile services. It amounted to using the state in a sort of enabling function – and it assumed that the 'poor' would remain a relatively small section of society.[20]

The Minimal State Project

This vision of minimal government – that governments should do only what cannot be done in the market, no matter the success or failure of said market – was, until the 1990s, just that: a vision, a distant goal. Certainly the late 1970s and 1980s saw a major tilt in the US political world (and consequently in Britain) away from social democracy and towards the market. Ronald Reagan and Margaret Thatcher gave political leadership to a conservative movement that used simple and populist terminology to get its anti-state case across. Politically powerful sound bites – such as 'get government off the backs of the people' and 'government is the problem, not the solution' – skilfully associated the state with bureaucracy, officialdom, 'red tape', inflexibility and, most witheringly of all compulsion.

Thatcher and Reagan also led an *intellectual* revival. Unlike many of the more centrist presidents and prime ministers who preceded them – most of whom who took a managerial view of leadership – they saw the long-term power of ideas. They used their offices to introduce to a wider public a host of classical liberal theorists who, marginalised during the postwar social democratic consensus, finally came into their own. Ludwig von Mises, Frederick von Hayek, Milton Friedman and Karl Popper, if not exactly becoming household names, did become the new gurus of the age (taking over from John Maynard Keynes and John Kenneth Galbraith).

A new generation of free-market 'conservative' intellectual leaders emerged in the think tanks and universities – economists such as George Stigler and George Gilder, sociologists such as Charles Murray, public choice theorists such as Mancur Olsen and J. M. Buchanan, and philosophers such as the former socialist Robert Nozick. In Britain, in an intriguing parallel eruption, theorists such as Arthur Seldon, Madsen Pirie, Anthony Flew and William Letwin, economists such as Samuel Brittan, Peter Bauer, W. H. Hutt, Patrick Minford, Gordon Tullock and Alan Walters gave Thatcherism a vibrant intellectual underpinning. These Reaganite and Thatcherite intellectuals wrote with verve and confidence, and with a sense that they were part of a new tide of ideas. And indeed they were. It was a period in which the governing social democratic consensus was seemingly breaking down, and the left's response to these insurgent thinkers seemed tired and bereft of fresh thinking.

One intriguing aspect of this renaissance of the 'free-market' was the number of former socialists and social democrats who began to break cover and support market solutions and a reduced role for the state. The initial issue for many of them was non-economic – they supported the defence build-up during the Cold War and rejected what they considered to be their fellow socialists' growing anti-western attitudes. But this was a time when the social democratic consensus – built by Roosevelt in the USA and the Attlee government in Britain – was seemingly failing on the economic front. Big government welfare had not solved the American inner-city problems which were literally going up in flames; and in Britain many of the country's economic problems were put down to the 'over-mighty' public sector – with its powerful 'over-mighty' public sector unions. It was an environment tailor-made for a systematic critique of the mainstream left's assumptions, not just about defence and NATO, but also about the role of the state and the market. And the list of 'left' public intellectuals who moved across to associate themselves with many aspects of the broad Reaganite and Thatcherite 'revolution' was considerable. It included Robert Nozick, Peter Berger, Norman Podhoretz, Paul Johnson, Evan Luard, Irving Kristol and – less so – Sidney Hook, Daniel Bell, New York Senator Daniel Patrick Moynihan and European Commission President Roy Jenkins.

A new, somewhat misleading, political term took hold to describe these former left-of-centre thinkers. They were called 'neoconservatives'. And, although they varied in their approach to social and economic policy, they succeeded in playing a major role in the 1980s in moving the centre of political gravity towards a more market-based world.

Two magazines became the home for this transatlantic generation of 'neocons' – as they came to be dubbed by the British and American media. In the US the American Jewish Committee's *Commentary* magazine – edited by the redoubtable Norman Podhoretz – not only focused on winning the Cold War but also, month after month, systematically attacked the social and economic agenda of the American 'liberals', including what they considered to be the overblown US welfare state. In Britain, *Encounter* magazine, led by the equally redoubtable Melvyn Lasky, did not set itself against social democracy quite so strongly (in the early 1980s it supported the social democrats' political exit from the increasingly leftist Labour Party), but it did provide a platform for serious arguments from Thatcherite economists and social scientists.

As well as these social democratic allies, the anti-statist market revolution secured support from another, somewhat surprising, quarter. Traditionalist conservatives – numerous in Britain and Europe, less numerous in the US – were always suspicious of individualism and consumerism, tended to be neutral about the power and reach of the state, and saw the market as destructive of traditional values and ways of life. Yet a number of these British 'paleo-conservative' thinkers – such people as Roger Scruton, John Casey and Peregrine Worsthorne – were swept up in the market revolution and rode shotgun with the free-market conservatives who if they saw real contradictions between the new, raw, global capitalism and Tory tradition rarely spoke up about it. (Worsthorne, a former editor of *The Sunday Telegraph*, was an exception: he was later to resolve the 'conservative contradiction' in favour of the state, and the European Union state at that!) During the 1980s *The Spectator* magazine began to straddle both this traditional conservatism (often with a very 'county' twist) and the new, more 'neocon', American meritocratic capitalist agenda. In the 1990s, under the Canadian mogul Conrad Black's proprietorship (and Frank and Boris Johnson's editorship), it essentially threw its lot in with both Wall Street minimal state capitalism and the 'neocon' idea of an American empire.

Lower and Lower Taxes

The intellectual case that sustained the market revolution was both systematic and, in an era witnessing the collapse of socialism, appealing. But the war for the market was really won on the more practical, and populist, terrain of taxes. Market politicians noticed something that the socialists and social democrats of the 1970s and 80s had ignored. One of the most pronounced social changes since the 1950s was the hugely increased number of people paying taxes. Low, and even average, wage earners were not really in the income tax brackets in any numbers until well into the 1960s. But as they, and the growing army of women in the workforce, flooded onto the labour market in the 1970s the anti-tax appeal of conservative politicians achieved a previously unknown resonance.

But it was the world of business that harboured the real resentments against the high-tax regimes of governments. And as globalisation developed, tax competition by governments, anxious to keep and attract global capital, assumed serious proportions. The name of the game was to keep companies sweet. So, from the late 1980s onwards the tax rates for companies fell throughout the world. It has been estimated that between 1991 and 1995 Europe's largest engineering conglomerate, Siemens (including its subsidiaries), was able to reduce its worldwide taxes from 50 per cent of its profits to 20 per cent. This new power relationship between corporation and nation-state was summed up neatly in 1996 by the reported comments of Daimler Benz chief Jurgen Schremp, who announced that he did not expect his company to pay any more taxes on profits in Germany, and told parliamentarians bluntly that 'you won't be getting any more from us'. Schremp summed up the clear, new, market capitalist idea that companies, not the state or society, have the ultimate right to ownership of money and resources – it is 'our' money, not 'yours'.[21]

So successful, so total, was this victory of business over government on the issue of taxes that by the turn of the century not a single politician in the West was even trying to associate him or her self with a regime of higher taxes. Gone too was the mid-1990s rhetoric – tried out for a bit by 'left-of-centre' politicians like Tony Blair, Bill Clinton and Gordon Brown – about how public services should come first even if it meant slightly higher tax rates. New Labour's public sector spending did involve tax increases – the so called 'stealth' taxes – but business pressure for lower taxes continued into the new century, and was only contained so long as growing amounts of tax money was being spent on the private sector through the growth of outsourcing.

In 2006, towards the end of his premiership, at the CBI conference in London, prime minister Tony Blair was still acting as a cheerleader for the low tax regime desired by business; and he was selling it by appealing to the well-worn formulae: We must, he argued, 'keep our tax system here competitive...with the new economies as well as the more traditional economies against which we compete.'[22] In other words, 'globalisation', which we must 'accept', demanded it. It was still difficult for any aspiring politician to say otherwise.

Minimum Welfare

Of all the projects of the minimum state, reducing welfare was the most difficult to sell. Most of the leading continental European nations, including Britain, had serious welfare states that, though reformable at the margins, were (are) so entrenched that any dismantling – particularly in health provision – would lead to political revolt. In Britain, the Thatcherite governments from 1979 to 1997 were constantly straining to make 'neoliberal' reforms to the welfare state, but in the end made no real structural changes, and Margaret Thatcher herself argued that the NHS was safe in her hands. New Labour added an interesting twist to the welfare argument: the idea was that the universal welfare state (which it supported) and an increasingly free – and global – market went together. Thus, a market economy and a marketised society would increase economic growth out of which welfare could be sustained. In a specific example of such thinking New Labour would give the City of London free reign (a regulatory 'light touch') and in return the burgeoning finance sector would contribute to the tax revenues. It was, though, a strategy that was completely dependent on boom times continuing. What would happen – both to government spending and to tax revenues – in a bust was hardly contemplated.

In the push for a minimum welfare state market fundamentalists argued on two levels. On the moral and ideological level they continued to assert that there was simply more dignity in providing for yourself than relying on 'handouts' from the state. Those relying on welfare become supplicants. This argument was spelt out clearly by a leading free-market theorist, who argued that the welfare state turned 'paying customers in the market' into 'importunate supplicants in the political process'. It represented a clear contrast with the traditional social democratic view, set out by Will Hutton, that 'the vitality of the welfare state is a badge of the healthy society; it is a symbol of our capacity to act together morally, to share and to recognise the mutuality of rights and obligations that underpins all human association'.[23]

Yet at the heart of the minimalist view of welfare was the question of efficiency and cost. Minimalists fervently believed that the four main services of the welfare state – education, medical care, housing and pension income in retirement –

could be provided much better by the private sector – through insurance and charging – than by the state through taxation. Indeed taxes are the real point here. Capitalism used to be able to sustain a welfare state through taxes on businesses – the so-called 'social costs'. Yet with the growth of demand in some welfare areas – such as health and pensions – the same level of service can only be provided by increasing taxes, and in the absence of punitive taxes on consumers, that means raising these 'social costs' on businesses. And the minimalist reformers of the welfare state argued (argue) that such social costs are no longer sustainable – certainly not at the level operating in continental Europe in the so-called 'European social model'. Unless prices or employment take the strain, then by eating into profits they threaten share performance.

In the 1990s, with global finance's minimalist-state campaign against Europe's welfare capitalist system in full swing, British and American supporters of the new capitalism regularly focused on late-twentieth century France as the prime example of the unsustainability of this 'high social cost' model. In 1997, under a headline 'Will Europe Face Up to Coming Reality', the American-owned *International Herald Tribune* investigated a French decorating company, BDM, in the Normandy town of Bray-et-Lu and found that 'employing a worker at a gross monthly salary of 10,111 francs ($1,702) ends up costing a total of 15,306 francs, or an additional 51%'. The paper revealed that these 'social costs' go towards family allowances, low-cost housing loans, unemployment insurance, work accident compensation, pensions and professional training, and even towards reducing the social security budget; and the clear implication emerged that in the Anglo-American market model much of this kind of provision cannot be expected to be funded by businesses.[24]

In the future minimalist state envisaged by neoliberals there would be a trade-off between welfare and unemployment. If social costs remained high then companies would simply lay off workers in order to keep profit margins high. A leading French banker argued in 1997 that 'if costs in America were the same as in France...perhaps 25% of Americans would be unemployed.'[25] Of course, in such a regime the minimal state would not be able to afford much in the way of unemployment benefits. So low-remunerated – very low-remunerated – part-time work for millions of people might be the answer. And in the late 1990s, at least in Anglo-America, in Britain and in the USA, widespread low wage, part-time work was indeed becoming the answer, and the grim reality.

Minimal Regulation (of the Banks Too!)

This minimal state would also be a minimal regulator. The minimalist revolutionaries based their deregulation agenda on the need to 'free up' business from the 'dead hand' of state regulation – a freedom that would lead, in financial services as much as elsewhere, to higher levels of innovation and productivity – and profits. One of the leading voices behind the campaign for deregulation was the American Nobel laureate and minimal-statist George Stigler who argued that regulation too often ended up favouring the regulated through cosy deals between the private and public sectors and led business into the inadequacies and corruptions of the political process.[26]

In the Anglo-American world in the 1990s the deregulators won the battle. In both Britain and the US the so-called 'light regulatory touch' ruled the day particularly in the banking and financial sector. And it was this 'light touch' that, in essence, opened the door to the massive overleveraging that, over a decade later, was to lead to financial catastrophe. So powerful was this push for deregulation that, even after 2007 – even after the banking failures, and even after the fallout from Enron and WorldCom – the voices of the minimalists could still be heard from Wall Street to the European Commission urging a new round of deregulation – this time in the labour market. And even as late as October 2007, when it was clear that something had gone seriously wrong with the financial sector, Hector Sants of Britain's financial regulator, the FSA, was still committing the agency to a 'principles-based' regulatory, seen by many as meaning a 'light touch' regime.[27]

A key demand of the minimalists had been a deregulation of the labour market – in order to create a 'flexible' workforce. And the key point of the 'flexibility' advocates was the need to establish a legal ability of corporations to hire and fire at will so they could respond quickly to changing profit margins caused by changes in demand. Some extreme supporters of these 'reforms' saw an endgame in which corporations not governments would determine the labour market, and would be free not just to hire and fire but to employ a whole range of labour – full-time, part-time, hourly, full benefits, no benefits, and so on. 'Reforming' the labour market – making it more 'flexible' – was a policy propounded far beyond Wall Street, most prominently by the European Commission.

If the power of a religion can be measured in adversity, then the religion of the market – and its central doctrine of deregulation – was strong indeed. For, even by 2008, when it was clear that deregulation had been a major contributor to bringing low the western financial system, and with it the living standards of the West, the true believers were still believing. The God of the market was still very much in his heaven – and was receiving souls. In the US, Democratic presidential candidate Barack Obama may have edged towards blasphemy when he argued, in a speech in March 2008 to the Cooper Union in New York, that 'a free market was never meant to be a free license to take whatever you can get, however you can get it'. But, at the very same time, and in the midst of the 2008 banking crisis, the then Treasury Secretary Hank Paulson was still in a deregulating mood. He brought forward proposals to further deregulate some SEC functions, and still refused to force hedge funds and banks to hold capital proportionate to the risks they were taking.[27]

Even the new Labour administration in Australia was, some months into the banking crisis, still buying into the necessity to deregulate. On 26th February 2008 Lindsay Tanner, the incoming 'Minister of Finance and *Deregulation*', no less, accused Australia's Conservatives of 'letting the deregulation agenda in this country lie dormant for most of their eleven years in office' and believed that 'relieving businesses and consumers of the burden of inappropriate, ineffective or unnecessary regulation will build Australia's productive capacity...'[28]

Globalism and the Minimalist Breakthrough

Market extremists and 'minimalists' did not, though, have it all their own way. Although possessed of a considerable *esprit de corps*, and a sense of being on the winning side, for most of the 1990s they were ascending rather than ascendant. They were never fully able to dislodge the mechanisms of social democracy – the state, the welfare society, or the mixed economy. Even under Margaret Thatcher public spending remained high (although it was increasingly spent by the private sector, through contracting and outsourcing), indeed at the end of her term, and that of her successor John Major, public spending was as high as that bequeathed by Labour in 1979 – and, as has been noted earlier Mrs Thatcher was enjoined to declare that 'the National Health Service is safe in my hands' (as it was). In the US, President Ronald Reagan presided over a huge budget deficit, and, no matter the rhetoric, also saw public spending remain high as a percentage of the US economy.

What is more, as the 1980s progressed it became clear that the European social model was still intact – as was the Japanese model – both representing something of a beacon for those who wanted a more cooperative public-private (and manager-labour) system, and an active, involved, and enabling, welfare state.

Even the marked growth of privatisation, which was particularly dramatic in late 1980s and early 1990s Britain, did not fully marginalise the state. It weakened the public sector by depriving it of the assets of ownership. Yet at the same time the newly-privatised companies paid taxes to the state, and when they reduced their workforces the state was still there to pick up the social security bill. By the end of the free-market 1980s most western states were, intriguingly, taking as much in taxes as they had at the beginning of the decade; and of course the state was still a power in the land by virtue of the huge military budgets – and the payrolls it still deployed.

It was not privatisation, but rather 'globalisation', that made possible the real breakthrough for the minimalists. Although privatisation deprived the state of assets, the state could still tax them. 'Globalisation', or the mobility of capital, meant that assets could move. During the 1990s – almost overnight, as it were – capital, freed from nation, began to establish a marked ascendancy over the state. Capital mobility, or the threat of mobility, allowed the market, for the first time, to punish and reward nation-states according to its requirements. It weakened the state *vis-à-vis* the market more effectively than any proselytising or privatising by Thatcher or Reagan and their army of market intellectuals.

And a Minimal International Political Order

The key prize for minimalists always lay beyond the water's edge. For in order to succeed they needed to weaken government. Their very best possible world was one single global order comprising no government at all. But they would settle for a world in which a host of states were all competing with each other for capital's favour.

A type of global governance existed during the post-World War Two Bretton Woods regime, when the world financial system – with its fixed exchange rates, regulated financial markets and currency risks borne by the public sector – provided some form of political, and thus democratic, authority as a balance against markets. This era ended when, in response to the pressures of the early 1970s, the US government decided to dump Bretton Woods; during the following two decades exchange controls were abolished, domestic limitations on cross-market access to finance were removed and controls on credit were scrapped. During the 1980s, amidst a quantum leap in speculative financial flows, financial risk was privatised and a global market in monetary instruments emerged. And in the 1990s this flow became a tide.

Supporters of capital globalisation, though, sought a world order that is far more minimalist than Bretton Woods – and one that is also far slimmer than the *ad hoc* internationalism of the earlier era. And, until the crash, they were getting it. With the state weakened at the national level, their aim was to ensure that the it could not regroup at the global or regional level – that the world order remained fragmented into a host of states, none of them too big to establish political authority over global finance, and all of them competing with each other for capital's favour.

It remained at once both a bold and a dangerous vision. It sought a world in which international relations – between nation-states – will, in all but a rudimentary, residual sense, cease to exist. In its place we will inhabit what John Burton, way back in 1972, described as a 'world society'. And 'the units of the system [of this 'World Society'] will not be billiard ball states but can be corporations, overlapping ethnic groups, classes or even individuals'.[29] There would, of course, be no off-setting global government. And thus no global democracy. In fact, no democracy at all.

The American business economist Joel Kotkin also caught the flavour of this modern global vision when he introduced the idea of global tribes – he talked of the British, the Japanese, the Jews, the Chinese and the Indians – establishing global networks 'beyond the confines of national or regional borders'. And, as for global tribes, so too for global corporate units and global individuals – our super-rich. In this idealised global society there is no government. The state is not minimal; it is non-existent. In short, no one is willing to regulate the casino.

As things stood at the turn of the twenty-first century, to believe in a future for this 'global society' – a society without effective global government and therefore effective regulation – was certainly not an unrealistic dream. Nor was it completely over the top for neocons to believe in the goal behind the vision: that the only serious form of government in this 'global society' would be that of the one superpower, the government of the United States of America. And with the US government as the only state with any power in the world, business and the dollar would rule.

In the late 1990s the newly-elected British New Labour government, and particularly Tony Blair, understandably believed that a Wall-Street led and American-dominated 'global society' (with minimal government and welfare) was indeed the wave of the future – a future that any government needed to accommodate to.

BRITAIN, BLAIR AND AMERICAN POWER

Over time Blair did more than accommodate to American power; he became a true believer – a believer, that is, in a future globalised world dominated not just by American economic leadership and military power but also by American liberal values. Blair's view of the world was classic Fukuyama – a future predicted a decade earlier just after the fall of communism by Francis Fukuyama in his book *The End of History*.[30] Fukuyama has subsequently changed his mind, virtually denouncing his own earlier analysis, but the British Prime Minister remained a true believer. Blair's strengthening worldview was to be reinforced after September 11th when the United States decided to develop a forward military posture and invade both Afghanistan and Iraq. Not only was American-led economic globalisation going to change the world, but also America was going to police this world through military power and the huge Pentagon budget. Wall Street and Washington (finance, Congress and people) were finally as one.

Blair was determined to get in on this act as were large sections of British elite opinion – in politics, journalism and business. Britain, under Blair, had become a neoconservative nation – as was revealed when parliament itself gave support to Blair over the invasion of Iraq. New Labour's support for 'global free markets', neoliberal economics, Wall Street economics and freeing up the City of London, needs to be seen in this broader political, geopolitical and ideological context.

The British Elites and Iraq

On the morning of September 11th 2001, just as the planes were about to explode into the twin towers of the World Trade Center, Britain's Prime Minister, Tony Blair, was in the southern English seaside town of Brighton preparing to address the Trades Union

Congress. He was about to deliver a watershed speech which would open the campaign for Britain's joining eurozone. It was to be a campaign that would finally resolve the country's long, awkward relationship with Europe, and help Britain to fulfill what Blair had called her 'destiny' in Europe.

But just before Blair set off from his hotel to the conference centre, the chairman, Bill Morris of the TUC, announced that a plane had struck the World Trade Center in New York and that Blair might be delayed. In the event, Blair cancelled his speech, returned to London, appeared on television to announce that Britain would stand 'shoulder to shoulder' with the Americans; and, fatefully, also put Britain's European campaign on hold.

It was a campaign that was not to be revived – for the atrocity in New York profoundly altered New Labour's whole approach to Britain's future role in the world. In Washington the reaction to 9/11 allowed a stalled Bush administration to develop a new, and aggressive, foreign policy. The influential, but previously-contained, neoconservatives clustered around the American Enterprise Institute and the Pentagon ready to seize their moment. The 'Statement of Principles' of the Project For a New American Century (signed by Dick Cheney, Donald Rumsfeld, Paul Wolfowitz, Elliot Abrams, Norman Podhoretz and others in 1997) was dusted off, and for a time became the handbook of President Bush himself. It was highly critical of Clinton's foreign policy, sought a new defence buildup, and called for a new global vision based upon 'military strength and moral clarity.' This political takeover of the US government led to an aggressive unilateralism – including an extraordinary bid for global supremacy which included the invasion of Iraq, a Middle Eastern nation that did not threaten the United States.[31]

The raw assertion of US power had real implications for Britain, for it gave the Prime Minister a subordinate but special, role in which Downing Street as junior partner would be a global advocate of US policy. It was a role perfectly suited to Tony Blair and to many in the British intelligence services and military. After a half-century of global decline – with America now off-balance and seeking a sidekick – here was a rare and real chance to place Britain at something near the centre of world events. And Blair took it.

For some time before 9/11 the British Prime Minister had seen himself as a global, rather than European, player – a posture made more credible when Britain stood alongside the Americans rather than as one of many amongst the Europeans. The Kosovo crisis had been a turning point for Blair. Here were America and NATO, without a UN mandate, laying down the rules for the post-cold war world. And he went even further, seeing himself, as a remaker of the world in tandem with Washington. In a strange, somewhat discordant, speech in Chicago in April 1999, during the air war over Kosovo, he went so far as to outline a new international doctrine. He declared that 'Bismarck had been wrong' to say that 'the Balkans was not worth the bones of a single Pomeranian Grenadier'; he singled out Slobodan Milosovic and Saddam Hussein as 'dangerous men'; and, more importantly, he attempted to overthrow the basic UN doctrine of 'non-interference' in other country's affairs in favour of a new idea of 'regime change'. It amounted to a call for a new world order in which western intervention and 'regime change', on western terms and for western reasons, was now acceptable.[32] For Blair, America (with Britain at her side) would lead the charge – in what was nothing less than a rationale for a new updated liberal – or neoliberal – imperialism. With 9/11 as its galvanising force, this new western assertiveness ended in the invasion of Iraq.

Only days after 9/11, with the wind in his sails, Tony Blair returned to this theme at the 2001 Labour Party Conference when he displayed a relish for the coming business of, in his own words, 're-ordering the world'.[33] The formula – which was being worked up in Washington as Blair spoke – was clear: the mission would be couched in liberal tones – 'bringing democracy' – but Washington (with London in tow) was going to 're-order' the world on western terms. And it was going to do so by a combination of western military power (to be put on show in the invasion of Iraq) and the ongoing westernising process of globalisation.

On the ground in Britain, though, the public remained hostile to the prospect of an Iraqi invasion. At the time, and for years afterwards, the British public could simply not understand why Blair had sided with Bush and joined in the fateful 2003 invasion. It was, after all, a bizarre, slightly unreal, decision for a Labour Prime Minister to take. All the opinion polls showed decisive majorities against the invasion, an opposition made manifest by a massive march and rally in central London; the main European partners were against it, the intelligence was not clear-cut; and the UN could not be squared. Yet, in the face of all this, Britain's left-of-centre progressive-minded premier went ahead and committed British troops to the American-led war.

Blair thus nailed his colours, and with them his legacy, to the mast of a conservative Christian Evangelical Republican President. Former Cabinet Minister Chris Patten could write that 'history will judge Blair as a defender of Bush's agenda above Britain's'.[34] It was a coruscating verdict. Blair had taken the 'special relationship' to a new level.

Invasion: The 'Special Relationship' In Action

By March of 2003 the whole British political class – Tony Blair and his cabinet, the majority of New Labour MPs, and the vast majority of Conservative MPs – took the fateful decision to sign up with George W. Bush and invade Iraq. And the British did more than just support the Americans in the UN, they also sent troops – the largest contingent after the US. And following the invasion the British, for the first time since imperial days, took over the military occupation of Arab lands (in the south of the country around Basra). Indeed, to the late twentieth-century British mind the very idea of British troops occupying a heartland Arab nation after having toppled its government would have seemed an act of blatant imperialism, a return to interwar mentalities, and wildly far-fetched.

The Iraq war was a 'defining moment' for Britain's relationship with the Arab world, but also for Britain's 'special relationship' with the United States of America. It was a rare and decisive either/or moment in the Anglo-American relationship. The Americans badly wanted British support, but were mainly interested in full-hearted diplomatic support in the run up to war. At no time did they insist upon Britain's sending large numbers of troops. The American Defence Secretary, Donald Rumsfeld had always had misgivings about the need for British – or any other – troops to support 'Operation Iraqi Freedom', and on the eve of war went as far as publicly stating that they were not needed.[35] Again on the eve of war, with Blair's continued premiership in some doubt, the President himself made a last minute friendly offer to let him off the hook. Bush suggested that Britain need not send troops should it lead to the Blair government falling. Yet even given these opportunities, Blair, in an act of breathtaking eagerness to please, sent the troops anyway.

Britain had some clear choice before it in the run-up to war. It could have sided with France and Germany and stood aside – a course which would have put at risk the country's relations with Washington. But Washington would have tolerated – some in the Pentagon would have preferred – Britain's simply supporting the US politically and diplomatically without sending troops (as Harold Wilson did during the Vietnam war despite pressure by President Johnson to go further). The Americans would also have accepted a British decision to send only a very small, token, non-war-fighting force. That Blair decided to go the 'Full Monty' of an invasion and occupying force showed his utter determination both to please Washington and to play a global role. From Downing Street's perspective, once the decision to support the US politically had been taken, then the damage with public opinion had been done. There was nothing to lose from sending significant numbers of troops, and much to gain in the scramble for reconstruction contracts in the occupation phase.

The spring invasion of Iraq in 2003 was the culmination of an extraordinary phase of Downing Street-directed British foreign policy in which the British PM and some of the higher echelons of the intelligence and military establishment not only took momentous decisions but also took real risks with Britain's geopolitical position in Europe. By siding with invasion and occupation Blair took Britain into the potentially momentous 'clash of civilizations' as he alienated Britain from Arab and broader Islamic opinion perhaps for generations. He also divided Europe by breaking with its two senior members, France and Germany. Whilst Germany and France led the opposition to the war, New Labour PM Tony Blair was joined by conservative Prime Minister Jose Maria Aznar of Spain and ultraconservative Prime Minister Silvio Berlusconi of Italy, and the leaders of a host of Eastern European candidate countries, in supporting the Bush White House.

Why?

In the months following Blair's fateful decision, large numbers of British people – both within and without the Westminster village – were asking themselves one question about their Prime Minister. Why did he do it? Why did Tony Blair take his country to war in Iraq when no apparent immediate British national interest was involved? Why did he put at risk his relationships with his fellow EU leaders? And why – a question asked after the revelations that Saddam had no useable weapons of mass destruction – was he prepared to deploy exaggerations and half-truths in order to do it?

Yet, as the dust settled following the invasion, the answers to these questions, although never stated, became progressively clear. It became obvious that, from Blair's Downing Street's perspective, once George W. Bush had made up his mind to go to war, the British Prime Minister – any British Prime Minister – had no alternative but to support him. In sum, Britain's 'special relationship' demanded it; when an American president goes to war, and asks for Britain's support, such support is normally given.

This time too it was automatically given although there were new factors. There was a split in the western camp. In all previous great global crises – during the Korean war, the Cuban missile crisis, the Vietnam war (when western differences were kept low profile), the first Gulf war and air war over Serbia – the West had been politically united. But over Iraq the major continental powers not only opposed Washington, they campaigned against her in the UN. Blair was forced to choose between America and Europe. But for Blair it was not a difficult or agonising choice. From Downing Street, the western geopolitical power correlation looked clear. Washington was still the stronger of the two western contestants. Bush was adamant and committed, would go to war anyway. And although an intriguing (particularly so with Russia as an ally) new security core was developing between Germany and France, it was in its infancy.

Martin Kettle, a commentator with good connections to Downing Street suggested that Blair supported the invasion, and the postwar US policy in Iraq, for quite straightforward reasons – he argued bluntly that Blair believes that 'what happens in the US defines the limits of the possible for Britain.'[36] According to this Blairite thesis, it was simply 'impossible' not to support the USA.

It was difficult though to sell such a raw idea of subordination to the British public – so a more palatable posture was struck. It had been outlined decades before by Sir Pierson Dixon, Britain's UN Ambassador at the time of the Suez Affair. He had argued ruefully that 'if we cannot entirely change American policy, then we must, it seems to me, resign ourselves to a role as counselor and moderator.' And he added that: 'It is difficult for us, after centuries of leading others, to resign ourselves to the position of allowing another and greater power to lead us.'[37] Half a century later, Tony Blair might not have put it exactly that way; but Britain as America's 'counselor' and 'moderator' was a role he had openly advocated as Prime Minister.

So, as the tension rose in the run up to invasion, the official British line became what the well-informed columnist and author Peter Riddell came to describe as a 'hug them close' strategy – the idea being that by 'hugging them close' Britain would secure greater influence with the Americans than by breaking with them.[38] Blair put out the word that his closeness to Washington was calculated: that in return for his support Bush was agreeing to support a revival of the stalled Middle East 'peace plan' which would secure a long-term Israeli-Palestinian agreement. Four years later, as Blair, again, lent his support to the US in the Israeli-Lebanon-Hizbollah war, he was still allowing it to be known that he was imminently set to get Washington's 'green light' for a new 'peace initiative'.

Tony Blair: American Conservative

Tony Blair's support for the United States in the Iraq war was simply the tip of an iceberg, a symptom of a much deeper commitment. For, by the time of his second term as premier he had basically adopted the whole Bush-American worldview. So much so that, like Margaret Thatcher before him, he came to identify with the US more than he did with Britain. On the 18th September 2005 the British media was abuzz with details of an intriguing and revealing comment by Blair about the New Orleans hurricane tragedy – seen at the time as a turning point in the standing of President George W. Bush. The BBC reported that Blair had told Rupert Murdoch that BBC reporting of the New Orleans hurricane tragedy had been 'full of hate at America and gloating about our [sic] troubles.'[39] The use of 'our' was highly revealing. It revealed not just where the British Prime Minister's true affection, if not loyalty, may have lain, but also that he saw the Bush Presidency and his premiership as conjoined, as one political unit with common friends and common enemies.

Blair's identification with the USA had, though, a considerable prime ministerial pedigree. Winston Churchill identified with America – after all he had an American mother. So too did Margaret Thatcher who had a close personal and ideological relationship with President Ronald Reagan. Yet, the Americanisation of Tony Blair was less easy to understand. Blair had no similar blood or ideological ties. His ties were with the Presidency: he was very close to *both* liberal-moderate Bill Clinton and conservative cum neoconservative George W. Bush. It was his relationship with the Texan that was somewhat odd, and may reveal that Blair's love affair was, at root, all about power – the power and celebrity of the American Presidency.

Yet, over time, the love affair with the Presidency turned ideological. Having begun his premiership in 1997 ostensibly as a European social democrat – with an 'ideology' roughly similar to Gerhard Schroeder's SPD, and slightly to the left of Clinton's 'third way' Democrats – he later morphed into a full, red-blooded American radical conservative. Blair, breathtakingly, signed on to each of the three components of Bush's brand of conservatism – global neoliberal 'free-market' economics, global political rule from Washington, and Christian-based 'family values'. It was an ideological package that took him into an unlikely political stable – one populated by Wall Street, the Pentagon and the Christian Right and, in Europe, by Berlusconi of Italy and Jose Marie Aznar of Spain. Blair was the lone supposed European social democrat in such company.

Blair became the chief European advocate of the need to accept 'globalisation'. When used by politicians, 'accepting globalisation' was code for the need to accept a business-driven, cost-cutting agenda. To survive in the global economy – so ran the argument – nation-states need to ensure that their costs, that is wages and taxes, are competitive. Labour markets should also be competitive – that is, flexible enough to make it easy to 'hire and fire'. In the age of globalisation, if governments don't so oblige, then global capital will go elsewhere – principally to lower-cost China and India. In an article in Newsweek in 2006 Tony Blair pulled no punches: 'complaining about globalisation' he said 'is as pointless as trying to turn back the tide. Asian competition can't be shut out; it can only be beaten.'[40]

Since the end of the Cold War there had been a quantum leap in the power of mobile capital over state and labour and neoliberals argued that governments needed to yield to these 'realities'. Blair was in the forefront of such yielding – constantly arguing that the British people should welcome 'globalisation', not resist it, nor even attempt to shape it. All any government could do was to help the population adapt to the inevitable by helping them to compete – primarily by providing suitable skills and education – the origin of Blair's catch-phrase policy priority: 'Education, Education, Education'. Of course, in this future low tax regime governments would not be able to fund the future welfare state and thus the welfare systems needed 'reform' (with a bigger private sector).

Blair – just like the Wall Street economists who propounded this doctrine – was sustained in it by a sense of almost righteous inevitability. There was, they, and he, argued, 'no alternative' to this global capitalist dynamic. Those who went with the flow, like neoliberal New Labour Britain – would be 'winners' – whereas the 'sclerotic' eurozone economies would be 'losers'. It was an American message, but increasingly, during the first few years of the twenty-first century, an American conservative message (as some US liberals in the Democratic party, worrying about out-sourcing jobs, began to flirt, and more, with protectionism). The message was clear: the West would need to 'accept' losing jobs in its manufacturing sector, but would see its service sector grow to make up for the loss, and it assumed that China and India would continue to demand western services. And the message had a warning – that any attempt at trying to use trade or other policies to staunch the loss of jobs in the west was 'protectionist' and self-defeating. It was a message that New Labour, no matter its moral and intellectual roots, could sign up to.

The fact was that Tony Blair's government came to believe – with some justification – that Britain depended on the City of London with its worldwide links. Hywell Williams, one of Britain's most perceptive writers, put it starkly. 'The power of capital over New Labour, with its superstitious veneration of money created Britain's most consistently business-friendly party' he argued; and this business-friendly party, as it promoted 'globalisation', found that, for Britain 'all that is left is the power of the City – the true governor of Britain, with a worldview of global markets that has ended British independence.'[41]

Blair's New Labour also adopted a key underpinning idea of the American economic conservative movement – the notion that western societies needed to live with growing *gross* inequality – as a price worth paying for private capital formation. A tolerance for inequality – and for a growing class of super-rich and mega-rich people – had been a feature of several eras of American history, and particularly so in what economist Paul Krugman has called the 'new gilded era' of the post-1980s world.[42] Such tolerance of *gross* inequality had not been present in Britain, certainly since 1945, and not really even during the premiership of Margaret Thatcher – when the stress was on creating a vibrant middle class.[43] But Blair broke with the British postwar consensus, and adopted a much more American approach. In a remark, unthinkable for any social democrat, Blair declared to interviewer Jeremy Paxman just before the 2001 general election, that he simply did not worry about growing inequality, or about the growing class of the super and mega-rich. 'It is not a burning ambition for me that David Beckham earns less money' he revealed.

This key American conservative idea – that inequality does not matter, that social problems are not caused by social divides or even poverty, but rather by issues arising from 'family breakdown' – helped further the idea that the tax bill for welfare could, thus, safely be reduced. In the 1980s, the American sociologist Charles Murray was hugely influential in this attempted divorce of economic inequalities from social problems, locating them instead in lack of family stability and personal inadequacies. And reportedly, Rupert Murdoch's aide, Irwin Steltzer, played a role in introducing Charles Murray to Rupert Murdoch and thus to British opinion formers and public through *The Sunday Times*.[44]

American conservatism won yet another battle in its takeover of New Labour when ideas about Christian 'faith-based solutions' began to appear in New Labour thinking. Throughout his premiership Blair was not bashful in proclaiming his Christian views, although he balked at journalists who suggested that his relationship with Bush was based upon a shared Christian faith (He deflected questions about joining hands in White House prayer meetings.) But he was less open about his growing Roman Catholicism (or his Catholic wife's influence on him); and the word from Downing Street was that he would make public any conversion to Catholicism only when he left office. In any event, although Blair's 'faith schools' schools programme chimed well with Bush's 'faith-based initiatives', they stood out awkwardly in secular Britain – particularly in secular New Labour (or, for that matter, in Old or Middle-Aged Labour as well). Yet, the New Labour Prime Minister continued to introduce them, and even appointed a member of Opus Dei to the sensitive post of Education Secretary.[45] Again, more intriguing perhaps than Blair's own American conservative belief system – from the Iraq war to economic and social policy – was the fact that it was tolerated by the bulk of Britain's Labour MPs. (Not one MP ever raised in public the issue of Blair's *systematic* support for the American conservative agenda.)

Murdoch Over Britain

This embracing of American-style radical-conservatism by Tony Blair was more than an act of true belief. It was also about hard-nosed domestic politics. For, as it happens, Blair's conservative agenda squared nicely with the worldview and global interests of the media mogul, the Australian-American Rupert Murdoch., owner of News International and *The Sun* newspaper. Blair decided very early on in his career as opposition leader that he needed, at the very least, to neutralise *The Sun*, which he believed had hurt Labour decisively in previous elections.

The power of *The Sun* was based upon its mass circulation. It outsold every other daily. It developed a clear and concise political message that, particularly following the Falklands conflict in 1982, associated Thatcherism with patriotism and national success and the left with the failed politics of national weakness, trade union militancy and liberal 'softness' on crime. And its political journalism had a knack of articulating basic populist views and appealing to the often-hidden resentments against the 'liberal elite' and their 'politically correct' attitudes of its relatively low-income and undereducated mass readership.

News International became a major player in British politics (in foreign as well as domestic policy) during the crises of the 1980s as Margaret Thatcher won her battle with Britain's powerful trade unions. Initially, Murdoch's empire was part of the broad anti-trade union coalition; and it also developed a radical, and seemingly progressive, meritocratic edge which, under the influence of *Sunday Times* editor Andrew Neil took as its targets traditionalist Britain – old money aristocracy, the monarchy and royal family as well as the trade unions.

By the late 1980s it turned into a support system for The Conservative party's campaign for a business-led economic and political culture under the banner of the 'free market'. It also began its systematic, high-volume opposition to the European Community and Union, and Britain's place in it. Murdoch's opposition to a European destiny for Britain had little in common with the chauvinism and nationalism exhibited in his papers, particularly *The Sun* (Murdoch, in fact, was an egalitarian

Australian, and a cosmopolitan globe-trotter who was to marry as his third wife a young Chinese woman). Rather, Murdoch's key concern was what he perceived as the anti-business culture of the EU and its highly regulated, high-tax welfare societies – a culture that he saw as hostile to his own media interests as well. His pro-business, anti-Europe, values were bound sooner or later to draw Murdoch to the USA. Murdoch and conservative America were a love affair waiting to be consummated. During the 1990s Murdoch built up considerable media interests in North America and, centering his business there, he became an American citizen on 24th August 2003. The successful political journalism of *The Sun* (and of Thatcherism) translated well to Bush's America. As Murdoch invested in newspapers and television (particularly the Fox News Channel) the key tunes of Thatcherite pro-business patriotism laced with strong law and order played very well indeed. Murdoch's Fox News Channel added to this 'Thatcherite' 'core' appeal the values and concerns of the American Christian-right – the so-called three G's, 'God, Guns and Gays' – that had been missing from Murdoch's British operation.

Tony Blair first met Rupert Murdoch in 1994 – privately, over dinner in the Belgravia restaurant Mosimann's. During this get-together Blair suggested that media ownership rules under Labour would not place Murdoch in a worse position than he was in under Thatcher and Major. For his part Murdoch indicated that his newspapers were not 'wedded to the Tories'.[46] In July 1995, Tony Blair, then the new leader of Her Majesty's Opposition (as official Britain still quaintly called the Leader of the Opposition), boarded an aircraft and travelled 24 hours to a remote island off Australia where he would attend a News Corporation Management conference.[47] From this time on, Blair would continue to seek, and to get, Murdoch's support for his premiership. On the 18th March 1997 Murdoch's *Sun*, which had supported the Conservatives ever since Murdoch took over, announced that 'The Sun Backs Labour' – incidentally on the very day that the Murdoch-funded neoconservative magazine *The Weekly Standard* declared that US radical rightist Newt Gingrich was not right-wing enough![48] Blair went on to win not only in 1997, but, with Murdoch's support, in 2001 and 2005 as well.

Murdoch's backing for Blair may help explain the latter's own transformation from European social democrat into American radical conservative. Irwin Steltzer was a key aide to Rupert Murdoch, an intellectual guru and advisor, and a major player in transatlantic Murdoch politics. He epitomised American radical conservatism, and, like many Bush neoconservatives possesses an articulate and knowledgeable universalist bravura that gives him the gift of proclaiming – with great confidence – the right course for countries other than his own.[49] Steltzer met Blair on many occasions both before and after he became Prime Minister, and became Blair's advocate in the US. He saw early on that the Labour leader shared many ideas in common with the American conservative right. 'I know Tony Blair…' he once said 'Blair is one of Thatcher's children. I think he knows it.' And he saw Blair's Christian beliefs as potentially linking him – beyond Clinton and the American secular-liberals – to the conservative right. Steltzer could assert perceptively that 'one thing is clear…the leader of Britain's left-wing party finds it acceptable, politically, to profess his Christianity and to look to the new and old testaments for a central core around which to develop his political program. Of necessity, that requires a cultural stance not very different from that of America's Christian Coalition.'[50]

Whereas Murdoch may have only facilitated Tony Blair's growing American conservatism, he and his newspapers and television stations were decisive when it came to Blair's European policy. Blair had come into office in 1997 with very positive views about Britain's joining the eurozone, but was never, throughout the whole period of his premiership, able to act on them. Before the 1997 general election he was forced into pledging a referendum of the issue for fear of Murdoch support for Major in the campaign. After entering Downing Street euro-entry remained an objective of his government, but fearful of Murdoch's media influence in any referendum campaign, he was never confident of winning a vote. Thus, a vote was never held, and Britain stayed outside. *The Mail on Sunday* even claimed that in the original, uncensored *Diary of a Spin Doctor*, Downing Street official Lance Price had written that 'apparently we [Downing Street] promised News International [Murdoch's corporation] that we won't make any changes to our European policy without talking to them'.[51]

Another clear, and stark, example of Murdoch's power over New Labour – particularly on the European issue – came in July 2006. Blair's premiership was clearly reaching its final phase, and Gordon Brown's team was preparing for the future transfer of power. Speculation was rife about Brown's political options. Into this vacuum Murdoch issued what amounted to a public 'ultimatum' or 'warning' to Brown. He was told flatly not to try for a quick general election but rather to stay around for eighteen months during which the electorate could judge his merits alongside those of the new Tory leader David Cameron. It became clear that Murdoch, ever the vigilant Eurosceptic, was worried that Brown might hold a quick election, get a new mandate, and then be free to develop his own European policy. At the time it was becoming clear that a new joint German-Italian-French constitutional initiative was possible and might well be launched after the French Presidential election in the summer of 2007 just after Brown had taken over. Murdoch feared that a new PM Brown might well sign up to it. Murdoch let it be known that *The Sun* newspaper – the only paper New Labour's leaders cared about would not support Brown in any quickly-called election campaign. Should he try such a maneuver it would support Cameron.[52]

An intriguing aspect of this intervention in British politics from a media organisation run from the USA was not its blatant nature. Rather, it was the nonchalant way it was received by New Labour, the British political class, press and commentariat. There was hardly a peep of protest or a riposte of any note. After a decade of New Labour, and three decades of Thatcherism, Rupert Murdoch, an American citizen, domiciled outside the UK, had become accepted as an arbiter of Britain's future. He had become as powerful as the whole British cabinet combined.

Murdoch's press empire was, though, by no means the sole pressure behind New Labour's growing extreme pro-Americanism. There was also a general pro-US bias amongst other powerful sections of the media world – not least the output of *Daily Telegraph* and *Spectator* owner Conrad Black. The nexus of media and politics which Murdoch and Black bestrode was, in fact, the world inhabited by New Labour – and, later, by David Cameron's Tories too. Blair's team, and Cameron's too, were not strictly 'political' in the classic sense. Mixing the political with modern communications techniques they took the world of the media very seriously indeed and they treated media barons as legitimate policymakers. British politics had come a long way since the early 1970s when it was the trade union leaders who were the 'over-mighty subjects' and held similar power over an earlier Labour administration.

In this process New Labour had ceased to act like a traditional left-of-centre British political party. Rather, with cabinet and party weakened, Blair's team resembled a highly sophisticated public relations company that, media-friendly, and brand and image-sensitive, cut out the party (its factions, its MPs, its trade unions, and its activists) and made direct contact with the voter. As New Labour embraced this party-less, American-style, politics it automatically became more and more dependent upon media support and approval, and upon business and private money for its campaigning. And the media-cum-business community demanded of New Labour business-friendly policies in return.

It was an embrace that as one commentator put it 'created Britain's most consistently business-friendly party'.[53] And a 'business-friendly party' was an American-friendly party. For New Labour increasingly acted as an amen chorus for the US economic model and as a pressure against British integration in 'social' Europe. And a key part of the business-friendly US economic model was the opening to a global marketised world with its pressures for 'competitive', low cost, low wage, low tax economies with flexible labour markets. As New Labour entered this world it began – often with relish – to join in the Wall Street barrage of criticism against the European social model with its 'inflexible', regulated – indeed 'sclerotic' – economies and hugely 'debilitating' welfare states. So powerful was the hold of this business-led consensus in Britain that even the downturn of Wall Street and the puncturing of the hi-tech bubble in 2000 and 2001, the huge and dangerous financial imbalances of the US economy, and the corruption scandals of Enron and others, did not shake New Labour's conviction that neoliberal economics was the way forward for Britain.

Mandarins, Spies and Submariners

New Labour's love affair with America, though, was not simply about business-friendly and media-mogul friendly politics. For, as well as the Americanised business and media class, Whitehall's traditionalist 'establishment' was also very much on board for the US connection. 'Atlanticism' ran deep in the corridors of Whitehall. When this Atlanticist faction joined up with the Eurosceptic business class in promoting the 'special relationship' it became a formidable pressure group.

An archetypal foreign office Atlanticist was Jonathan Powell, an Oxford contemporary of Tony Blair, who became Blair's chief of staff in 1997 and saw him every day sometimes at least a dozen times. Picked out by Blair whilst at the British Embassy in Washington, Powell (an affectation has it pronounced 'Po-ell') is a 'devout Atlanticist who is not much bothered about Europe'.[54] Indeed, pro-American Atlanticism runs in the family, for Powell is the brother of an even stauncher pro-American Atlanticist, Lord Charles Powell who was Margaret Thatcher's chief foreign policy advisor.

The Powells are in one sense very representative figures – representative, that is, of the governing official mindset of top political Britain. Like Tony Blair himself they are the product of old-fashioned public schools and, again like Blair, have just a touch of the old imperial manner, and of its attraction to power – in this case to the power of superpower America. Like the foreign policy establishment they represent, their 'Atlanticism' is ingrained, made so by the historic success of NATO during the cold war years.

Below this top political level – where the Atlanticist 'special relationship' was held as an act of faith – there were the more pragmatic pro-American Whitehall interest groups: the spies and submariners. Britain's intelligence community had a real 'special relationship' with Washington – based on intelligence sharing, not offered to other European nations, which had continued beyond the cold war years; Whitehall continued to please Washington for fear it would be cut off. This may help explain the seemingly determined behaviour of John Scarlett, the Chair of the Joint Intelligence Committee, who, throughout the great post-invasion controversy about Britain's intelligence, and the Hutton enquiry into the strange death of a weapons inspector, stood one hundred percent by Blair and his policy even though at least one other intelligence chief was reported as having severe misgivings about the war.[55]

The role of the intelligence services is shrouded in mystery, but they have two clear and obvious advantages in Whitehall's power struggles. They are the sole possessor of 'knowledge' and 'information'; and they have total and regular access to the Prime Minister's office, more so than top cabinet ministers.

The other Whitehall pressure group highly supportive of Washington is the British Navy, which ever since the late 1960s has played host to Britain's nuclear weapons which, together with the missiles, are carried in the navy's submarines. To many in Whitehall this 'British bomb' remains the central nervous system of British power and thus the key to the British establishment's 'world role'. Yet, as befits this British nuclear 'world role' Washington is indispensable. For the United States – first through the Polaris and then through the Poseidon agreements – provided and provides indispensable servicing requirements for the submarine force and crucial satellite targeting systems. The British bomb is independent but only if the British government wants to launch a 'spasm' response. A proper, targeted, response needs American input and allows for an American veto over its use whereas, by contrast, the French nuclear weapons system is genuinely independent.

These umbilical intelligence and nuclear ties to Washington may explain, perhaps much more clearly than any of the more geopolitical and theoretical attachments to 'Atlanticism' (and 'NATO-think'), why exactly it is that Britain's top leadership needs the Americans and needs to 'hug them close'.

In 2007 Britain's elites were still 'hugging them close' when Wall Street lending crashed. It was a crash that was to take down with it American global economic and political supremacy and American-style 'economic globalisation' – and thus destroy the validity of the three decades long pro-American national strategy of Britain's political and financial class. The 2007 crash was a terrible blow for Britain.

CHAPTER FOUR

THE GREAT CRASH

August 2007 was a real turning point for the American, and therefore the global, and the British, economy. During that fateful month the strains on the American economy – principally the global imbalances and the mountainous private debt linked to the housing bubble – could no longer be contained. What bankers were calling the sub-prime mortgage crisis finally spilt out into the wider banking industry as American and then other western banks stopped lending to each other (except, that is, on terms of prohibitive rates of interest). Banks looked vulnerable for the first time since the 1930s.

This debt-bubble covered the world – or, at any rate that part of the globalised world run by banks and financial institutions. Its global dimension was soon revealed when news came through of banks in trouble outside the US. In Britain the Northern Rock bank had to be nationalised (by a market-friendly British government); banks from Spain, France and Germany, and Asia, including the Peoples Bank of China, were all in trouble. It had the feel of major global crisis about it.

This sudden 2007 crisis may well have been triggered by the French bank BNP Paribas whose board took a fateful decision in early August to junk its toxic debts in the US – for reasons that are still unclear, but may have ultimately been cultural (a Gallic antipathy to Wall Street's 'Wild West' lending practices, or a reluctance to risk-take with sub-prime mortgages). In any event the board of the French bank found itself unable to properly value the assets of three sub-prime mortgage funds – and refused to play the game any longer. But, by not playing by the rules that were keeping the Wall Street bubble intact, BNP set off alarm bells all over the global banking system, directly leading to the August 2007 shutdown in global interbank lending. The European Central Bank, seeing the potential for a run throughout the system, immediately stepped in by opening $130 billion in low interest credit.

The Wall Street bubble burst over Switzerland too. At the height of the housing/debt mania UBS, the giant Swiss bank with $31 trillion in assets, had taken a large slice of American mortgage debt (reckoned to be around $80 billion dollars worth) and, when the bubble burst, was forced to write down $37 billion of that debt. This was a bigger write-down than American banks Citigroup and Merrill Lynch. 'What happened here is a scandal' declared local lawyer and shareholder Thomas Minder at the shareholders' meeting in Basel Switzerland in early April 2008. 'You're responsible for the biggest loss in the history of the Swiss economy' he thundered, and, adding a political postscript, demanded that the board 'put an end to the Americanisation of the Swiss economy.'[1]

An important part of the new capitalist global debt bubble was the so-called 'carry trade' in which speculators and investors borrowed from low-interest countries, like Japan, and placed their money in higher interest countries, like Iceland, Turkey, or the Baltics. Enormous amounts of money were involved. Iceland became what one commentator called a massive 'Nordic hedge fund masquerading as a country', a fund that invested throughout the world in such enterprises as Woolworths, Hamleys Toy Shops and West Ham Football club. The asset base of the Icelandic banking system was a world-record 8 times GDP. But it was always fragile. Max Keiser likened the small, debt-laden country to a money geyser awaiting an eruption. In a television documentary aired just two days before the western debt bubble burst (on 7th August 2007 when bank debt literally dried up overnight) he told the story of Iceland and the carry trade – and the global financial imbalances that it represented. In the same programme, Dr. Paul Walker of GMFS argued that 'the buying up of US debt has been a key component of the global imbalances' and that 'central banks kept putting off the day of reckoning…but the longer they put it off the more serious it will be…and it will come.' It came two days later.[2]

Previously, high inflation and a trade deficit would have brought the bubble to an early and abrupt end. This time, however, the low cost Chinese would keep the system going and the American consumer buying. Americans took on huge debt and the Chinese built up massive reserves. These 'global imbalances' represented a dangerous and fragile balancing act, but even as American debt levels reached Himalayan proportions 'neoliberal' policymakers in Washington, Wall Street and London remained confident and upbeat. A soothing thesis was delivered: the Chinese were recycling their reserves into the western system (including the US government) and would never allow their great new market to contract. In reality, though, the whole Wall Street global edifice was shaking.

It all represented a major defeat for Wall Street and, by extension, the City of London – and the 'neoliberal market' capitalist economy they represented and had been vigorously promoting. The crisis led to much public soul-searching about the causes and responsibilities. One thing was clear. The crisis had been triggered by lending to 'sub-prime' (i.e. lower income) people who could not afford to pay back the debt – either because the teaser interest rates suddenly rose or because of job losses or income weakness. And the banks – the lenders – were in the dock both for 'predatory' lending and for parcelling up the 'bad loans' in collective debt packages known as 'securitisation'.

Surprisingly, the bankers' bank, The Bank For International Settlements, became a harsh critic of the Wall Street-led banking establishment. Indeed, it 'startled the financial world' by pinning the blame firmly on the US central bank for what it considered to be its lax monetary policy, arguing that 'cleaning up' a property bubble once it had burst was not easy. A year later the BIS, in the form of its 78th annual report written primarily by its chief economist, Bill White, stated 'the magnitude of the problems we now face could be much greater than many now perceive. It is not impossible that the unwinding of the credit bubble could, after a temporary period of higher inflation, culminate in a deflation that might be hard to manage, all the more so given the high debt levels'.[3]

NORTHERN ROCK, BEAR STEARNS

On the 13th August a Bank of England loan to the British bank Northern Rock PLC was made public and this led to the first time there had been a run on the deposits of a British bank in living memory – with the new 24-hour-news channels broadcasting pictures of the lengthy queues outside Northern Rock around the world. Four days later the Treasury guaranteed the deposits of the bank; four and a half months later it was nationalised.

Bear Stearns was a Wall Street institution. Founded in 1923 it grew to become one of the largest investment banks on Wall Street with a sizeable equities business. It employed over 15,000 people. At the beginning of 2007 its total capital was well over $65 billion and it had total assets of $350 billion. The public got to know of trouble when in 22nd June 2007 it sought to save one of its funds which was trading in the collateralised debt obligations. It was in real risk of bankruptcy when on 14th March 2008, in a highly unusual deal involving the Federal Reserve Bank (of New York), JP Morgan Chase provided Bear Stearns with a mammoth emergency loan. And on 16th March JP Morgan effectively bought Bear Stearns.

The Federal Reserve had 'tossed out the rulebook when it assumed the role of white knight', temporarily bailing out Bear Stearns with a short-term loan 'to help avoid a collapse that might send other dominoes falling'.[4] Just days before, the Fed had announced a $200 billion lending programme for investment banks and a $100 billion credit line for banks and thrifts. And in what the NYT called a move 'unthinkable until recently' the Fed agreed to accept risky mortgage-backed securities as collateral.

Hard on the heels of the Bear Stearns crisis, the spotlight returned to Britain. The giant British bank, Royal Bank of Scotland (RBS), appeared to be in trouble, and in late April 2008 announced a massive £12 billion rights issue. The day before, in response to the obvious dramatic weakening in interbank lending and to help with the growing overhang of illiquid assets (assets they could not sell or secure borrowing on), the Bank of England had announced a special scheme by which £185 billion of Treasury bills were to be lent to the banks to improve liquidity and confidence.

A week later HBOS announced a $4 billion rights issue and two weeks after that the much smaller British bank Bradford and Bingley announced a £300 million issue. And then, a month or so later, in late June, Barclays joined the party and announced a £4.5 billion share issue. With two of the country's great 'universal' banks, RBS and Barclays, in trouble the Bank of England's special liquidity scheme window saw a lot of traffic over the summer of 2008; but the growing British arm of the worldwide crisis was contained – at least for a few weeks.

FANNIE, FREDDIE, AIG AND THE DISAPPEARING INVESTMENT BANKS

In July the crisis moved back to the US and to the mammoth lenders Freddie Mac and Fannie Mae. On the 13th the US government made the extraordinary announcement that they would bail out the tottering companies. Freddie and Fannie were hybrid organisations – they were stockholder-owned but government-sponsored. More importantly, they controlled just about half of the US home loan market – a total market amounting to $12 trillion. The Bush administration agreed to an unspecified and unlimited credit line, borrowing privileges at the discount window and, incredibly, a capital injection into the companies if needed in return for which the US government would receive shares.

So severe was the financial crisis, and the panic, that these measures were introduced swiftly in the Congress and signed with a sigh of relief by the conservative Bush administration. The US government had ditched decades of history – not to mention half its belief system – and guaranteed the debt of a private company. With the 'full faith and credit of the US' taxpayer behind them they were just one step away from socialist nationalisation – indeed, to all intents and purposes they were in fact nationalised but with shareholders continuing to take the profits – should there be any.

Later, in September, the US government went further. It effectively nationalised both Freddie and Fannie by taking them into 'conservatorship', sacking the top executives, and placing the two companies under the management of The Federal Housing Finance Agency.

Later still in September two other investment banks, Lehman Bros. and Merrill Lynch, effectively collapsed. Following an historic meeting in which the US Treasury brought all the top US bankers together, Lehman was forced to file for bankruptcy and Merrill was engineered (by the US government) into a sale to Bank of America. The very next day the 'free market' Bush administration was forced into rescuing (effectively nationalising) the huge insurer, AIG. This outright state takeover was a measure of how dire the US financial system had become: for, without it, the US, and the world, may well have faced an immediate financial meltdown as the now all-important foreign holders of US dollars rushed to unload. The Chinese government was particularly interested in how the US was going to deal with the Fannie and Freddie bankruptcy – as, according to a National Public Radio report on 7th September by Adam Davidson, almost one tenth of China's GDP was invested in the outcome.

BRITAIN'S BANKS ARE RESCUED

The collapse of Lehman Brothers amounted to a US government-backed default, and its repercussions were to be felt worldwide amongst an array of counterparties, not least in the UK financial sector. On the 18th of September the British government forced Lloyds TSB and HBOS to merge (a deal finalised in January 2009) and the British regulator, the FSA, announced a ban on short-selling. Ten days later, on the 29th, Bradford and Bingley joined Northern Rock in becoming a nationalised bank (with Abbey (Santander) having bought its retail deposit book). And then on the 13th of October the British government took on a great and unprecedented new burden as further details were released about a £37 billion operation of government support for the recapitalisation of RBS, Lloyds and HBOS – all of this just after the UK had announced that, in the wake of the Icelandic banking collapse, it would protect British retail depositors.

November saw the UK government formalise its extraordinary socialising (basically, nationalising) of Britain's major banks when it set up the UK Finance Institute (UKFI) to manage the government's investments in the banks. After a lull, January brought yet another quantum leap in socialising the City with the announcement of the government's Asset Protection Scheme, asset-backed securities guarantee scheme and the extension of the CDS draw-down window.

By March of the following year the banking system of the City had been stabilised – at least for the moment – and the Brown government then turned its attention to the broader economy – with a singular and dramatic new policy. On the 5th the Bank of England introduced a new term into the vocabulary of socialised finance by announcing that it was organising a 'Quantitative Easing' (QE) of £75 billion. This was later to increase to over £175 billion by August, and then again to over £200 billion by November 2009.

A RECKLESS AND IRRESPONSIBLE ELITE

This socialising of the debt by the Brown government may well have temporarily stabilised the banking system, but it led directly to a growing financial crisis for the British government itself – a phenomenon that was to become more widely described as a 'sovereign debt crisis'. In short, the British taxpayers had bailed out the British banks; but this had put such pressure on the public finances that there was a danger that Britain itself could go bust. The country, no longer a global imperial power, was simply too small to carry these huge, overextended global banks. The overextension of RBS told the awesome story: for, by the end of June 2008, this one bank had a balance sheet of almost £ two trillion – whereas its backer and seeming guarantor, the UK, had a GDP that amounted to just £ one and a half trillion.

It was clear that this continuing imperial mindset of Britain's political/financial elites – with its hubristic over-importance and its consequent financial overextension – was coming home to roost. The irresponsibility of allowing such overblown, global, finance was breathtaking.

The economist Willem Buiter could argue that Britain's political/financial establishment had acted as recklessly as that of another island with an egregiously overextended global banking system – Iceland. 'Returning from Reykjavik last night was like coming home from home. Allowing for the differences of scale...there are disturbing economic parallels...Relaxation of regulatory norms was consciously used by the British government as an instrument for attracting financial business to London, mainly from New York City. Fiscal policy in both countries became strongly pro-cyclical during the boom years... Households were permitted, indeed encouraged, to accumulate excessive debt – around 170% of household disposable income in the UK, over 210% in Iceland.'

And on top of this irresponsibility, there was another, related one: the British had allowed, indeed encouraged, the 'Dutch disease' to take hold – that is the crowding out by the financial sector in the City of London, and the housing and construction sector, of other sectors of the British economy. It was a highly short-sighted national strategy leading to a deadly imbalance in the economy; and all this on top of the imbalances created by Britain as an oil economy – the petro-dollar economy – that had been built up since the discovery of North Sea oil. As Buiter could argue, referring again to Britain and Iceland, "in neither country have the responsible parties (the prime minister, the minister of finance, the governor of the central bank and the head of banking regulation and supervision) admitted any personal responsibility for the disaster'.[5] The 'responsible parties' named here would therefore include: Tony Blair and Gordon Brown, Alistair Darling, Eddie George and Mervyn King, and Callum McCarthy and Howard Davies – although their 'responsibility' needs to be placed in the context of a generally supportive political/financial elite.

'ANGLO–AMERICA' FAILS

Of course, the British crisis as it unfolded in 2008-9 was but part of a more general crisis of the 'Anglo-American' economic and geostrategic model. During Tony Blair's premiership Britain remained out of the eurozone and instead increasingly bound itself to the American Wall Street-led way of doing economics, the so-called 'Anglo-American model'. It joined the US in both constructing and operating the new global financial capitalist system as it evolved during the years since the collapse of communism. The old maxim used to be that 'when America sneezes Europe catches a cold'. Now it had become 'when America catches a cold Britain catches pneumonia'. Indeed, the story of Britain's 2007 ongoing financial crisis cannot be told without placing the country's plight in the broader context of her earlier choice, a choice not made by France or Germany, to take part in the American-led global debt scam – that is the pursuit of an economic model with stagnant wages, no savings and huge personal credit based upon a housing bubble, indeed of a people living beyond their means whilst funded by rising, low-cost, Asia. In other words, by 2007 Britain had got caught up in a broader unfolding disaster – that of the growing weakness of the American-led Anglo-American economic sphere, American imperial decline, the rise of China, and the stalling and eroding of 'globalisation'.

Living Beyond Her Means

The American banking and credit crisis that spread to Britain during the fateful year of 2007, serious though it was (is), was a symptom of a deeper structural economic problem facing the United States. For the explosion of domestic credit had been but a part of a policy that allowed Americans to live well beyond their means. Ever since the early 1980s – when mobile capital and 'free trade' began the process of hollowing out western jobs, and wages became static or fell – American living standards were kept high by the singular, dramatic, and ultimately deadly, growth in debt. This massive indebtedness took many forms. Two of the most dangerous were the private debt of households (causing the housing bubble) and the huge US current-account deficit which for many years remained a wonder of the world.

The country's growing current account deficit, particularly its trade deficit and the interest payments on debt to foreign investors, measures the extent to which America has been living beyond its means. And the trend has been all one way, and disastrous: for the USA was in surplus for 18 of the 22 years between 1960 and 1982 but has been in deficit every year since (except for 1991). These 'imbalances' have been a subject for urgent discussion for some years, but usually, though, only in academic circles. The Washington and Wall Street establishments have, in public at least, dismissed the idea that they represented an inherent instability that could unravel with disastrous consequences. One top official in the Clinton administration was moved to observe that 'there is something odd about the world's greatest power also being its greatest debtor.' They were indeed treated as an oddity rather than a danger.

Economists tended to deal in technical talk about 'imbalances', and the new century saw the beginning of a public debate about these imbalances, but, as with all economic problems after 9/11, they were relegated to the back burner as fears about security dominated the agenda. By 2004, though, the question of debt was beginning to surface. *The Atlantic Monthly* magazine, under the title 'America's "Suez Moment"', a reference to Britain's invasion of Egypt in 1956 and its humiliating rendezvous with its loss of global power, published an article which argued that 'America is like no other dominant power in modern history – because it depends on other countries for capital to sustain its military and economic dominance.' In the same year the prescient analyst NYU Professor Nouriel Roubini set out the magnitude of the problem: that the current account deficit was set to rise to 7 per cent of GDP in 2006 and that the US's net investment debt was set to equal about 50 per cent of GDP and to equate to about 500 per cent of US export revenues.[6]

By 2004 Bill Clinton's former Treasury Secretary, Larry Summers, was issuing warnings. In his Per Jacobsson Lecture he reiterated his serious concern about whether the foreign financing of the huge US debt could continue indefinitely. And he coined the dramatic term 'balance of financial terror' to describe the co-dependency between the foreign lenders and the US – as the US relies 'on the costs [to China and others] of not financing the US debt as assurance that financing will continue.'[7]

By 2006 the US current account deficit was topping $800 billion, representing 6 per cent of US GDP. China's current account surplus was $250 billion, which amounted to almost 10 per cent of China's GDP. East Asia's surplus continued to rise during 2007 – making any global adjustment more difficult by the month. In expert testimony on 26th June 2007 to the House Budget Committee Brad Setser, a Senior Economist at Roubini Global Economics, again raised the question of American vulnerability to foreign holdings of US debt. He reported that 'since 2000, total foreign holdings of US debt have increased from $4.3 trillion to close to $10 trillion while US lending to the rest of the world has increased from $2.9 trillion to an estimated $4.6 trillion'.[8]

These huge amounts of debt revealed the full illness of the ailing heart of the US economic system – a system that the British elites had over the previous two decades seen fit to bind themselves, and their people, into.

The Good Life Courtesy of China

And then, in late 2007, as the banking and housing boom began to burst and unravel, the full importance of China to the West, and particularly to the USA, was revealed. The difficult truth was that it was China's integration into the global market during the 1990s that had allowed Americans to live beyond their means. It did so by fuelling the American (and western) private debt bubble, which in turn was only made possible because of the worldwide low inflationary environment – itself made possible by the low cost (cheap labour) economies of Asia.

It worked like this: Asian and Chinese low costs fuelled a broader global low-inflation regime which, crucially, provided the low-interest environment for the great US-UK mortgage-based housing boom. Americans (and Brits) saw their house prices rise whilst their wages were stagnant. In the US wages as a percentage of personal income fell from around 76 per cent in 1979 to 62 per cent in 2005; yet during the same period consumer spending as a percentage of wages had risen from around 120 per cent to 160 per cent.

This decline in wage income for Americans, however, was more than offset by the growth in credit – fuelled by the 'wealth effect' of higher house values. It was this credit rush which allowed a boom in consumer spending – a boom which became the life-blood of the American economy in the 1990s and into the twenty-first century.

It was this credit rush that allowed Americans, and through the US growth machine, the Brits, to live well beyond their means.

Starting around 1995, and lasting through to 2007, the mechanism for such living was an expansion, and explosion, of low-interest credit fuelled by a bonfire of regulations across the credit industry. As the then Chairman of the US Senate Banking Committee, Phil Gramm, asserted, 'freedom is the answer'. A top lawyer for Citibank who had pushed for the deregulation of the credit-card industry later argued, 'I didn't realise that someday we might have ended up creating a Frankenstein'. The sheer size of this American private debt bubble slowly revealed itself. A year or so before the bubble burst, leading American political scientist Kevin Phillips was virtually alone amongst his peers in predicting real trouble ahead. He conjured up the arresting image of the 'indentured American household' with Americans becoming 'indentured servants' or 'sharecroppers' who were, in effect, spending their working lives labouring on behalf of whip-holding creditors – be they 'credit-card companies in the US or dollar-holding central bankers in Asia'. It was, as he admitted, an analogy that did not strike a popular chord. Not then.[9]

But by 2008 it was becoming accepted wisdom that debt was at the heart of the unfolding American economic tragedy. So dire was the debt situation that it moved Ambrose Evans-Pritchard of The Daily Telegraph to write that 'the capitalist system is deformed by debt' and 'how did we ever let matters reach this pass.'[10]

'ChinUsa', the 'lone superpower', which a generation of British leaders had hitched their country's destiny to, had become the 'lone super-debtor'. And the super-creditors were in Asia. In the first few years of the new century the Asian dimension of this foreign deficit and debt was becoming alarming. East Asian countries' reserve holdings rose at an alarming rate: Japan's from $220 billion to $834 billion, China's from $143 billion to $610 billion between 1997 and 2004. East Asian countries accounted for 80 per cent of central bank purchases of dollars and Treasury securities in the last two quarters of 2004. The US was indeed becoming locked into what amounted to a co-dependency system with Asia, and particularly with the emerging Asian giant – China.

Not surprisingly during the boom times these global imbalances were unaddressed by the politicians in Washington. They, and most commentators, still saw this system as 'mutually profitable and stable'. Yet it was becoming accepted wisdom that a correction – some kind of a resolution – was ultimately needed. Few wanted a sudden resolution – with all the attendant dangers of a collapse in confidence. The danger was that any domestic crisis could trigger a bigger Asian-US crisis.

In any such crisis few doubted that the global geopolitical tectonic plates would begin to move. And by 2007 this US-China co-dependency had become so pronounced that there seemed to be only two ways out – both fraught with danger. The first would be a rupture of the relationship. This would likely follow a precipitate act by one of the parties – say the US Senate passing a bill signed by the president that significantly upped tariffs on Chinese imports. This protectionist measure might well lead to counter-protectionism with a spiral that ultimately ended in political tension, even conflict.

Alternatively, though, a crisis could lead in exactly the opposite direction. The US and China, faced with such a break, would find it all too daunting – and pull back from the brink and deepen rather than weaken their ties. The crisis would thus be resolved by a further and deeper integration of the two dependencies. The American consumers and the Chinese producers, the US debtors and the Chinese lenders, would solidify rather than shatter their ties – and become so bound together that in effect the two economies would become one. And like the European Union, but perhaps without the formality of rules, a single market would be born and currency pegs would, over time, morph into a single currency 'ChinUsa' would be born. 'ChinUsa' would, of course, never, but never, be acknowledged. But the reality would be that the two governing leaderships in the USA and China, would, forever be constrained by Larry Summers's 'balance of financial terror', and would always act to avoid conflict even if it should mean a deeper and deeper co-dependent relationship.

Sovereign Wealth – OK As Long As It's Foreign

And China was not the only foreign power able to provide a shock to the US financial system. For should the Gulf states, or even Saudi Arabia, adjust the dollar share of their foreign portfolios they could also shake the foundations of the US financial system, and through it the City of London, leading to a dramatic lowering of the dollar. Throughout early 2007 the financial world was replete with rumours of imminent changes of holdings out of dollars and into euros.

Chinese and Arab leverage on the mighty US – through its economy – was also highlighted by the growing controversy (and panic) over 'sovereign wealth funds' a term given by the finance industry to mobile capital owned by governments and invested abroad – much of it in the West. And there was a sudden dawning that these kind of funds were, in essence, 'political' funds, accumulations of capital controlled not by private equity owners but by such regimes as the Chinese Communist party or Middle Eastern sheiks and dictators. These 'sovereign wealth funds' were another name for funds ultimately controlled politically – by authorities ranging from basic dictatorships and to communist parties (one such being the Peoples Liberation Army Pension Fund). With continental European governments still wary of these 'sovereign wealth funds' the British government put out an official statement welcoming them; and, as of writing (2010), in the US, Citigroup and Merrill Lynch were attempting to raise $21 billion from foreign banks in Asia and the Middle East, and the Government of Singapore Investment Corporation announced a stake in Citibank.

In a US banking committee hearing, Democratic Senator Sherrod Brown from Ohio had some fun when he asked Treasury Secretary Paulson why the Republican administration got so worried about nationalisation of banks but seemed quite willing to accept national 'sovereign' capital – as long, that is, that it was provided by foreigners. The very same question of course could have been asked in Britain. For London's financiers, worried about British government money in the banks, were apparently not similarly concerned when at the height of the crisis foreign (Arab) sovereign wealth helped bail out Barclays Bank. And Larry Summers also sounded an alarm. He argued that the motives behind these 'sovereign wealth funds' might be questionable. Whereas capitalists invest and own companies in order to maximise their profits, any other motive distorts the proper functioning of capitalism – and he suggested that the motives behind these funds could be political, or even geopolitical. He pointed to George Soros's 'short position in the British pound in 1992' and his speculative attack on the British currency as a warning of what a sovereign wealth fund – should it have been in the same position – could have gotten up to. 'This is not conducive to the successful relations between nations' he argued.[11]

An early sign that these 'sovereign wealth' funds possessed a political content emerged when in early 2008 it was revealed that governments in Asia and the Middle East were resisting western-led IMF attempts to establish a 'code of conduct' setting out 'best practice' for their operations. It is not without irony to observe that some neoliberal western governments remain hostile to nationalisation at home but welcome – as saviours – nationalised money from dictatorship and authoritarian regimes.

THE STALLING OF 'GLOBALISATION'

Post-World War Two American economic expansion and British economic growth was inextricably bound up with the more general process of 'globalisation', a rising tide that turned into a flood post-1989. Yet by the turn of the new century this wider project of 'globalisation' – used here to mean largely economic transformation – was in trouble, beginning to look somewhat frayed at the edges. An important change in the mood surrounding 'globalisation' had taken place – it was no longer seen as the wave of an 'inevitable' future.

For a start, by the early years of the new century there were signs of growing opposition to 'globalisation' at home – amongst the publics of the West, particularly in America, but also in some of the large southern EU nations like Italy and France. The western nations faced a catalogue of problems – manufacturing job losses, stagnant wages, unsatisfactory healthcare benefits, illegal immigration, and dangerous levels of Chinese imports – all of which, fairly and unfairly, were becoming associated in the public mind with 'globalisation'. Harvard academic Jeffry Frieden, in a comprehensive account of the history of globalisations, argued that today's globalisation – the present one he suggests stretched from 1939 to its zenith around 2000 – is losing its allure and that dissatisfaction with the latest bout is now widespread. He cites the 2006 polling results about globalisation and reported that when EU citizens were asked whether globalisation is a 'threat' or an 'opportunity', 47 per cent chose a 'threat' and only 37 per cent saw it as an 'opportunity'.[12]

Following the attacks on the twin towers in 2001, US opinion detoured into an overriding concern with security, but the evidence shows that even before the atrocities Americans were turning decisively against globalisation and in favour of some kind of protectionism. By early 2008 a decided shift in American opinion away from a belief in the virtues of globalisation had been detected, as had a growing support for protectionism. One of America's leading surveyors of public opinion, Norman Ornstein, the elections expert and political analyst at the American Enterprise Institute, has monitored this shift. He has suggested that 'globalisation has had a significant impact upon public optimism about the economy and public confidence in the future. 'It's given people the sense that their safety net's been shredded' he argued. And Joseph Stiglitz, the Nobel Prize-winning economist, suggests that 'we're paying the price today for the overselling of globalisation, the fact that those who pushed globalisation in both parties were unwilling to face up to the downside risks and take actions to mitigate them.'[13]

Indeed, in recent years dangerous divisions about the merits of economic globalisation have opened up between western publics and western elites (including the super-rich elites) who, shielded from its ravages, remain insistent about its merits. Not surprisingly the lower down the income hierarchy the more hostile to globalisation people become. Asked whether they support 'a policy of restricting foreign imports in order to protect jobs and domestic industries' 53 per cent of those with advanced degrees, 61 per cent of those with College degrees, 61 per cent of those with 'some college', 71 per cent of those with high school degrees and 73 per cent of those with 'less than high school' agreed with the proposition.[14]

During the early years of the twenty-first century the evidence of serious disenchantment with global free trade was all around us. In the western world it could be seen in the high-profile middle class youth protests during the gatherings of world leaders. It could be seen also in the growing opposition from within the American political establishment to the trade regime established by successive free trade administrations. Indeed protectionist proposals from US Senators Schumer and Graham – in 2005 they introduced a bill to raise tariffs on Chinese goods in retaliation for Chinese currency policy – continues to lurk menacingly in the Senate wings.

Opposition to globalisation has many facets, and there is one such in the resistance present in the economic policies of European countries as they continue to resist globalisation's imperatives to lower their welfare provisions and tax regimes (even though, by so refusing, they risk becoming 'uncompetitive' in the global environment). Also, in the US presidential campaign of 2008 the three leading US Democratic candidates all felt the need to compete with each other in developing anti-globalisation themes – for instance, in attacking the excesses of NAFTA and promising

to review US trade agreements and even US membership of the
WTO. And in Europe, country after country – France and Holland
in 2005 and Ireland in 2008 – found that anti-free trade opinion
was a powerful factor in the serial rejections of EU treaty reform.

'Blowback' And The End Of Free Trade

Resistance and opposition to globalisation outside the West
became so pronounced, and sharp, that a term was coined for it:
'blowback'. The concept was originally introduced by the CIA to
describe the 'unanticipated consequences of unacknowledged
actions in other people's countries' and it was popularised
by Professor Chalmers Johnson, in a book published in 2000.
It soon spread to describe a whole host of global reactions –
cultural and social as well as political – to the standardised
global world that was being created.

In a sense the biggest 'blowback' of all was the increasing
rejection by governments of its central doctrine of 'free trade'.
Although 'free trade' remained the mantra, it was more and more
often honoured in the breach. A big turning point was the death
– announced in 1998 during the Asian financial crisis – of the
five year long OECD-led Multilateral Agreement on Investment
(the MAI). This agreement was pure 'globalisation' created
to perfectly suit global capital's needs. It was bold and to the
point, guaranteeing in treaty form that foreign investors 'would
receive treatment no less favourable than the treatment [which
a country] accords its own investors and their investments with
respect to the establishment, acquisition, use, enjoyment and
sale or other disposition of investments'.[15] It sought nothing less
than what Thomas Friedman had described as a 'flat world'.

Yet nation-states – on behalf of their peoples and job
programmes – were not seeing it the same way. One such was
Malaysia in 1988 when it simply gave up on the globalisation

process and rules – and to most everyone's surprise, prospered. More importantly, China itself, often considered an integral part of the globalised world, was only superficially integrated into its processes – allowed essentially to act strategically (that is picking and choosing amongst globalist and protectionist policies), an intelligent approach which allowed the Asian giant to remain intensely resistant to opening up many of her markets to western suppliers.

DID 'GLOBALISATION' EVER EXIST?

By the end of the first decade of the new century there was some clear evidence that 'globalisation' is no longer the dominant dynamic in the world economy. And, looking back, perhaps 'globalisation' was always the wrong word for the new international economic relationships that developed after the fall of communism. For there never was a true 'globalisation'. The figures make the point – for most of the rise in trade in the world seems to have been between the trilateral areas of America, Europe and Asia, with the rest of the world – what used to be called the developing world – not really getting a look in. And, as I argue throughout this book, the whole story is not really about the rise of a 'globalised' world, but, rather, about a much more precise development – the adhesion of Asia (and primarily China) to the western trading and financial system. And it is also a story of how, no matter its other beneficial effects, China's rise – and the western elite's support of this rise – has been the principal cause of the economic and social dislocations of the western world.

THE END OF AMERICAN ASCENDANCY

The world at the end of the George W. Bush presidency was very different from that envisaged at its beginning. At its start, on Inauguration Day, 20th January 2000, Americans – and most of the world – still saw an ascendant America at the heart of a global economic system. The driver of this economy was something called 'globalisation' – an essentially Americanising dynamic that was fashioning the world's economy on American economic lines with American capitalist values and rules. It was also seemingly a global economy in which the US consumer was the engine driving global growth.

America was also ascendant politically. In January 2001 American influence was still spreading east through the NATO expansion into Eurasia that was inaugurated by Bush's father and continued by Bill Clinton. Poland, Hungary and Czechoslovakia had joined in 1999 and even the Baltic countries, former states of the Soviet Union, were slated to join. They were all very pro-American, seeing Washington as their liberator. And with successes in the first Gulf War and in the Kosovo campaign against Milosevic, the US stood tall. So tall that George Bush during his election campaign could promised a 'humbler foreign policy' and in his inaugural could suggest a global engagement 'without arrogance'.

But eight years later, as the Bush presidency drew to its momentous close, the promise of American ascendancy had shrivelled. The reckless 2003 attempt to remake the Middle East had failed, and the American political class was divided about how to extricate its troops from Iraq. And both big and small nations were no longer listening to the US as carefully as they used to. Iran (as of writing) was successfully rebuffing the US over its potential for gaining a nuclear arsenal; The EU leaders had turned down an American request to bring Georgia and the Ukraine into NATO; Russia was reasserting its Soviet-era influence in the Caucasus as it pressured the American satellite nation, Georgia, to disgorge two of its regions with majority Russian-speaking populations – all whilst the US was unable to offer any serious counterpressure; and China was determining its own economic path – and had refused to revalue the renminbi even after insistent American pressure.

And on top of all this the American economy was in deep structural recession. For the first time since 1945 American power in the world was becoming a live issue – and a question could well be asked: what kind of superpower was it that was no longer economically independent, relying for its very financial stability and living standards on another power? Of course, few were openly asking this question. London University Professor Iwan Morgan was an exception. He was suggesting that America was an 'indebted empire' and prophesied that 'when Asia stops buying dollars, the American economy will experience problems that will have implications for America's global power'.[16]

After any turning point the times that went before can, with hindsight, look very different. And, looking back – from a vantage-point in 2008 at the end of the Greenspan/Bush regime – the great era of 'globalisation' did indeed look rather different. It looked far less comprehensive than it appeared during the heady days of expansion. In fact, it began to look as though it may never really have existed at all – at least not in the sense that the world was becoming a single global system.

What had, though, decidedly existed was a 'partial globalisation', if such a phenomenon was possible. This 'partial globalisation' amounted to an increasing trilateral integration and economic lift-off across North America, Asia, and Europe (and parts of Latin America, Brazil certainly), but it left huge swathes of the world outside the system, still without an industrial or commercial base or internal market.

What was also increasingly clear was that, whatever the precise dimensions of the power and influence of the various players in the coming multipolar world, the 21st century was not going to be the second American century.

BAD NEWS FOR BRITAIN

This was very bad news for Britain's political and financial elites who had progressively from Margaret Thatcher's third term onwards hitched themselves both to American power and to the American way of doing things. By the turn of the new century this choice was assuming the proportions of a fatal and fateful British blunder.

CHAPTER FIVE

DEBT DISASTER FOR THE BRITISH

DEBT, THE JOBS CRISIS AND THE BRITISH HOUSEHOLD

DROWNING IN DEBT

The crash of 2007-8 revealed Britain's serious economic vulnerability – the mountainous debt levels of the private and household sector. For 25 years neoliberal free market economics allowed the City to run wild and private debt reached fantasy proportions. By the time of the crash the British people had amassed the highest amount of debt of any European country, accounting for about one third of all EU private indebtedness.

In 2001 personal debt in UK was estimated to be an astronomical £1,000 billion, much of this mortgage debt; between 2001 and 2005 average earnings grew by only 22 per cent, while mortgage debt increased by 94 per cent. Five years later the indebtedness was even worse. In 2010 average household debt was £57,888; excluding mortgages it was £18,784 so the average owed by every UK adult was £30,226. Total UK personal debt stood at £1,459 billion.[1]

However, during the 1990s for any commentator to raise this issue as a potential threat – certainly to raise it as a problem that the market could not rectify – was considered somewhat crankish. The Bank of England, the Treasury, the political class in Westminster, and most financial journalists all missed its significance. Yet debt was building up huge problems for the British. As economists Larry Elliott and Dan Atkinson, amongst the first to warn about it, could argue, somewhat understatedly, 'astronomical levels of personal indebtedness will, we believe, prove a millstone around the economy's neck in the decade to come'.[2]

Britain saw two private sector borrowing booms, one following the other. In the late 90s corporate liability grew rapidly during the dot.com bubble and the so-called 'new economy'. Then, following the dot.com crash, the authorities, with help from low inflation derived from low costs in Asia, kept interest rates low – and the great 2002-7 housing boom was born.

But Britain's debt disaster was two pronged – for whilst British families were borrowing at home, British-based financial institutions were borrowing abroad – big time! By the time of the banking crash Britain's external debt was causing serious credibility problems and was by far the largest of all the western economies. This debt – private and public owed to non-residents repayable in foreign currency, goods or services – amounted to a staggering $9,191,104 million or $150,673 per (British) person. This was almost four times that of the USA (only $42,343 per person), three times that of Germany (with $54,604 per person) and well over twice that of France ($68,183 per person). Britain's debt to foreigners as a percentage of GDP was 365 per cent, a very high percentage compared to that of the USA (95 per cent), Germany (160 per cent) and France (211 per cent).[3]

Britain's banks were the most overextended of all the banking systems in the advanced economies and were increasingly being compared to Iceland and Ireland, two countries whose banks were too big for their respective nations to support. So when the crash threatened the UK's entire banking system, the government bailout had to be substantial. The Treasury footed part of the bill – with consequent high levels of government liabilities and the Bank of England began a money-printing operation, euphemistically called 'Quantitative Easing'. In the process Britain's central bank became overextended. Central Bank balance sheets told the story: for between September 2008 and July 2009 all the major central banks expanded their balance sheets – the ECB with a 39 per cent increase, the Swiss National Bank with 80 per cent, the US Fed with 119 per cent but the Bank of England with the largest of all, a 127 per cent increase.[4]

DEBT AND HOLLOWING OUT

So during the neoliberal era – and aided and abetted by the financial districts in London and New York – the British, and their financial institutions, were progressively drowning in debt, primarily in the private sector (and, following the crash, facing a great 'de-debting' and 'deleveraging' crisis). However, this mountainous level of liability had not been built up accidentally, or by chance. It had been a key part of public policy promoted by governments and central banks and financial industry lobbyists. For a generation of British politicians the 'financialisation' of the economy had become the easy way out of an increasingly difficult economic dilemma caused by Britain's lack of competitiveness in the heavy industrial and manufacturing sector, the changing global order and the shift of wealth to low cost Asia.

Britain saw its future in services. A key component of the Thatcherite revolution was the breakup of old Labourist Britain with its full employment policies and its large 'uncompetitive' manufacturing and industrial base. In the era of globalisation the country should concentrate 'on what it does best', and financial services was one such area. This strategy dominated British government thinking from 1979 right through to 2007. Blair's New Labour was a particularly enthusiastic supporter of adapting to the global market, rejecting 'industrial policy' and emphasising a future based upon financial services, 'the creative industries' and 'the knowledge economy'. During the 1990s other western economies, though not France and Germany, were developing along the same lines, but Britain was an extreme case.

This great strategic switch to a service-based, knowledge-based, economy, though understandable, had two deadly effects. First, the economy became seriously unbalanced.

The domestic economy was becoming overly-financialised: for although British people 'selling insurance to each other' made good business during a boom, it added little to long term economic well-being. More importantly the country became far too dependent upon the burgeoning global financial services industry in the City of London, which, though benefiting the country in good times, was to become a catastrophic burden in a downturn. Although it was clear from the early days of 'globalisation' that China would not really open her vast market to Britain's finance and service sector, the British elite remained fixated by 'free trade' and the stubborn belief that the East, and particularly China, would become a big and lasting market for British services. It was another example of the complacent, conceited nature of British strategic thinking which was based on the assumption that 'Chinamen could not do banking'. So, by 2007 both the downturn and the emergence of Asian protected markets was creating real trouble for the City and its global debt industry.

Another deadly effect of the great three decades-long gamble on services was the obverse side of the policy – the increasing 'hollowing out' of the country's manufacturing jobs, and the prospect of lower or stagnant living standards for large swathes of its people. During the nineties and noughties, average wages (as a percentage of GDP and relative to profits) were stagnant, and in the US were actually falling. Harvard academic Robert Lawrence set the fall in American wages in its proper historical context – he argued that for over a hundred years, between the 1870s and the 1970s average real wages in the US doubled every thirty-five years, and that consequently 'each successive generation lived twice as well as its predecessor. This was the basis of populist idea of the 'American dream', but it no longer holds. Nor can the, always less vivid but still powerful, 'British dream'.

As the full force of economic globalisation hit the British economy some incomes began to fall and average incomes also fell. Real median earnings were £228 a week in the spring of 1993 but had fallen to £225 by the spring of 1996. As a Labour party spokesmen, obviously not yet fully Blairised, argued 'These bleak figures were the result of well paid full time jobs… over a period being replaced by badly paid part-time jobs.'[5]

In Britain (as well as the USA) the credit bubble saved many of these increasingly-strained family and household budgets. And they needed to be saved – not least for macro-economic reasons. The troubling fact was that the fabled 'economic growth', upon which the British boom depended, was wholly consumer-led. Both Tory and New Labour governments – needing to keep 'growth', and thus income, up, conveniently used debt to fill the income deficit. And in the process the households of the West, and the banks of the West, were ensnared. They became, in Kevin Phillips' arresting phrase, indentured. They were to become ever more dependent.[6]

The crunch came when the debt bubble finally burst – in the form of the sub-prime mortgage crisis with bad debts in the American housing loans market overwhelming the system. Banks were affected, and the interconnectedness of the global financial system spread the instability to London. As economic confidence started to wane and the City of London shed jobs, people were facing a real downturn. And because the British had got used to living on debt for so long the average household had little or no savings to speak of to help them through the crisis. It was a real economic emergency with potentially explosive social and political consequences. Alongside the emergency measures to save the banks, the authorities eased household budgets by dragging interest rates lower and lower (rates which translated into historically very low mortgage rates). The Bank of England's base rate, which stood at 5.75 per cent in August 2007 (when the banking crisis first broke) had by March 2009 fallen five times to an exceptional 0.5 per cent.

WASTING NORTH SEA OIL

Debt was not the only bonanza of the neoliberal years – the revenues from North Sea oil added to the sense of well-being. Indeed, some have suggested that the Thatcher revolution could not have sustained itself without it. In 1979 Britain received the first serious income – half a billion pounds – from the new North Sea oil revenues. In the mid-Thatcher years, 1984-7, revenues peaked at a very healthy level (£12 billion in 1984-5, £11,348 billion in 1985-6), but thereafter revenues fell to an average of around £2.5 billion per year.[7] The new millennium has brought a general rise in oil prices and the government has seen these revenues shoot up again, averaging over £6 billion per year from 2001-7. In an extraordinarily lucky break these revenues reached £12 billion during the crisis year of 2008;

but they are due to fall back dramatically as the oil runs out.[8] There can be little doubt that the fortuitous discovery of oil in the North Sea was invaluable to government finances during the 1980s when, rising unemployment put pressure on the social security budget.

Looking at the neoliberal era overall from the early 1980s to 2007 – there is little doubt that without the debt bonanza, and North Sea oil revenues, Britain would have seen a fundamental lowering of living standards. But both these were temporary and distorting. By 2010 North Sea oil was running out, and the debt bonanza was over and deleveraging the new order of the day.

At the end of the first decade of the new millennium Britain was like a ship of the line going down in the heat of battle. It had been holed below the waterline by the 'hollowing out' of real jobs during globalisation but had been stabilised by infilling the holes in the hull with larger and larger bundles of debt, both private and public. The only problem was that the debt was so heavy the ship was sinking.

THE GREAT JOBS CRISIS

The great British debt crisis was part of a deeper underlying structural change in the British economy as it adapted to globalisation. It amounted to a three-decades-long, slow, imperceptible, weakening of real employment levels – and thus of incomes, certainly when compared to profits, capital and inheritance. This 'jobs crisis' or 'hollowing out' started with Thatcher's market reforms, but gathered pace under Major and then, powerfully, under Blair. And because it was slow-burning, and living standards were held up by rising debt and oil revenues (and real employment figures were difficult to properly assess), for many commentators 'hollowing out' was, at any one time, hardly discernible – and, after all the leaders of media corporations and many of their journalists were high net worth individuals and continued to do well, shielded from facing the growing strains on normal family budgets.

The 1990s saw a radically changed environment for labour, and for work more broadly. The new globalised capitalism ensured that labour was both less secure and less valued. Increasing job insecurity followed naturally from the progressive introduction of the 'flexible labour market' – one of the central pillars of the new globalism, an approach lauded across the Anglo-Saxon political spectrum from Ronald Reagan's conservatives in the 1980s through Tony Blair's New Labourites in the late 1990s. Underlying the argument for a flexible labour market was the not unreasonable notion that no one should expect a job for life.

However, although the postwar 'American dream' was never based upon a job for life, for most middle-class Americans in the pre-globalisation era relatively secure work was certainly an expectation; as was the ability, if the family was prepared to move to a new location, to find equally well paid or better paid work elsewhere. And umbilically linked to this secure work – an integral part of the job, indeed often a recruiting tool – was a package of benefits, including healthcare and pension coverage. In Britain, too, relatively secure, adequately paid work, with the support of state health and pension benefits, was also an expectation.

Yet, the labour market created by the new era of global capital brought to an end these expectations. It did so by systematically replacing full-time work by part-time, thus creating a huge 'contingent' workforce. The growth in a 'contingent workforce' was most pronounced in the US. During the 1990s temporary worker agencies – such as Kelly Services and Manpower – grew twice as fast as the nation's GNP.[9] It has been estimated that all kinds of 'contingent labour' – contract and temporary workers, involuntary part-timers, employees of subcontractors, and homeworkers – grew by a staggering 120 per cent in the first half of the 1980s.[10] The US Bureau of Labor Statistics has noted that the number of part-time workers rose to 19.5 per cent of the workforce in 1994, up from 14 per cent in 1968, but according to Susan Houseman of the Upjohn Institute, such data fails to account for the 'growing number of Americans who hold *two* part-time jobs, or a full-time and part-time job. They appear instead in the official count as full-timers, working a total of more than 35 hours per week.'[11]

In Britain, the other major 'neoliberal' economy, all types of households saw part-time work increasing: 5.9 million worked part-time in December 1992, rising to 6.3 million in September 1996 (five million of these being women). In Britain between 1979 and 1993 full-time work fell dramatically – by a huge 10 per cent. Will Hutton has calculated that between 1975 and 1993 the proportion of the adult population in full-time tenured jobs fell from 55 per cent to 35 per cent. And many of these, he argues, were not wholly defined by their income, which ranged widely from high to low, but rather by their insecurity.[12] And in both Britain and the US, as the economic boom of the late 1990s gathered pace – ahead of the inevitable recession – many new jobs were created, but most of these much-touted additions to the job pool were of the part-time, contingent variety. 'Contingent labour' is difficult to define properly – for instance some analysts believe it should include self-employed independent contractors (the kind of worker who is a victim of corporate downsizing). Even so, a 1995 US Bureau of Labor Statistics study, which defines contingent labour as individuals who do not possess an implicit or explicit ongoing contract of work, suggests that 15 per cent of wage and salary workers are contingent.[13]

In any event, the rise of contingent labour has produced a new pattern of corporate employment based upon an inner core and outer periphery of employees. In the summer of 1997 the *New York Times* ran a controversial series of reports from across the country on the effects of downsizing. It reported that:

> at many companies, an upper tier of full time core workers enjoys the best combination of pay, benefits, hours and job security that a company can offer. Below them is a second tier of less valued part-time, temporary and contract workers who, in addition to being less expensive, can be discharged more easily, giving corporate managers the flexibility that they say is essential to compete in an increasingly global economy.[14]

Of course this new system of contingent labour and, more generally, the flexible labour market demanded by the global economy does in some sense serve the needs of people, of labour as well as of capital. Flexibility and part-time working appeals to many women and some men because it fits in with their family responsibilities. And in principle labour flexibility is a highly appropriate mechanism for an advanced, complex society.

However the 'hire and fire' economy of the Anglo-American globalised system was not essentially a response to these changing social needs; rather it was a cost-cutting operation. Contingent labour relieves the employer from burdensome social costs such as expensive healthcare benefits or pensions. In the US this amounts to a major breach by capital and corporations of an unspoken social contract whereby the middle class, who could expect little or no state support for health, could rely upon their employer to provide healthcare as part of a relatively secure job contract. In Britain the plug has also been pulled on another social contract – the increasing army of contingent workers used to be able to rely upon a relatively adequate benefit system, but have seen it progressively eroded.

Flexible labour markets make it easy for capital to respond quickly to changing market conditions by being able to hire and fire easily. However this too often means that the employees, rather than the so-called capitalist 'risk-takers', bear the risks of the free-market system. What is more there is no evidence whatsoever that the hire and fire economies have been more successful than those with regulated labour markets.

Hidden Unemployment

Karl Marx famously coined the idea of a 'reserve army of the unemployed' acting as a weapon that could be used by employers to discipline workers. As the number of core workers has shrunk and that of contingent workers risen, modern global capitalism now has its own 'reserve army' available – and, in a sense unknown to Marx, on a global scale! Of course many part-time workers, unlike the unemployed of old, are not seeking full-time work and therefore cannot be counted as 'reserve' in the Marxist sense; however, many are, and with welfare being pared down, with more income needed in traditional households and with the growth of single parent families and people living alone (who need a proper wage, not a supplementary one), the demand for full-time, benefit-linked work will always be high.

Contingent, part-time work serves another function too. In this public-relations-dominated media age western government are constantly fighting a battle of presentation. The growth in part-time work hides the extent of unemployment. During the 1970s the unemployment rate began to rise across the OECD world – up from 3 per cent at the beginning of the decade to an average of about 6 per cent at the end. The 1980s saw unemployment rise further, denting the view that unemployment was a passing phase, linked to economic cycles.

In the early 1990s, with the corporate mania for downsizing in full swing, it became obvious that structural factors such as changing technology and footloose global capital in search of low costs were causing high unemployment. Harry Shutt has pointed to technology as being partly responsible for this higher unemployment, and as a reason for the new phenomenon known as 'jobless growth', particularly in Europe. He argues that 'taking the 1974 to 1994 period as a whole, there has been negligible growth in the numbers of employed people in the countries of the European Union at a time when the level of economic activity (GDP) has expanded significantly', and he pointed to the example of Spain, where employment fell by over 8 per cent during the period whilst the economy virtually doubled in size![15]

In the late 1990s the peak of the Anglo-American boom did create a tightish labour market and an American 'jobs miracle' was proclaimed. But the high employment figures hid the fundamental – and grave – changes that were overwhelming the world of work. For included in the employment numbers were millions and millions of employees who were not in full-time, secure work, were not in adequately paid work and – more harrowing even than that – were not in work that provided adequate social benefits. In fact, included in US 'employed' figures are 'day labourers and people who survive on odd jobs', for 'all it takes to be listed as "employed" is to have one hour of work a week'. This American 'jobs miracle' was a statistical con game. And at the heart of the myth of late 1990s 'full employment' was the assumption – accepted by most of the Anglo-American media – that high employment meant high living standards. The *New York Times* issued a contrarian position when it argued that 'a lower jobless rate means little if a $15 an hour factory worker is fired and earns only half of that in his next job'.[16]

Rarely was the question asked of the new millions of low-paid workers in Anglo-America: would you prefer to be 'in work' in the US or Britain, or unemployed and on welfare in France or Germany? Millions of 'employed' in Britain or the US would have opted for the latter.

Nagging Insecurity at Work

But perhaps the most important consequence of the new 'flexible labour market' was the widespread and profound insecurity it engendered. Insecurity is indefinable, and its extent is not statistically provable. Yet over the last two decades it has been interwoven into the very fabric of the working populations of the 'free-market' economies. The signs of anxiety are there for everyone to see: employees work longer and longer hours, workers stay late at the office, not in order to finish necessary work but to secure their positions, and there is an increase in useless paperwork to justify jobs and salaries.

Of course job insecurity certainly keeps people on their toes, as well as on other people's toes, but there is no evidence that it produces higher growth rates than was the case in the more regulated and structured labour markets of the 1950s, 1960s and early 1970s. The jury is still out, and may always be out, on whether labour market competition and insecurity, or alternatively stability and cooperation, produce a more efficient workforce.

Aside from the economics of it all, there was the fact that in the new capitalist society insecurity was (is) unequally spread. Owning capital was supposed to be a risk-taking enterprise, but was increasingly becoming a more secure way to live than the world of work. Even in a financially turbulent world, even too in a financial meltdown, the risks to capital were becoming far less than the risks associated with holding a job, particularly in the private sector. Capital ownership provided many more real choices, and opportunities for diversification and manipulation, than did (does) a job. Investments are unlikely to do badly in good times, and even if shares and bonds plummet there is normally some capital left. Often the worst that can happen is a reduction from a lavish to a high living standard – from a large to a small yacht, from three Mercedes to one, from three or four homes to just two. Yet the loss of a job, particularly with few state benefits available, alters a whole way of life.

For most people in the West under pensionable age, income from employment remains the very foundation of their lifestyle, if not their life. Other sources of income – dividends from shares, interest from bonds, small inheritances, rent – may help out, but tend to be marginal. Jobs remain the name of the game – and the character of employment – particularly its security – becomes important. For the employed majority, if not for those who employ them, the new capitalism's destruction of traditional job security was a real blow. And by destroying the good secure job (with pensions and benefits) it was also destroying one of the building blocks of the American and western middle class.

Flexible, 'hire and fire' labour policies may also have caused some wider problems in society. The world of disposable jobs may well have induced a short-termism into the work culture that would feed through into broader social values. Richard Sennett, in his fascinating book *The Corrosion of Character: The Personal Consequences of Work in the New Capitalism*, argues that this connection is very real. It appears that 'when people talk in earnest about family values, "no long term" is no way to raise children. We want them, for instance to learn how to be loyal; a management consultant told me he felt stupid talking to his children about commitment, since at work he does not practice it.' Sennett also argues, intriguingly, that hire and fire labour flexibility may undermine the work ethic: 'the classic work ethic was one of delayed gratification: coping with immediate frustration usually requires a sense of sustaining purpose, of long-term goals. The flexible work ethic undermines such self discipline; you must seize the moment, delay may prove fatal.'[17]

The Devaluation of Work

The British (and western) middle class was forged on the work ethic. The capitalist system of the twentieth century, which created this middle class, differed from the old aristocratic system it replaced by elevating productivity and creativity – that is, work – over lineage. And by mid-century almost everyone – the medium and small businesses, the professional classes, even the big corporate bosses – was defining themselves by their work, and by securing their money 'the old fashioned way' – by earning it.

Yet the new globalised economy, and the new capitalism it created, was turning this value system on its head. Work itself was becoming devalued. Earning, as opposed to 'making' or having, money was becoming more and more difficult. It was a stark fact that in the 1990s earned income (wages and salaries) actually fell as a percentage of total income. Global capitalism was at least becoming clear about its priorities: lower rewards from work, higher rewards from investments and inheritance. And there were big rewards too for going into debt. The average Briton no longer worked to pay for a house – you could buy it, and sell it, for a huge profit, all in the same week by the clever use of debt.

Profits were outstripping wages. By 1995, as globalisation was getting underway, US wages were stagnating or declining for the vast majority of the workforce. And this was during a time when profits were at a postwar high. For instance the average after-tax profit rate for non-farm businesses was 7.5 per cent in 1994 compared with an average 3.8 per cent in the 1952-79 period. 'By the close of the second quarter of 1995, the return on equity for Standard and Poor's list of five hundred major blue chip companies was running at an annual rate of 20% – the best ever for corporate America.'[18] Another estimate, reported in the *Wall Street Journal*, was that corporate profit margins in the US rose between 1989 and 1996 from 6 per cent to 9 per cent.[19]

The same trends were observable in globalising Britain. Looking at the same issue from a different vantage point, income from employment (wages) diminished as a ratio of all household disposable income from 90.4 per cent in 1977 to 73.3 per cent in 1994, while income from rents, dividends and interest grew from 10.7 per cent to 13.6 per cent and even benefits rose as a proportion of income.[20] An IFS study in 2006 reported that since 2001-2 household earnings had barely risen in real terms, while at the same time self-employment incomes had fallen considerably, a startling decrease of 30 per cent over the same period.[21]

Wages Versus Investments

One look at the riches and rewards created by investments – as opposed to wages and salaries – shows the advantages in the new economy of investing for a living over working for a living. Charles Handy calculated that 'a £10 million investment, for example, which is made on the expectation that it will recover its costs in ten years' time and provide a 20 per cent compound return, will, in the next ten years, if the expectation is met and if things continue the same, earn an extra £26.4 million, and even more in the years following.'[22]

Of all the income coming into all the households in the British and US economies during the height of the new global capitalist boom the share of pay went down and the share from interest, dividends and straight gifts (inheritance) went up. Of course much of this was concentrated at the top. Take shares. In Britain there remained a marked difference between the wealth holdings of the top 1 per cent and the rest – the top 1 per cent holding almost half of their portfolios in shares whereas less wealthy groups held progressively less and less in shares.[23]

Inheritance payouts are also concentrated at the top but are now becoming increasingly widespread. Inherited wealth is very big business, perhaps the biggest business of all in today's global capitalist economy. The British free-market Conservative government in the 1990s talked approvingly of a future economy dominated by inherited wealth as wealth 'cascaded down the generations'. As the new capitalist era got underway in the early 1990s Robert Avery of Cornell University predicted that 'we will shortly be seeing the largest transfer of income in the history of the world'.[24] And around the same time political scientist Kevin Phillips also argued that inheritance is 'about to become a critical component of the younger generation's future, *something America has never before experienced*'.[25]

The Working Poor: The Wonderful World of McJobs

Perhaps the single most powerful illustration of global capitalism's devaluation of work, and of earned income, is the growth on both sides of the Atlantic of the working poor. These are the millions of people who put in 'a fair day's work' but end up without 'a fair day's pay'.

In the early years of the new century the American 'new economy' retailer Wal-Mart became the symbol of such low pay and conditions. There were even reports that in parts of the Wal-Mart empire their workers were depending on federal food stamps and the use of hospital emergency rooms for basic medical care. From being the darling brand of the new 'flexible economy' in the 1990s Wal-Mart's labour practices became highly controversial – so much so that by 2007 Democratic politicians in the presidential campaign found the company an easy target.[26] In the US, the Bureau of Labor Statistics defines the working poor as 'persons who worked (or were looking for work) during twenty-seven weeks of the year, and who lived in families below the official poverty line'.[27] Where this 'poverty line' falls is obviously contentious, but what is not in dispute is the fact that large numbers of people in work are paid very low amounts – in 2005 42 per cent of individual Americans had an income of less than $25,000 per year and about 20 per cent (40 million people) had an income of $12,500 or less.[28]

In Britain, where there is no *official* 'poverty line' or count of the number living in poverty, low pay, in reality 'poverty pay', is also a feature of the employment landscape. In 1991 a staggering 28 per cent of those with *incomes of less than half the national average* were in households in some kind of work, including a third who were self-employed.[29] Over a decade and a half later – with 'low pay' now defined as 60-70 per cent of median pay – around 20-30 per cent of *all incomes* were designated as 'low pay'.[30] The low value set for the minimum wage in both the US and Britain tells the whole story of poverty pay.

Of course for some, poverty pay is simply an addition to family income. As Paul Gregg and Jonathan Wadsworth have reported about Britain, 'new jobs – often McJobs – are taken disproportionately by those with another household member already at work'.[31] For others low pay is acceptable as a step on the ladder to higher pay. And for some, work, any work at virtually any pay, will suffice because of the need to be in a working environment. However none of these arguments outweighs the damage that low pay does to the work ethic. If work is underpaid it will ultimately be undervalued. Nor do they justify the extreme differences between the top of the income scale and the bottom. It is difficult to argue that the gap between the ability, creativity and dedication of the millions of working poor and that of the top earners (let alone the top 'unearners') is large enough to begin to justify the unacceptable gap in income and wealth.

BRITAIN'S DIVIDED SOCIETY

Britain's late twentieth-century experiment with financialised capitalism was supposed to create a stable and prosperous middle class society. It was certainly sold as such by its proponents. They predicted that by sweeping away postwar social democracy and the industrial society it represented we would also sweep away the old 'us and them' frozen class divisions of Britain – the entrenched class warfare between the paternalist business cum aristocratic class at the top and the large traditional highly unionised working class. Instead, and over time, the market would ensure social mobility and we would all become 'middle class'. It would also, necessarily, be a society with big disparities of income and wealth, but this would not matter for it would also be a society in which, broadly speaking, 'all ships were rising' with the tide of growth. As long as 'all ships were rising' we would be at ease with ourselves – and we would not particularly care, we would be 'supremely relaxed', about the super and mega rich. And so, particularly during the early years of Blair and New Labour, when for a few years average wages were rising, we were. Issues of inequality began to seem like yesterday's debate.

It was a beguiling prospect. But by the turn of the millennium, and after two decades of full-on marketised capitalism, British society was not evolving as envisaged. For a start, there may have been many 'rising ships', but there were also many ships in the fleet that were sinking, and many more that were taking water. The fact is that Britain has seen a marked increase in economic inequality over the three decades of the neoliberal period, and by 2010 these inequalities had become striking. In January of 2010 a report, commissioned by the Minister For Women and Equality, Harriet Harman and chaired by Professor John Hills, stated that 'inequalities in earnings and income are high in Britain, both compared with other industrialised countries, and compared with thirty years ago.' The report also showed that disparities in wealth were even more striking. It argued that 'for some readers the sheer scale of the inequalities which we present will be shocking' and then concluded, dramatically, and rather ruefully, that 'whether or not people's positions reflect some form of merit or desert, the sheer scale of the differences in wealth, for instance, may imply that it is impossible to create a cohesive society.' And an IFS study published in 2009 at the very end of the neoliberal period reported that 'income inequality has risen for a second successive year, and is now equal to its highest-ever level (in 1961)'.[32]

Entrenching Inequality

But it was only after the crash, and the bankers' pay and bonuses revelations in 2008, that Britain's unequal society was firmly back in the spotlight and with it the issue of the super and mega rich. As I outlined in Chapter One a mega- and super-rich class (with income deriving from inheritance and investment rather than work) has become an embedded feature of British and western society. The economist Paul Krugman has argued that the much vaunted 'Anglo-Saxon' new capitalism model is not only not producing a middle class of so-called 'knowledge workers'; but rather the model is generating 'the rise of a narrow oligarchy' with 'income and wealth becoming increasingly concentrated in the hands of a small privileged elite.'[33]

The problem now, though, is not just growing 'concentration' of wealth and income, or growing inequality – it is much deeper, and much more worrying. For what the three decades of neoliberal capitalism has wrought in the 'Anglo-American' market economies, in Britain and the USA, is the *entrenching of classes* and the virtual end of mobility. During the those years virtually every political tendency in Anglo-America, from right-wing conservative Republican to left-wing socialist Labour, could at least agree with the aim of 'equality of opportunity'. Yet, even achieving this meritocratic objective, long promised by market enthusiasts, was not so easy. Indeed, from the 1990s onwards things may have gone into reverse. In 2009 the New Labour Blairite meritocrat par excellence, Alan Milburn, issued a report called 'Unleashing Aspiration' which was greeted with praise from many quarters (including from London Mayor Boris Johnson and neocon Tory *Telegraph* commentator Janet Daley).[34] Milburn argued that 'the huge growth in professional employment that took place after the Second World war was the engine that made Britain such a mobile society. By opening their doors to people from a rich variety of backgrounds, the professions created unheard of opportunities for millions of men and women' Yet, in a devastating admission of failure he also argues that 'in the decades since then, of course, social mobility has slowed down in our society. Birth, not worth, has become more and more a determinant of people's life chances.' Yet, as the Harman report in 2010 argued achieving this objective 'is very hard when there are such wide differences between the resources which people and their families have to help them fulfil their diverse potentials'.[35]

So, in a startling reversal, it is continental Europe's so-called 'sclerotic' societies that are arguably more socially mobile that those of the 'dynamic' 'Anglo-Saxons.' Even after the crash Britain's neoliberal elites, however, were finding this proposition very difficult to accept.

Global Capital and Inequality

This failure of neoliberal economics to deliver on its central promise of a socially mobile society was becoming its Achilles heel. And this failure was slowly turning opinion against 'free-markets'. Yet there was a related, deeper, cause. For it was not markets as such, but, rather the global capital market, or what was called 'economic globalisation' that was to blame. By the early years of the new century the evidence was becoming overwhelming – that the economies that that were more exposed to the dictates of economic globalisation, that is the 'Anglo-Saxon' new capitalist economies of the USA, Britain, New Zealand, had clearly generated greater inequalities and social divisions than their, less globalised, continental European counterparts.

It was during the 1980s that first signs of a difference between 'Anglo-Saxon' inequality levels and continental Europe became apparent. There were, in fact, increases in the measure of inequality for all leading western nations, with the intriguing exception of France. In the US the Gini index rose from 31 to 34 (compared with 27 to 31 for Britain, 25 to 27 for the Netherlands and 23 to 23.5 for Belgium). OECD figures also show that the US had the highest percentage of low-income persons of any of the OECD countries. And in the 1990s – as 'globalisation' grew apace – an in-depth OECD study of inequality in the leading western nations, published in 1995, showed that the US was leading the world in terms of inequality, with Canada second, Australia third, Britain fourth and New Zealand and France joint fifth. Interestingly, most of the continental European nations – those shielded from the full impact of 'globalisation' by a social market or social democratic tradition – came well down the field, and Norway, the Netherlands, Belgium, Finland and Sweden would have had to more than double their inequality ratios to match those of the US.[36] Latest figures for 2007 show the United States with a co-efficient number of 45, the UK of 34, and France and Germany both 28.[37]

During the 'Thatcher revolution' the UK immersed itself in the emerging global economy more fully than any other western nation. Indeed Britain became the most 'globalised' of all major economies – and virtually a laboratory for testing the future of 'market globalisation'. Thatcher argued that 'there is no alternative' to 'globalisation'. But her victory was bought at a price: a new era of growing inequality. Before 1976, and Britain's revolutionary 'adjustment' to global economics, life in the country had been becoming more and more equal in terms of both income and wealth. After thirty years of social democracy Britain was probably a more equal society than it had ever been before, and may ever be again. According to John Hills, inequality (measured by income after taxes) fell significantly between 1949 and 1976. But from the mid-1970s, as the social effects of 'globalisation' began to take hold, the inequality index (the gini co-efficient) rose dramatically (from 25 points to over 35 points by 1990 and by 60 per cent, over 1978, by 2008). According to Hills, 'the rise in inequality after 1978 is more than large enough to offset all of the decline in inequality between 1949 and 1976-7, and almost large enough to take it back to 1938'. Similar trends towards inequality have been reported for New Zealand, another globalised 'free market' country made defenceless against 'globalisation' in the 1980s. Between 1981 and 1989 the New Zealand equality index (Gini coefficient) rose by almost three points – from 26.7 to 29.5, a larger percentage rise than that of the US in the 1980s.[38]

In the US itself, the primary driver behind, and host to, global capitalism, inequality also rose sharply in the 1980s and 1990s, a trend made more remarkable by the fact that it had also risen during the 1970s. In 1994 the Council of Economic Advisors reported that 'starting some time in the late 1970s income inequalities widened alarmingly in America'. In the 1980s the average income of the poorest fifth of American families actually declined by about 7 per cent whilst the richest fifth became about 15 per cent wealthier. This left the poorest fifth with only 3.7 per cent of the nation's income and the richest with a little over half by 1990! Amongst all advanced countries where data for the 1980s are available, the US showed the most dramatic expansion of inequality, a social division that one American scholar argued was 'lethal to our middle class way of life'.[39] By 1994 the share of the US income cake held by the poorest fifth of Americans had declined to 3.4 per cent. Between 1992 and 1996 American families in all the lowest income groups – those earning less than $10,000 a year through to those in the $50-75 000 category – received a smaller share of the nation's total pretax income whereas those in the higher categories – $75,000 to $200,000 or more, received an increase. One sure sign of increasing inequality within the US was the diverging income shares of the middle quintile and the top one per cent of the US population. Between 1987 and 1998 the income share of the middle quintile fell from 16.3 per cent to 14.3 whereas that of the top 1 per cent rose dramatically, from 8.3 to 13.5.[40] By 1998 even official predictions foresaw increasing inequality. Labor department data showed that if current trends continue America's income gap will resemble that of Mexico by 2043.[41]

However, the essential tale is told by the figures on the eve of the crash – for the 2006-7 period – in the inequality index: they show globalised Britain standing at 36.0, the globalised USA at

46.6. and the less globalised France and Germany at 32.7 and 28.3 respectively.[42]

Wealth Inequality

Of course income inequality is only one measure of the social division in western nations. Wealth also counts. And the story of wealth distribution in the highly globalised 'new capitalist' states of Britain and the US since the late 1970s is a striking one. We have already (in Chapter One) recorded the egregious wealth of the mega-rich; but the extent of wealth *inequality* in the Anglo-American world in the last two decades is, perhaps, an even bigger story.

The situation in the 1990s is illustrated by the fact that in 1995 the mega-wealthy (the top ½ per cent, or 500,000 families) controlled 24.2 per cent of assets and 27.5 per cent of net worth, the top 1 per cent of American households (about one million) possessed 31 per cent of assets and 35.1 per cent of net worth, the next 9 per cent (the affluent) possessed 31 per cent of assets and 33.2 per cent of net worth, and all the rest (over 89 million households) only possessed 37.9 per cent of assets and 31.5 per cent of net worth.'[43]

By 2004, wealth inequality had grown even further, and there was evidence that the mega – and super-rich were leaving greater and greater gaps between themselves and everyone else including the merely affluent. Figures show that the top quartile (25 per cent of people) owned 87 per cent of the country's wealth, the upper middle owned 10 per cent, the lower middle 3 per cent and the bottom zero. They also show that between 1995 and 2004 the gap between the top quarter and the 'lower middle' quarter had risen by almost a third. A 2007 report from Harvard University argued that 'by the early 1990s, the United States had surpassed all industrial societies in the extent of inequality of household wealth'; and it also argued that the economic growth of the most recent decade or so, from 1995 onwards, had seen 'growing inequality [of wealth] accompanying [this] wealth growth.'[44]

Not surprisingly Britain increasingly resembled the US in this 'wealth gap'. In Britain an unhealthy concentration of wealth is not new. In the 1930s the top 1 per cent owned as much 58 per cent of all the country's wealth while the mass of Britons were capital-less and property-less. As R. H. Tawney poignantly argued, Britons who fought during the First World War on the Somme and at Passchendale 'probably do not own wealth to the value of the kit they took into battle'. In the first seven decades of the twentieth century there were significant – indeed dramatic – changes to the wealth of the top 1 per cent which declined from 68 per cent in 1911 (for England and Wales) to 20 per cent in 1976 (for the UK as a whole). This half-century-long spreading of wealth, primarily the product of progressive tax policies, amounted to what Charles Feinstein has called 'a major economic and social revolution'.

However, in a clear measure of the reactionary effects of the new global market capitalism, this wealth 'revolution' stalled as the British economy became more globalised during the 1980s and 1990s while wealth distribution remained static. By the end of the 1980s – after a decade of Thatcherite market radicalism – the top 10 per cent of adults owned 45 per cent of the wealth, and 30 per cent of adults still had less than £5000 in assets. In the early 1990s the British super-rich – the top 1 per cent of the population, with an average wealth of $1.3 million each – owned a huge 18 per cent of the country's marketable wealth and the top 5 per cent owned a staggering 37 per cent of all wealth.[45] Even after Thatcher's 'popular capitalist' revolution (with its rhetoric of 'spreading the wealth' beyond the traditional landowning class) wealth and land still tended to go hand in hand. In the most sophisticated analysis available, John Scott has described the 'top twenty' of the British league of wealth as 'a mixture of urban and rural rentier landowners and entrepreneurial capitalists'. Scott argues that because research into this very murky area can only concentrate on relatively visible sources of wealth, and is often unable to penetrate into the anonymity of most shareholdings and bank accounts, rentiers, whose assets are concentrated in such anonymous investment portfolios, are normally underrepresented in any hierarchy of wealth holders. Even so, he argues that land and entrepreneurial capital remained the major sources of really large fortunes in the 1980s, and that 'the wealthiest landowners are the long established landowning families of Cadogan, Grosvenor, and Portman, most of whom own substantial urban estates as well as their country acres'.[46]

THE COMING MISERY OF THE MAJORITY

The future can rarely be depicted with any precision. But *should today's trends continue*, and the global market still rules whilst public spending is cut, then one thing is certain: Britain will see emerging a new social structure in which the lives now lived by its poorest people will be the future of more and more citizens, and maybe even a majority.

So, should global capital still set the rules, this misery of the British majority will, though, likely exist side by side with a wealthy and self-perpetuating globally-oriented 'aristocracy' who will define themselves by their ownership of capital.

It is a combustible prospect for it will exist in an era, unlike any before, in which this poor majority will also be assertive. The social and political deference to 'authority' that existed at the beginning of the twentieth century is, at the beginning of this century, as dead as a dodo. Indeed, in Britain the irony is that Thatcherite culture has, by promoting individualism and consumerism, added a further dimension to the collapse of deference. So it would seem likely that such a future majority will demand major, even revolutionary, changes in the economic and political system.

It amounts to a classic pre-revolutionary situation – as critical and as dangerous as the last time – in the 1930s – when the West faced economic collapse and total political change. Britain had a relatively benign depression in the 1930s, certainly when compared to Germany or the United States. Then it was protected by an imperial economic system, and the blows were somewhat softened. Today, though, the country is much more exposed. It is seriously globalised, and its relationship with Europe – inside the European Single Market but outside the eurozone – remains ambivalent.

DEBT AND DISASTER

By the late 1990s, the gathering problem of stagnant – or falling – real incomes was becoming urgent. The politicians certainly knew of it. Yet, strangely, with so many family incomes in trouble, consumption levels remained high, and were fuelling what seemed to be endless economic growth.

There was a nagging question in the air: how, in these circumstances, could this extraordinary consumer boom be maintained? It remained a mystery. And no one, least of all western policymakers, was in a mood to answer it. For this was the time of the 'dot.com revolution' – in which America was leading the West into a new hi-tech world, a 'new economy', indeed a 'new paradigm' with new rules. The 'revolution' was in reality a 'bubble', and it was to burst. But soon thereafter there was another massive distraction when, after 9/11, security from terror dominated the scene.

Yet the answer to the question was not difficult. The consumer boom in Britain was floated by the stagnant incomes of the middle and lower middle class being massively supplemented by bags and bags of debt. Nationally it amounted to a mountain of debt – a mountain of Himalayan proportions. Britain's financial industry organised a private debt bonanza the size of which had not seen before in the country's history. And it was engineered through the British love affair with home ownership. Millions of cheap mortgages (kept cheap by the low inflation environment) allowed millions of families to access cash and to borrow money as never before because of their rising house prices – the so-called 'wealth effect'. The much-vaunted British economic growth rates (compared that is to the continent) were underpinned by a consumption binge as Britain's consumers used loans and credit cards mainly for holidays and shopping.

By 2010, in the aftermath of the crash, Britain's hard-pressed families were still drowning in debt. Credit had become much tighter, but many households were saved from penury by historically very low interest-rates – a purposive act of policy specifically aimed at keeping mortgage rates low. Should these rates ever rise then, outside of another housing boom, millions of Britons would simply be unable to afford the homes they lived in and household budgets would be stretched to breaking-point. This looming catastrophe was the measure of Britain's great debt disaster.

CHAPTER SIX

THE UK'S BROKEN CAPITALISM

A 'SOCIALLY USELESS' SYSTEM

A 'SOCIALLY USELESS' SYSTEM

By the autumn of 2009, only a year after the collapse in Wall Street and the effective nationalisation of the British banks, criticism, and bitter criticism, of the working of financial capitalism was commonplace. Even the country's erstwhile super-confident financial establishment was beginning to buckle under the pressure. Attacks upon the very system that only a few months earlier had been so stoutly defended became a regular feature of comment. On the 20st October, no less a figure than the Governor of the Bank of England, Mervyn King, launched what amounted to a fundamentalist critique. He argued that 'to paraphrase a great wartime leader, never in the field of financial endeavour has so much been owed by so few to so many. And, one might add with little real reform.' The reform he called for was radical: in essence, and shorn of its carefully constructed official English, it amounted to a call to break up the large 'too big to fail' banks; the Governor was readily supported by the Conservative party's Treasury spokesperson, George Osborne, who called the speech 'persuasive'.[1] King's attack on the system came fast on the heels of one, even more blistering, on the City by the City regulator, the FSA Chairman Lord Turner. He described much of the City's activities as 'socially useless' and questioned whether the whole financial services industry had grown too large.[2] On top of these 'official' critiques, re-assessments and *mea culpas* were coming thick and fast from London's erstwhile financially orthodox commentariat – not least from erstwhile doyens of the neoliberal consensus like Martin Wolf in *The Financial Times*, and Anatole Kaletsky in *The Times*, who became as eloquent in their denunciations of capitalist finance as they had earlier been in their support.

The leading lights of the British financial establishment were, however, somewhat slower, and less fulsome, in issuing their *mea culpas* than were their American counterparts. Larry Summers, whilst Treasury Secretary under President Bill Clinton, had been instrumental in the repeal of Glass-Steagall and had helped construct, and cheerlead, the whole Wall Street excess; but during the presidential election campaign of 2008, as he became an Obama supporter, he reversed himself and issued a public apologia. (Summers was to join the Obama administration and roundly condemned the 'bloated financial system'. He endorsed his boss's efforts to regulate Wall Street.) And the former Fed Chairman Alan Greenspan himself (whom only a few years previously the British establishment had treated as the wisest of the wise) delivered his own half-apology as early as October 2008. 'Those of us who have looked to the self-interest of lending institutions to protect shareholders' equity (myself especially) are in a state of shocked disbelief' he reported, and he also conceded that he was 'partially wrong' to resist regulation of some securities.[3] These remarks, coming from the author and architect of the long debt boom, himself, were revealing; for they were a sign that something very serious had gone wrong with financial capitalism.

These 'official' voices may well have conceded that banks and finance now needed a radical overhaul, but they always stopped short of attacking the fundamentals of global capitalism itself. Yet, the fact was that the Wall Street/City collapse, and its aftermath of rising unemployment and crises in public expenditure, had placed the whole 'new capitalist' system – the 'new capitalism' that is of global markets and global finance – in question.

Moral condemnations of the new capitalism were now commonplace. The 1990s was being called 'the greediest decade in history', an era of excess neatly captured by a series of high-profile business scandals. The most sensational of these had erupted in early December 2001 when the mega-global company, Enron, filed for bankruptcy. The scam had involved the creation of offshore units which were used both to avoid taxes and keep losses off the balance sheets. So shocking was the revelation that it also destroyed the Enron accountants, Arthur Anderson, and even led a traumatised Congress to more properly regulate financial business through new legislation known as 'Sarbanes-Oxley'.

Yet the bedrock legitimacy of western capitalism – and the worldwide appeal of the West – had not rested on capitalism's ethical standards, Rather, it had been based on the delivery of prosperity – more precisely on mass middle class prosperity. But now, the first time since the 1950s this mass prosperity was no longer a firm expectation. The middle class was fragmenting (both up and down), 'all ships' were no longer rising with the tide, and many were sinking. The living standards of millions of middle class people were falling. And, as discussed in the last chapter, a new ugly, 'un-American', feature was emerging: a rigid class system with little upward mobility. As the crisis unfolded during 2008, Main Street's troubles (mainly the collapsing housing and mortgage market) were beginning to rock Wall Street too. So much so that the banks and financial institutions were running to the erstwhile derided state for life-support.

Clearly, something had gone wrong with the economy. And the question that no one had thought possible was now arising: was there something wrong with the system itself? Can Anglo-American free-market capitalism any longer deliver? Alongside this nagging question, and just as important for capitalism's future, and for its long-term popular legitimacy as an economic model, was its moral and ideological standing. Post-1945 capitalism – the Roosevelt-LBJ 'social democratic' model – had for a time secured a popular consensus behind it. It was seen as stable, as delivering rising living standards to a mass middle class, and, crucially, as furthering American values – it was both *democratic* (certainly more so than the command economies in the East) and *meritocratic* (instilling the positive values of work and merit).

And when in the 1980s Ronald Reagan and Margaret Thatcher took western capitalism into its new rawer, and more globalised, phase, they also sought to justify it beyond its appeal as a material success story. They promoted their new brand of 'popular capitalism' as being virtuous as well as efficient. It would deliver 'freedom' as well as prosperity. Indeed, capitalism and freedom went hand in hand, and capitalism was uniquely able to preserve western liberties. This idea drew upon a deeper body of thought that saw capitalism as an historically progressive force – having broken the bonds of feudalism in the middle ages. It was not only the ally, but also the begetter, of political liberalism and democracy, indeed of the modern liberal world itself. The heroes of the 'new capitalism', economists like Frederich von Hayek and Milton Friedman, were touted as the incarnation of John Locke and John Stuart Mill.

One major success of the Thatcher-Reagan revolution was to associate modern capitalism with 'freedom' and with 'markets'. And according to its 'free-market' supporters, the key virtue of the capitalist system, what allied it to 'freedom', was that it was not based upon 'commands' – unlike in the 'command' economies. The theory was that every action in 'the market' – buying and selling – was purely voluntary.

Advocates also argued that access to capitalism and the market was both free of prejudices and unlimited. Traditional barriers based upon class and background, race and religion were all irrelevant criteria for membership of capitalist society. It was 'the colour of your money' not 'the colour of your skin' that counted. And although access through money limited the numbers who could properly participate, the great capitalist growth engine would, by 'trickle-down', allow more and more people to participate. Thatcher made 'popular capitalism' a political slogan and promised wider and wider access to capitalism and the market, based upon the idea of wider and wider shareholding.

As it turned out, though, modern global capitalism, like its nationally-based predecessor, is hardly teeming with participants. Shareholding has certainly burgeoned; yet most of this growth is through pension funds – at one remove from and with no participation by those whose money is used. Just as tax dollars and pounds support programmes of which the taxpayer may not approve, so in today's global capitalist system the people's pension money might easily be supporting companies and industries of which many do not approve. (A recent advertisement by the Calvert Group in an American newspaper highlighted this problem: it asked 'Does your retirement money go places you never dreamed of?' as part of a campaign against tobacco.) Real shareholding – in which the participant knows what he or she owns and can direct his or her money to the desired location – remains a decidedly minority affair both domestically and globally, and shares remain a small proportion of the portfolios of the vast majority of those who own them.

it is difficult to describe global capitalism and its markets as 'democratic' when the vast majority of western people still come to the market with next to nothing, putting them at a great disadvantage compared with those who bring substantial financial resources to the party. As I will argue later, the claim that modern capitalism – particularly when it is shorn of the balance provided by the state – is dynamic and progressive now rings hollow. Indeed modern capitalism (and the 'markets' associated with it) has become a force for stasis and tradition in that it gives a huge advantage to those with established wealth rather than those whose talent and merit will make wealth.

Some imaginative 'market theorists' have acknowledged this problem of limited access to the markets. Jeff Gates has argued that modern capitalism needs to be more inclusive but seems unable to make enough capitalists. In order to create a better system he suggests a whole series of reforms, including bank credit without collateral, conditional tax relief on capital gains and a re-engineering of estate taxes to advance broad-based ownership.[4]

Others seek to rectify this deficiency in modern capitalism by using state money for vouchers or indeed cash rather than services. 'Give em the money' as a one-off in order to increase access to the markets. As Arthur Seldon suggested in the context of how to fund education, health and pensions, 'the obvious alternative [to state funding] was to provide purchasing power in cash, general or earmarked, rather than services in kind'.[5] This provision would presumably come from taxes, and be subject to downward pressure every year as the low-tax regime developed. But not even the most radical policy of income redistribution would provide those outside the capitalist world with the asset base necessary to seriously join it – to become 'a player'.

'Popular capitalism' will thus remain a pipedream as long as the global system has no way of opening itself up to mass involvement. The fact remains that mass asset ownership without a revolutionary programme of *asset redistribution* – from the asset rich to the asset poor – is well nigh impossible. Only a political programme to break up the accumulated asset base of families and companies could achieve this objective. However, no 'pro-market' theorist, not even the radical and adventurous Seldon, has proposed such a dramatic departure from the norm. The idea of an existing political party's taxing wealth in order, say, to fund mortgages for the young is utterly fanciful. Hardly anyone today – left or right – sees a role for government as an agent of widening the distribution of *capital*. Few supporters of the new capitalism see anything wrong with one man owning wealth equal to whole nations, or any problem with one man personally owning huge tracts of Britain's capital city – as does the Duke of Westminster. The 'new capitalism' has no use for Huey Long's cry of 'every man a King!' or Lloyd-George's aim of everyone owning an 'acre and a cow'.

THE DEGENERATION OF DOMESTIC CAPITALISM
The Lost Work Ethic
In her campaign for 'popular capitalism' Margaret Thatcher also portrayed capitalism as a system which protected and enhanced the Protestant virtues, including the work ethic. Certainly this idea of the 'work ethic' – that hard work, application, delayed gratification, and making sacrifices is good for economic growth –

has consistently been espoused as public doctrine by supporters of Protestant, liberal capitalism. In their famous works both R. H. Tawney and Max Weber argued that Protestantism, and specifically Calvinism – with its belief in the value of work – was a crucial ideological ingredient in the rise of capitalism; and many contemporary American economic historians, like Talcott Parson and Herbert Gutman, have also tended to associate the work ethic with the US's economic success.[6]

Whilst she was prime minister Margaret Thatcher made the Weberian case for the capitalist work ethic by evoking 'Victorian values'. She argued that hard work, thrift, delayed gratification, and the like, built self-reliance and independence; and she counterpoised all this to what she described as the 'dependency culture' – the socialist welfare state – in which hard work was replaced by inducements to idleness and sloth. Intriguingly there was no similar rhetoric from 'market' supporters about the problematic values of the 'idle rich'. Yet, interestingly, such criticism had been a prominent feature of pro-capitalist Victorian radicalism.

Yet, in today's economy justifying capitalism by reference to encouraging the work ethic is difficult. The popular idea that there was a link between hard work and income – that those with high incomes earn their economic rewards because they work harder than others – was always fragile; but may well have been broken altogether by the publicity surrounding some of the very large rewards 'earned' by private sector executives. These egregious salaries and 'packages' enjoyed by top executives in the corporate world have raised the issue of the proportionality of work to reward, and the powerful question of 'how much is enough?' Furthermore, it is now more difficult to defend huge salary 'packages' for failing executives like chief executive Roger Smith of General Motors who received a rise of half a million dollars a year following the collapse of the company's market share and the huge reduction of its workforce or those who were corrupt like the top Enron executives, paid lavishly whilst the company was cheating the public.

The work ethic, particularly delayed gratification, has been systematically eroded by the commercialism of modern capitalism, by the personal greed promoted by the advertising industry, and by the search for short-term financial gain, which is now almost endemic.

The Loss of Merit

The work ethic and the idea of 'merit' tend to go hand in hand. British Prime Minister Tony Blair, declared on entering Downing Street in 1997 that he sought to create a 'society based on meritocracy' and that 'the Britain of the elite is over...the new Britain is a meritocracy.' This term 'meritocracy' was taken from the title of Michael Young's famous 1958 work *The Rise of The Meritocracy*; and although Young was to say 'I wish Tony Blair would stop using the term', Blair, like Thatcher before him, and like many others, saw 'opening up...old structures to uniquely reward merit and meritorious individuals as one of the key attributes of the new 'market capitalism'.

Of course the core institution of capitalism, the market, is not meritocratic at all, for the market exists specifically to cater to the public's wants and needs, those of the majority not the meritocracy. However to use the market effectively in supply side economics requires some degree of merit of business acumen; this requires ability, rather than position and intelligence, not social standing.

The problem for contemporary capitalism is that the rewards for merit (and work), though extant, are no longer as substantial as they were. Rewards from other than work and merit – most particularly from the inheritance of capital – are today often much greater, enough to secure a very, very good standard of living indeed. Without providing a real system of rewards for merit and work, the very legitimacy of modern capitalism may falter.

Conformity Rules

Alongside hard work and enterprise, individualism has been at the heart of the value system of old-style capitalism. Calvinism, with its commercial values, believed in the individual having a direct line to God. 'Grace alone can save, and this grace is the direct gift of God, unmediated by any earthly institution.' And other supporters of capitalism and private property – the great English liberal thinkers like Hobbes and Locke and Herbert Spencer, the American founding fathers in the new world, the New Liberals at the turn of the century and the 'neoliberal' globalisers of today – all, irrespective of their differing views about the exact role of the state, have placed 'the sovereign individual' at the very centre of their worldview.

In the contemporary era, this ethic of individualism has been favourably compared to socialism, and even social democracy, which according to supporters of the capitalist system have weakened the individual through the conformity that, they argued, collectivism inevitably induced.

Yet today this polemic is increasingly difficult to sustain. The free enterprise system no longer has a lock-hold on individualist values. Indeed, how can it when it was the ancestors, and not the present economic players, who were the individualists and who, by hard work, enterprise or even sharp practice, amassed the wealth? And how can individualism be such a highly prized virtue when, in our economy of inherited wealth, it is increasingly the family unit, and not the lone individual, from which all good things, primarily riches, flow?

What's more, modern capitalism can hardly be the engine for individuality. Its primary institution, the large corporation, promotes conformist corporate cultures and hierarchies that, instead of rewarding individual flair and creativity, induce all the opposite attributes such as safe, bureaucratised, routine thinking, and lack of imagination and risk. These latter characteristics are highlighted in William H. Whyte's classic work *The Organisation Man*, published in 1956 – and he had corporations, not just public sector organisations in mind! With corporations now triumphant and more powerful than ever, we can expect a further quantum leap in the deadening conformist hand of corporate bureaucracy. It is not a system in which the creative individual will flourish.

Risk (Or Lack of It)

In today's capitalism the decline of creativity and the individual has gone hand in hand with the decline of risk. Risk was always the great capitalist value; and risk-taking was always the prized hallmark of the entrepreneur, the lifeblood of the daring, the unusual, and those who stood out from the crowd and deserved their riches.

Yet more and more critics are now asking a question – perhaps the most subversive question of all. Who, in the modern global capitalist economy, is actually taking the greatest risks? Capital or labour? Corporations or employees? Today when companies have problems they can switch their investments abroad with minimal losses. Or, as in the credit crunch, they can be bailed out by governments for fear of a more general collapse of the system. On the other hand, in the age of 'flexible labour markets' and 'downsizing', employees lose their jobs, and the loss of a job is everything, a total loss, to the individual and the family.

In the modern capitalist economy it is now the employee who increasingly bears the risks. For when the gamble of investment fails, those without capital are laid off (or casualised) whereas those who make the investment decisions are protected against loss. It is a topsy-turvy, perverse, world and another reason why modern global capitalism has lost its moral edge.

Global investors are also able to shed risk. When markets collapse it is the state and the taxpayers which stand ready to save the investors; the bigger the investors the greater the state bailout. When investors are vulnerable for millions in low cost foreign markets, such as Latin America in the 1980s or Asia in the 1990s, the taxpayer-backed IMF was needed. As Martin Wolf has argued, 'unregulated flows of short-term international capital are a license to rack up losses at the expense of taxpayers'.[7]

The 2007-8 banking and debt crisis, still unfolding as this book was written, demonstrated how the 'entrepreneurs' of the financial business class suddenly ceased to be society's risk-takers. As the crisis unfolded some super-rich bankers and hedge fund operators lost money, but many other 'risk-takers' have turned to the much maligned state for salvation. Worries about 'moral hazard' – the bailout of risk-takers – have been cast aside.

The collapse of Bear Stearns in March 2008 is a good example. Bear Stearns incurred reckless and irresponsible debts which came home to roost. But instead of letting the risk-taker go bankrupt, the debts of Bear Stearns were effectively nationalised in one fell swoop. The 'risk-taking' bankers at JP Morgan, who were chosen by the US government to take over the failing bank, were given a huge state subsidy; they paid next to nothing. The moral of the story: when Wall Street bankers were in trouble, they hardly batted an eye before running to the state for life-support, the same state – the US government – that Wall Street had for years been disparaging as too big, too prone to regulation and too interfering.

Vincent Reinhardt, a former Fed director of monetary affairs, spoke for many, not just market purists, when he criticised the Bear Stearns deal on the grounds that it would set a terrible precedent for future state bailouts. He recalled that in 1998 the Federal Reserve had saved the hedge-fund Long-Term Capital Management ; it had done so without using taxpayers' money but by coaxing its creditors to save it. This time, though, the Fed had gone too far. It had, he said, 'eliminated forever the possibility that the Fed could act as an honest broker' and that the next time a big Wall Street firm was in trouble they would expect government money to come to the rescue.

The earlier 1998 Asian financial crisis provides another illuminating example of how global risk is no longer borne by those who are supposed to bear it: the great western capitalist risk-takers, the lenders of capital – banks and financial entrepreneurs. Instead the losses fell on local Asian borrowers and peoples. As Edward Luce has argued, 'Apart from those who lost money on regional stock markets or bet the wrong way on currencies, most banks which lent money to the three economies (Korea, Thailand and Indonesia) will be repaid in full.'[8] And incredibly, following the IMF-imposed recovery programme, some creditors received a higher rate of interest than they had negotiated before the crisis occurred.

That tenacious critic of modern capitalism, *The Guardian*'s economics commentator Larry Elliott, focusing on this shedding of risk, reports with some glee Professor K. Raffer's 'wicked' idea that debtor governments should be able to seek protection from creditors in the same manner as US entrepreneurs are able to use the bankruptcy procedures of 'Chapter Eleven' in the US to avoid serious penalties for failure.[9]

The biggest banks, as well, are also in the risk-shedding business. During the bank and credit crisis of 2007-8 their full 'have it both ways' approach – particularly from the big investment banks – was on display. Whilst profits were secure, 'risk-taking' was encouraged and the banks shunned the 'fearsome' state, arguing for light touch regulation if any. But when in trouble they were no longer 'risk-takers'; they demanded successfully that the public sector bail them out.

A Return To Feudal Values?

An audit of corporate capitalism in the early years of the new century would not bring good news. The headlines tell it all: global imbalances, mountainous debt, runaway profits and growing social divisions. The old style capitalism that the postwar period so prized and which forged prosperity for the majority is, today, hardly discernable.

The truth was that today's capitalism has degenerated. It has become seriously regressive. And in its new deregulated, global, phase, it has unleashed a dynamic that is, incredibly, taking us back in time. Back, that is, to the values and society of the feudal world from which earlier capitalism set us free. This degeneration has many causes, but at its heart is a change in the means by which capital and wealth is made. About what values and skills, or lack of them, are needed in the money-making process.

As the old self-improving adage had it, 'he made his money the old-fashioned way – he earned it'. No longer. Now money is in large part a result of inheritance. Inheriting capital and money may be personally helpful to the recipient, but it erodes the value of work – of earning money as opposed to getting it. It has no connection with work – neither hard work nor Michael Rose's 'effective work' – or creativity. It is a reward for bloodline rather than merit. And in today's explosion of inheritance it is creating a class – or rather a caste – at the top of our western societies who have inherited, or stand to inherit, enough wealth and income to enable many of them to avoid work forever.

Historically work has been the key to productivity, both material and cultural. It may be argued that in advanced societies economic productivity (though not cultural productivity) can increasingly be fostered by improved technology rather than work. However, even if true, a society and culture that marginalise the importance of work, relying instead for rewards based upon inheritance, face the issue of the incalculable and intangible loss of human dignity.

Inheritance is very big business, perhaps the biggest business of all in today's global economy. In Britain the extent of inherited wealth often remains hidden, but its importance can be seen in the storm of protest that erupted when in 2010 the new coalition government, under Liberal Democrat pressure, decided to raise Capital Gains Tax on 'non business' capital such as second homes and estates. It could also be glimpsed in the pre-election Conservative party pledge to lower inheritance tax for what amounted to the 3,000 largest estates in the UK. In the US, Robert Avery of Cornell University, sensing a trend, predicted some time ago that 'we will shortly be seeing the largest transfer of income in the history of the world'.[10] In 1973, 56 per cent of the total wealth held by persons aged 35-39 had been given to them by their parents. By 1986 the figure for 35-39 year-old baby boomers had risen to 86 per cent, leading political scientist Kevin Phillips to argue that inheritance is 'about to become a critical component of the younger generation's future, *something America has never before experienced*'.[11] In one of the few studies of the inheritance transfers of the super-rich – in this case American millionaires – it has been estimated that, on present trends (in 1996) 'the number of estates in the $1 million or more range will increase by 246 percent during the next decade; these estates will be valued (in 1990 constant dollars) at a total of more than $2 trillion (that is $2,000,000,000,000). But nearly the same amount will be distributed by so-called pre-decedent affluent parents and grandparents to their children/grandchildren.'[12]

The amounts of individual wealth transfers by inheritance are staggering. Looking to the future, economist Edward Woolf has projected that if inheritance follows the pattern of US wealth concentration in the 1990s then in the early years of the new century the wealth going to each of the top 1 per cent of Americans will average $3 million, and the next richest 5 per cent (the 95-99 percentiles) will average $900,000 each. Also looking to the future, Kevin Phillips suggests that inheritance taxes might slightly alter the future social outcome, but that 'baby boomers would be the most polarized and stratified generation in US history', and that 'the overall pattern would be unmistakable: inherited wealth would create a hereditary caste; class lines would harden'.[13]

Yet these concerns are falling on deaf ears. The 'new market economy' politicians in both Britain and the US, particularly those who proclaim the merits of 'entrepreneurship' and 'hard work', are seeking the directly opposite outcome – to *increase* the pool of inherited wealth by lowering inheritance taxes even further, or removing them altogether. In Britain the free-market Conservative governments of the 1990s talked approvingly of a future economy dominated by inherited wealth as wealth 'cascaded down the generations'. And the New Labour government that succeeded it fell in behind the inheritance culture and in its 2008 budget raised the threshold before paying inheritance tax to £600,000 per couple. In the US the Republican party successfully demonised proposed inheritance taxes by calling them 'death taxes' – even though such taxes did not fall on the dead but on their estates (and did not apply to the vast majority of people, only to those with estates more than $4 million).

Intriguingly, the intellectual leaders of the new capitalism – in the Anglo-American economic think tanks and the 'neoliberal' university departments – have no objections to this new inheritance culture. Few 'free-market' theorists see any contradiction at all between growing levels of inheritance and the enterprise society they have been attempting to create. Even the great man of economic liberty, Frederich von Hayek, saw no reason to oppose, or even limit, private inheritance. He supported what he called 'the transmission of material property' because 'there is a natural partiality of parents for their children', and because if inheritance was seriously threatened, people would 'look for other ways of providing for their children'. In a very, for Hayek, defensive, indeed sheepish, mode of thinking he also argued that 'men being what they are, it [inherited capital] is the least of evils', and inherited capital is a 'lesser evil' to be tolerated.

In a further line of argument Hayek revealed his irrational opposition to the state when he asserted that 'those who dislike the inequalities caused by inheritance should recognise that the state will not be capable of splitting up inherited capital leading to its dispersal'. Why not? Isn't every redistribution, from inheritance taxes to lower income taxes, to welfare benefits, to road building programmes, to education, helping to split up inherited capital, and disperse it?[14]

The *Sunday Times* journalist Irwin Stelzer has recently broken ranks with many of his fellow 'free-marketeers' by suggesting that their opposition to taxes on inheritance is wrong, that 'revenues from [inheritance taxes] could be used to lower income tax rates, especially on low earners…This would reduce the tax on work by increasing the tax on the less productive activity of being around when someone dies.' He also argues that inheritance taxes do not deny children their 'endowments of family reputation and connection; [and] knowledge, skills and goals provided by their family environment'.[15]

Inheritance remains a decidedly under-researched and under-discussed subject in the debate about 'free markets' and modern global capitalism. Grossly unjust, unfair and unproductive – as it rewards lineage not merit or work, and undermines the enterprise culture – the conservative support for inheritance appears contradictory and hypocritical. So much so, that capital inheritance has become one of the intellectual Achilles' heels of 'free-market' theory, the 'guilty little secret' of 'progressive' modern global capitalism.

The New Inheritance Culture

Of course inheritance has always been part of the way of life in Britain in both its industrial capitalist and its pre-capitalist phase. Passing on wealth from one generation to the next (via primogeniture) kept relatively large accumulations intact, and was defended on moral grounds by virtue of the right of the giver to dispose of 'his' property as he saw fit. During the age of the mixed economy – in the mid to late twentieth century – inheritance taxes started biting into the inheritance culture, but at the same time inheritance became a feature of middle-class life, primarily through housing.

Now, though, with inheritance taxes falling throughout the globalised capitalist world – as part of the necessary 'competitive tax environment' – the actual amounts of money and assets being handed down from generation to generation are becoming larger. Also, during the neoliberal era it has been far easier to make these inherited accumulations grow than previously. To create a large amount from a smallish one used to involve considerable work and talent; now, however, huge fortunes accumulate as you sleep. In Britain this growth in unearned income has been generally welcomed by the political class – in particular by British Prime Minister John Major in his first speech as PM to the Conservative Party Conference in 1991 when he delighted in the idea of 'wealth cascading down the generations'.

Worse still, many of today's inheritances are becoming the sole means of income for the inheritors. A huge private dependency culture – dependence upon the family rather than the state – is being erected. American analysts – normally more acerbic about big inherited wealth than their British counterparts and more able to assess relevant statistics – have described this in derisive terms as 'economic outpatient care'. And such outpatient welfare is now massive.[16]

This super-rich welfare state involves the transfer from one generation to another of 'entire coin collections, stamp collections, payments of medical and dental expenses, plastic surgery' as well as straight cash gifts. It has been estimated that 43 per cent of millionaire parents fund all or a large part of their grandchildren's tuition at private primary and/or secondary school, 32 per cent fund their adult children's further education. 59 per cent give financial assistance in purchasing a home, 61 per cent provide 'forgiveness loans' (those not to be repaid) to their adult children, and 17 per cent give gifts of listed stock to their adult children.[17]

All of this is producing a new generation – children of the global super-rich who, because they are partly or wholly financially dependent upon their parents – even when they are well into their forties and sometimes their fifties – exhibit, and are likely to transmit to their own children, non-productive, idle and dependent values. And they are also likely to experience poor social relationships. As in any dependency culture, relationships can be distorted by inheritance. Reliance upon inheritance can induce animosity and squabbling amongst family members. As an analyst of the US inheritance scene put it:

> In fact, many [young thirty year olds] are unable to purchase even a modest house without financial subsidies from their parents. It is not unusual for these 'rich kids' to receive substantial cash and other financial gifts until they are in their late forties or even early fifties. Often these [young family members] compete with each other for their parents' wealth. What would you do if your economic subsidy was being threatened by the presence of your equally dependent brothers and sisters?[18]

And these cash gifts often go to the less financially successful and least independent children of the super-rich – daughters who have married and become homemakers, thus losing their earning power, or less successful sons. 'Consequently, an increasing number of families headed by the sons and daughters of the affluent are playing the role of successful members of the high-income-producing upper-middle class. Yet their lifestyle is a facade.'[19] This gift culture – which is an acceptable part of the contemporary capitalist system – represents not only a huge misappropriation of resources but also a distortion of values, elevating failure and unproductiveness over personal success, merit, work and enterprise.

Such a massive inheritance economy is already polarising western societies. It has been estimated that in the US, *in early 1990s money*, the wealth given to the top 1 per cent averages $3 million and that given to the richest 5 per cent (the 95th to 99th percentiles) averages $900,000, whereas the middle fifth (the 40th to 59th percentiles) on average receive $49 000. For those further down the inheritance is negligible.[20]

The western world, already divided between the skilled and non-skilled, is now also becoming divided between inheritors and non-inheritors and large inheritors and smallish inheritors. In this age of inheritance even those fortunate or talented enough to acquire skills may not prosper. For skills will continue to be much less well rewarded than capital or its associated professional services, and the gap between skilled employees and the rich and super-rich will continue to grow. The fact is that an economy that supports and nurtures inherited capital simply cannot create the right environment for skills to flourish. Global footloose capital, as it exerts downward pressure on the national tax regimes and hence the public education system, will inevitably limit investment in skills. And there is also some evidence to suggest that inheritance encourages greater consumption, less savings and investment and more dependence upon credit amongst those who receive it.[21]

The 'free-market' system, which rejects government interference in individual decision-making, *even at the point of inheritance*, is simply unable to act as the radical, democratic and 'classless' force some of its supporters claim it to be. Instead, under the pressure of globalisation it is now becoming a conservative force, an economic system for stasis, geared primarily for the protection and inheritance of existing capital and only secondarily for the creation of rewards for work, risk and skills. The ancestry of today's American millionaires points up the inevitably conservative, aristocratic, and unproductive character of the reward system of today's capitalism. The fact is that the American super-rich scene is still dominated by descendants of the early migrants to North America – the English (21 per cent), followed by the Germans (17 per cent), followed by the Irish (12 per cent) and Scottish (9 per cent).[22]

Indeed, in one sense, 'markets' are not just 'not progressive'. They are inherently conservative in their social and cultural consequences. For to 'leave it to market forces' of classical economics is not to submit to an impersonal and rational mechanism of allocation, but rather to ensure that *existing*, indeed traditional, patterns become entrenched. And Britain under the supposed radicalising impact of the Thatcherite capitalist revolution was a case in point. Privatisation and deregulation, regardless of the independent case for each of these measures, seems to have given an unexpected lease of life to the 'old money' conservative (and inheriting) class and culture.

The Return of Aristocracy

A progressive, liberal and dynamic economic system would not freeze existing social relations. However a strong case can be made that, socially, the neoliberal global market, although encouraging upward social mobility at the margins, *has* ultimately served to bolster fundamental inequalities not only globally, but within national communities as well. Indeed, this 'new economy' may have so improved the economic power of the western super-rich that they have become entrenched in their positions at the top. Working through institutions, primarily the big corporations, but also through private capital, they have been able to effectively neuter governments by bidding down taxes, particularly business and inheritance taxes, and bidding up the rewards to private capital.

In an historic irony this new global capitalism is creating nothing less than a return, on a global basis, to an older form of social life – aristocracy – the very system which the rise of capitalism ostensibly broke asunder.

If today's super-rich resemble the lords of medieval times, then the vast majority of peoples, billions worldwide, millions in the West, including many who count themselves as middle class, are increasingly like modern-day serfs, with either a minimal stake, or none at all, in the economic system. The political stake created for the masses by democracy – the regime of rights and votes – is still largely national and therefore is increasingly being either bypassed (by global corporations) or bought (by media corporations).

Just as in the feudal past, a few wield incredible power. These modern-day 'lords of the universe' do not, like medieval lords, exercise detailed, local control over most or every aspect of the lives of others. However their individual, personal command over the huge resources at their disposal, gives them inordinate power over people's livelihoods, if not their lives. It also gives them the non-economic power to construct politics, society and culture in their own image and according to their own needs, which sits ill alongside the pretensions of democracy.

From Noblesse Oblige To Raw Greed

Of course there are some major distinctions between the old European aristocrats and today's global rulers. The old aristocrats were, at their core, domestic, or 'national'. They identified with the nations they lived in, and rightly so, because they owned them. Their assets were based primarily upon land. Today's aristocrats are global, owing no loyalty or affection to any particular landmass or group of peoples. Their assets are financial and they make money as rentiers. French economist Alain Parguez has called the system they operate – lending to governments and companies – 'the international rentier economy' and the 'rentier welfare state'.[23]

The aristocrats' social outlook was that of *noblesse oblige*, not out of sentiment, but for sensible, prudent reasons. Even the American robber barons, such as the Rockefellers and the Carnegies, gave great sums to the arts and charity. The new 'aristocrats' have no such condescension (or, as some would put it, 'they could care less'). They have little or no social obligation – because they have no country. Politically, the old aristocrats were conservative – believing in organic development and incremental change, and even sometimes in moderate reform, viz the Whigs of England. The new aristocrats of global capitalism have no such social obligation or sense, and indeed, Gekko-style, are taught to be proud of their circumstances. Modern inheritors believe, in the words of the L'Oréal ad, that 'I'm Worth It'!

The old aristocrats existed in an environment in which capital and riches needed some kind of justification – usually religious in nature. Capitalism was not only productive, but also good. Indeed, the idea that private wealth accumulation is a sign of grace goes back all the way to the puritans, arguably the founders of American commerce. Benjamin Franklin's writings, particularly *The Way To Wealth* and *Advice To a Young Tradesman*, were cited by Max Weber in *The Protestant Ethic* as portraying the essence of this ethical aspect of capitalism, a moral case – at least for self-made capitalism.

Peter Singer argues in his critique of contemporary self-interestedness, *How Are We To Live?* that this puritanical religious justification for capitalism conjoined with a later, increasingly secular, ethic that also supported capitalism, the free market and the importance of wealth. Capitalism was good for character building, and good for the poor.

The idea that the market builds character was a theme pursued by Herbert Spencer, who saw a positive value in great wealth being accrued through exertion and risk – a viewpoint that, admittedly, would make him cast a suspicious glance at modern capitalism's inheritance culture. And it is 'ethical' because, as George Gilder argues in his influential book *Wealth and Poverty*, capitalism is good for the poor too. The wealth made by the super-rich will benefit all by 'trickle-down', and capitalism and wealth creates an incentive for the poor, who, he argues, 'need most of all the spur of their poverty.'[24]

Of course old capitalism's puritan values – independence, individuality, enterprise, risk, delayed gratification – may have told only half, or less than half, the story. Traditional capitalism was always Janus-faced, and the obverse face was of course a countenance of greed and selfishness. The late mid-twentieth century consumer culture – which spawned the label 'consumerism' – certainly emphasised material possessions and encouraged self-centredness. Critics of old capitalism made their anti-system pitches by painting capitalists – indeed even the ownership of small amounts of private property – as greedy. This criticism was often somewhat high-handed, for old capitalism, limited as it was by the state, had created a consumer society in which masses of people who had previously been shut off from life's material pleasures began to enjoy them. For the first time ordinary people were experiencing some limited, very limited, economic power.

New Capitalism, New Greed

Today's global capitalism has lost its erstwhile puritanism, particularly the value of delayed gratification. The huge amounts of super-wealth now being generated need to be justified, and in the process not only do such accumulations of wealth become morally acceptable, but so too does greed itself. Greed becomes good. As Ivan Boesky, the 'king of the Wall Street arbitragers', told students at Berkeley, 'Greed is alright…greed is healthy… You can be greedy and still feel good about yourself.'[25]

Greed had a good press in the 1990s when supporters of the 'free market' suggested that greed was healthy because it recognised human nature as it was, not as we wished it to be. Greed was also sold as a spur to activity and productivity. What is more, 'free-market' apologists propounded, with some truth, that 'greed...is the motive of mankind in all economic systems, socialist as well as capitalist', but that the capitalist system succeeds in releasing it and harnessing it.'[26]

This echoed an older rationale for capitalism that is no longer heard – that self-interest was positive and to be encouraged because it was efficient, and out of this efficiency would come a broader interest, some kind of 'general good'. The idea of the ultimate good being the prosperity of the people or some kind of 'general good' – achieved by an invisible hand – has disappeared under a welter of economism (of statistics, returns, performance indicators) and growing scepticism about whether such a thing exists at all. Market capitalists tend to see the general good as but a contrivance for some hidden self-interest. But if greed can no longer be justified by its contribution to the general good, then we are left with nothing beyond saying amen to individual self-gratification.

However, an insistent question about contemporary greed remains: how much money do the super-rich actually need? Is ten times the average wealth enough? Is a thousand times needed? As Bud Fox asks Gordon Gekko in Oliver Stone's movie *Wall Street*: 'Tell me Gordon...How many yachts can you water-ski behind? How much is enough?' It was a question beginning to be directed to Britain's top bankers – like Fred Goodwin of the Royal Bank of Scotland – when the salaries and bonuses where headline news following the crash.

The view of a leading social critic was that 'it seems safe to conclude that there is *never enough* for the very rich in our society – whether they are the chief executives of America's largest corporations, scions of the country's wealthiest families, or major recipients of the great bulk of stock dividends parcelled out each year'.[27] Another late 1990s view, surprisingly from a pro-'free-market' quarter, is that it may now be time to put 'a limit on greed' – 'now that these huge accumulations have reached what anyone would agree has no conceivable purpose other than to preclude others from the modest accumulations essential to economic self-sufficiency'.[28]

'These huge accumulations' not only raise questions about basic material greed, but also about greed for power: and about how much power is enough. Modern owners of capital are achieving inordinate amounts of power – power over individuals, power over families, power over society, even power to make history. The satirist Tom Wolfe's depiction of Wall Street financiers as 'masters of the universe' sums up this power aspect of big capital. Such power is even more concentrated than that in the hands of individual politicians – those usually associated in the public mind with the ownership of power. Politicians, however, have to live within the constraints of sharing power with competitors and opponents. Furthermore they are accountable to their electorates. The super-rich 'masters of the universe' are, theoretically at least, accountable too – to markets. Yet this accountability is vaguer than that of politicians, whose lines of authority – committees, cabinets, parliaments and ultimately voters – are clear. Financial and economic power is far less transparent and open to the scrutiny of the media than is political power.

GLOBAL CAPITALISM: A REACTIONARY FORCE

Yet, with these serious problems of capitalism building up throughout the 1990s, the British establishment's love affair with 'free-market' capitalism, and particularly with global financial capitalism, has continued unabated. So passionate was the love affair that the national zeitgeist had it that this new capitalism defined what it was to be British. Capitalism became synonomus with the history of Britain; it was the very best of British; it ran with the British grain, and what its elites believed to be its liberal tradition. Yet, the disturbing truth was that global market capitalism was turning into a deeply reactionary force, exactly the opposite effect of its proclaimed, and intended, consequences.

The image of the 'free market' implanted in many British minds by globalist intellectuals and propagandists during the 1980s and 1990s was that of a progressive force: open, liberal and democratic, reforming old institutions, making vested interests (primarily an over-weaning public sector) conform to consumer needs through the market. Neoliberal economics – as its very name suggests – was also associated with the 'liberal' side of politics. Adam Smith, and the Manchester School of 'free traders' and 'free-marketeers', in the nineteenth century were all liberals. This derived from the historical association between capitalism and Whig, then Liberal, politics, primarily in England, where the opponents of the market and the rising merchant class were often conservative and Tory.

The political ideas and values of today's leading contemporary 'free-market' neoliberals are more difficult to identify. The Frankfurt School of economists, clustered around the legendary Freiderich von Hayek, and the later Chicago School of monetarists, with Milton Friedman at the helm, were not only disdainful of the state but also of politics and most politicians. Seeking a minimal state and a small, sometimes tiny, role for politics, their social values were normally 'liberal' in that they tended to place the 'sovereign' individual at the centre, although they believed that this individual was best protected and enhanced by the market rather than the state and a programme of rights. Hayek himself made clear in a famous postscript to his major work, *The Constitution of Liberty* ('Why I am Not a Conservative') that he did not stand in the European conservative tradition. The latter, he argued, lacked principles and represented little more than a 'widespread attitude of opposition to drastic change'.[29] Hayek did not seek change for change's sake, but at the height of postwar social democracy – he did seek change, even drastic change.

Hayek saw himself as a liberal but not as a democrat, or at least not a modern democrat. Like his supporter, the monetarist Milton Friedman, he saw democratic politicians as demagogic, and elections as problematic because they tended to entrench parties committed to welfare and enlarging the state. In the 1970s and 1980s the politics of Chile became a testing ground for their proposition that limited democracy, or even its temporary abandonment, was sometimes necessary in the construction of a 'free-market' system.

Some of the disciples of Hayek were ultraliberal – indeed libertarian. They possessed a 'moral commitment to the idea of a polity that maximises the scope for individual human beings to give material expression to personal values and perceptions of self-interest' – a view that often led on to socially liberal policies on issues such as homosexual law reform and the decriminalisation of some drugs.[30]

During the 1970s and the 1980s this liberal and progressive image of capitalism made a lot of headway with intellectuals, journalists and the media. Leading Thatcherite Arthur Seldon was not a supporter of the Conservative Party and called himself 'Whiggish'. Thatcher herself presented some of her political battles as 'progressive' compared with the views of public school traditionalists in her cabinet, the hierarchy of the Church of England, even the royal family. Her rhetoric praised the liberal, 'open' character of the free market, and depicted the left as socially reactionary, as favouring the trade union power of the 1950s, the old British class divisions and a bureaucratic centralisation of the state that kept 'kept people in their place'. Her Conservative government – particularly Cabinet Minister Norman Tebbit – talked of 'upward mobility' as a positive social aim and saw traditionalist upper-class England as attempting to frustrate a new social openness. (Indeed most leading market economists would support the general liberal postulations in Karl Popper's *Open Society and Its Enemies*.[31]

The 'freer' market system Margaret Thatcher introduced certainly liberalised and modernised some aspects of traditional British society, for example its consumer laws and pub and shop opening hours; her privatisation programme led to a managerial flexibility and consumer consciousness that had not been present previously. Of course these liberalising changes in the 1980s were part of the deeper process of modernisation – of the sloughing off of the social stultifications of empire and class hierarchy – which would probably have taken place anyway.

In the US, Ronald Reagan backed his democratic opponents into a conservative corner: isolating them as supporting 'old-fashioned' spending plans and 'unreformed' welfare programmes. Part of Reagan's 'progressive' appeal was simply to do with vision. He and his 'free-market' supporters seemingly had a vision, while his political opponents, lacking anything new to add to New Deal economics, appeared stuck in the past, traditionalist and conservative. Reagan, like Thatcher, was continually counterpoising the democratic 'free market' system with the reactionary, indeed authoritarian, command economies of the Soviet Union and the Eastern Bloc (and with western leftists, liberals and social democrats who, may be more moderate, but also shared incipiently undemocratic instincts).

However, by the new century this perception that 'free markets' were more socially and politically progressive and liberal than the alternative models, had begun to look superficial. After almost a decade and a half of triumphant global capitalism, as the full hand of unchecked 'free market' globalism revealed itself, a different picture was emerging: on the fundamental questions – of prosperity and power in society – the supposedly 'free market' was turning out to be deeply conservative, indeed reactionary, in character.

The 'free market' had been touted as a challenging arena where competition erodes tradition and vested interests. But a clearer way to see it – with its deregulation and low taxation – was as a strategy for freeing up tradition, freeing up existing power centres and removing the forces that might threaten, challenge or change them. By removing the ability of politics, of the state, to encourage or institute change, it leaves existing institutions, classes and interests without challenge. Indeed, it offers them greater power. The great privatisation programme of the 1980s and 90s in Britain is a good case in point – for, although it allowed space for a small number of new capitalists and entrepreneurs the bulk of the freeing-up of state assets simply allowed those with existing capital, traditional money, to make more – much, much more.

The 'free market' rarely challenges existing institutions, classes, or interests, except at the very margin; rather it operates *in their favour*. Traditional capital – in the big corporate institutions and leading families – remains largely undispersed. And in crude terms, the position of those with money, with capital, is entrenched *vis-à-vis* those without. Those with money and position are not overly challenged, and in the absence of cataclysmic financial crashes they have to work very hard to lose their capital.

GLOBAL CAPITALISM'S THREAT TO DEMOCRACY

Perhaps, though, the biggest problem of all posed by the new capitalist aristocracy is what it is doing to our democracy. Democracy is ultimately all about power. Who has it? And who doesn't? With money and power in fewer and fewer hands, in a new ruling class no less, the rest of us are beginning to resemble the mass of powerless subjects before the age of democracy. There seems little doubt that the West's economic system – global capitalism – is ultimately on a collision course with the West's great political achievement – democracy. The inescapable fact is that democracy is located in nation-states – where people vote and have rights; but capital and business, by spanning the globe, are escaping democratic control – and also, by weakening the state, weakening democracy.

Yet from the Thatcher revolution onwards the British were consistently told that capitalism and democracy went together, and that capitalism, even new City/Wall Street capitalism, was part of the democratic story. A generation of British elites truly believed that capitalism and democracy, were necessary for each other. And they also believed that in Britain it was the growth of capitalism, and its idea of the market, that gave birth to the democratic society and way of life. Mrs Thatcher herself was a doughty exponent of this view. Half way through her government, at her 1986 party conference she declared, to great applause, that 'popular capitalism is nothing less than a crusade to enfranchise the nation...returning power to the people.'

For many on the right during the cold war years 'capitalism' and 'democracy' became synonymous, and both were claimed in the West to reflect their system against the communist or socialist (or totalitarian) systems of the Eastern Bloc. Indeed a strong case can be made that the history of capitalism is interlinked with the history of democratic development – in the sense that, by casting aside the feudal world, capitalism helped usher in modern democratic ideas of equality and freedom. And after three centuries of capitalism it is undeniably true that democracy has become the governing ideology, indeed the very spirit of the times, almost the religion of the West.

Just as capitalism helped forward a more democratic world, so for many it remains the best way to preserve it. Theorists of the market see it as providing more democratic safeguards than government ever can. They also see 'market democracy' as more real than 'political democracy', because they believe that political democracy, government or the state, unlike markets, are inherently abusive of power. When the classical liberal economist and founder of public choice theory, Professor J. M. Buchanan, presented his pioneering pro-market ideas to a British audience at the Institute for Economic Affairs in 1978 he set them in a democratic context, quoting John Stuart Mill against government. Mill had argued that 'the very principle of constitutional government requires it to be assumed that political power will be abused to promote the purposes of the holder...such is the natural tendency'.[32]

Thus, at the very heart of the more serious 'free-market' economists' worldview is, intriguingly, a *political* proposition: that the most important value of all is that of individual freedom – preserving, and enhancing, the freedom of the 'sovereign individual'. Market supporters suggest that only the pluralism of the market allows this sovereign individual to develop freely. This, they argue, is because the market, unlike the state, avoids compulsion. 'Free-marketeers' proceed from the proposition that the state compels us to obey its laws by force and gathers its resources forcibly. They argue that the state, unlike the market, is backed by the law, which in turn employs the sanction of punishment, indeed jail; and that, ultimately, what lies behind the power of the state – of the world of politics – is the military.

The central 'pro-market' contention here is that the resources held by the individual (money, property, other assets) are inalienably his or hers – and that, whereas in the market the individual releases these resources voluntarily and by invitation, the state and government compels their release.

On a propagandistic and polemical level this *compulsion* argument (or, rather, anti-compulsion argument) of the global free-marketeers is very appealing – particularly when the issue is tax. People naturally tend to believe that the resources they hold are indeed 'theirs', and the idea that 'my' money is being taken forcibly by the state's tax collector taps a populist vein. Public bodies (unlike private groups – even those in a monopolistic or oligopolistic position), are defensive about their use of taxpayers' money. For instance public bodies (such as the taxpayer-funded British Broadcasting Corporation) worry about accountability, whereas privately funded organisations (such as the commercial television companies) believe they are automatically accountable – to 'market forces' when, in fact, they answer to the whims and demands of 'market-makers' like advertisers.

An intriguing question remains to be answered: does not the private sector also engage in compulsion? To continue the television analogy: the idea that there is no 'compulsion' involved in the financing of commercial television, simply because it takes no money from the state, may be fanciful. The fact is that if the market determines television output, then in the real world it means that the advertisers – interpreting public taste – determine this output. Rarely are consumers or shareholders consulted by the advertisers on their month-by-month decisions, and these short-term decisions can be very important indeed. The advertiser then places the costs of the advertisement onto the price, which is passed on to the unwitting consumer in the supermarket. Thus in the real world of the real market, as opposed to the imagined 'free market', a host of little 'compulsions' are forced on the individual – acts that are, in truth, involuntary because of shortage of time, imperfect knowledge, rigging of market entry and all the other real world constraints. Compulsion is certainly present in the market and the private sector. It is simply more subtle and circuitous than that imposed on the individual by the state.

The Question of Compulsion

The global financier-turned-public intellectual, George Soros, (famous for his speculation against the British pound during the ERM crisis of 1992) has argued that the new global market system is not only undemocratic, but also represents a threat to what he calls – taking his definition from Karl Popper – 'the Open Society'.

The kernel of Soros's argument is that the global free market is not based upon the democratic interplay of supply and demand. 'The assumption of perfect knowledge proved unsustainable', he argues, 'so it was replaced by an ingenious device. Supply and demand were taken as independently given...[but] the condition that supply and demand are independently given cannot be reconciled with reality, at least as far as the financial markets are concerned. Buyers and sellers in financial markets seek to discount a future that *depends on their own decisions*.' (Nor can supply and demand be taken as independently given in areas other than finance; in fact there is hardly any economic activity at all in which supply and demand are 'independently given'.)

According to Soros, markets, and market players, 'have the capacity to alter the subject matter to which they relate'.[33] He suggests that market players are inevitably imposing their will

– in the form of their expectations, but inevitably also in their values and interests – upon the rest of us. Such an imposition – arguably as much a compulsion, as any conceived in the democratic world by politicians – affords a new view of the moral balance sheet between state and market.

It opens us to the little-heard proposition that 'the market' can limit freedom as much as can government, that the market can create a class system – now on a global canvas – as insidious as any created by old-time feudalism or the postwar political class.

In other words, contrary to the mantra of Britain's neoliberals, 'the state' – certainly the kind of western welfare state of the democratic age – is an essential player in the construction of a free and democratic society. It can be so by providing a balance to a big private sector, by acting as the last resort in a crisis (as in the the financial bailouts of 2008), and through its welfare function by *enabling* opportunity and social mobility. The problem with global capitalism is that, by eroding and demonising 'the state', it also weakens this bulwark.

BROKEN BUSINESS ATTACKS BROKEN POLITICS

One of the intriguing aspects of post-crash Britain was how Britain's broken business and financial class, complicit in the crash, was nevertheless still able during 2009-10 to launch a serious assault on the country's relatively innocent public sector. Of course, immediately post-crash, Britain's political cycle was out of kilter with the rest of the West. The country had a New Labour government that had been in bed with the City and an opposition party which was *even more* pro-city and pro-business in its inclination. Any political change from New Labour was therefore going to be tilted even more to the 'right' – even more business friendly, even more critical of the state than its predecessor. So, whilst post-crash US rhetoric, unleashed by President Obama, was seriously anti-big business and anti-bank and in Paris the French president was roundly denouncing financial capitalism, Britain's political mood was still very business friendly.

Certainly the banks and the bankers were not popular; and even in post-crash Britain a head of steam against bankers, financial capitalism, super-rich wealth and inequality was beginning to build. Yet, Britain's business class was still able to limit the damage to its reputation by a very skilful and highly successful media-led campaign which deflected blame away from the private sector, placing it instead firmly on the political class in Westminster.

And it did so through a highly successful *Daily Telegraph* campaign against the public sector political class in Westminster. In May 2008 the High Court had ruled in favour of releasing the details of MPs expense claims, and a year later the House of Commons authorities announced that in July 2009 these would be published with certain information deemed 'sensitive' removed. Yet on 8th May 2009 the *Daily Telegraph* newspaper began publishing details on a daily basis of MPs expenses (based upon a leak of the full records). These expenses were very small beer indeed when compared to the bonuses (and expenses) of the City's leading bankers. However, there was no question that many MPs had used their expenses system to make money during the housing boom (by manipulating the system the expenses for MPs second homes), and others had made outlandish claims for everything from duck houses to manure.[34]

These revelations were like manna from heaven for the privately owned press. For, even though the excesses of the private sector bankers were still in the public's mind, the press could continue, and deepen, their decades-long campaign against the public sector and politics in particular. All of this played perfectly into the anti-politics mood that had been growing in Britain – and the West – throughout the 1990s and into the new millennium.

By the time of the *Telegraph*'s campaign, the reputation of politics, never held in high regard, had already reached an all-time low. The decades-long Thatcher/ New Labour business-friendly ethos had so demeaned the public sector, the civil service and the life of politics, that 'public service' had no resonance, whereas a life in business was increasingly prized. 'Government' had become a dirty word, considered inherently inefficient, if not dangerous, whereas the private sector was regarded as competent and dynamic. Above all, there were no role models left in the world of politics – no heroes like FDR, Kennedy, De Gaulle, even Winston Churchill; they had been replaced by business celebrities like Bill Gates, Warren Buffet and Donald Trump, in Britain Alan Sugar and Richard Branson.

The reputation of politics and 'public service' had, of course, not been helped by the politicians themselves, above all by the sleaze surrounding John Major's government in Britain and Bill Clinton's 'Monica Lewinsky episode' in the US, and then the 'stupid white man' image of George W. Bush. But that was only a small part of the 'anti-politics' story. When, in the mid-1990s, the American social theorist Peter Drucker suggested that 'if this century proves one thing, it is the futility of politics' he was echoing a widely held view that politics had been made increasingly redundant by the business era. That in today's world change was no longer forged by politics, but rather by the growth of markets, the privatisation of assets and the globalisation of finance; and that it took place in new arenas – primarily economic and financial, but also technological and cultural.

'Futility' was of course something of an exaggeration. For even by the end of the 'greedy decade' with global capitalism rampant, politics and government were still important, and liable to be restored in importance. What it lost, though, was its *special* quality. Politics (like the state) has lost its *special* role as the arbiter between economic interests and as the court of final appeal between business and social interests. It is no longer the ultimate forum, or the overarching way of thinking about the public world.

That arch-priestess of global capitalism, Margaret Thatcher, summed up this toppling of politics from its special status with her famous dictum that 'there is no such thing as society'. She argued – and it was a powerful thrust – that politicians were nothing special, that they were little more than a vested interest like any other, an elite who evoked images such as 'society' and the 'public good' only in order to dress up their personal agendas in selfless language.

Above all the world of politics has come to be seen by influential supporters of the market as a mechanism for elitism – for the 'government of the busy, by the bossy, for the bully', while the market operated in favour of 'ordinary men and women'; the political process was constructed for elites and specialists 'in the arts of persuasion, organisation, infiltration, debate, lobbying, manipulating meetings...'[35] It was a polemical bullet that hit home, particularly in the 1980s in Britain, which had just witnessed the excesses of a minority on the extreme left in local councils and trade unions.

From this market vantage point, the world of politics has become an interest group like any other – no longer concerned with the best for the country, with 'the big picture' essentially no different from farmers, teachers, small businesspeople; politicians always have an axe to grind and a nest to feather; politics is lacking in virtue; public service is a sham, merely a cover for personal aggrandisement; the great political creed of 'rights' is a cover for selfishness (and more stress should be placed upon responsibilities). Even the political art of compromise is derided, and is often compared unfavourably – by the privately owned media – with the risk-taking of business.

It is little wonder, then, that during the high point of the victory of business in the 90s the authority drained out of politics. Political leaders are no longer esteemed, indeed the very word 'politician' has become a term of derision. The careful, contrived public language of politicians increasingly bores the public. The widespread use of public relations advisors – the politicians' response to the massive growth of the political media – tends to reduce politicians to little more than a branch of the entertainment industry. And, in the British and US systems at least, successful politicians are those who, like Prime Minister Tony Blair and President Bill Clinton, are 'PR conscious' and presentationally skilful – highly polished performers in front of the cameras, concerned to court the media elites. In a sign of the times Tony Blair as Prime Minister even agreed to a lower billing on a television talk show than that of a popular singer.[36]

By the late 1990s, therefore, the role and standing of the politician had changed radically, not only from the days of Churchill and Roosevelt, but also from those of Thatcher and Reagan. With the exigencies of the Cold War fast becoming a distant memory, the 'heroic' or 'mini heroic' style of political leadership – the attributes of distance, gravitas, character, vision – had given way to softer traits: warmth, concern, understanding, sensitivity. For the successful politician at the turn of the century 'doing the right thing', or thinking long-term and strategically is less important than the day-to-day management of the polity and society. Testing policies before they are advocated became a political must and a leadership skill: much of Tony Blair's and Bill Clinton's success with the electorate was down to Phillip Gould's and James Carville's political consultancy, GGC-NOP. An ear to public opinion – via the use of sophisticated polling techniques and focus groups – has become more important to a politician than a grasp of the details of policy, let alone a sense of history.

This collapse in the traditional standards of political leadership in part reflects lowering public expectations of its political leaders. So low had these expectations become that opinion polls in 1998 showed that although a majority of Americans believed that their president had lied under oath – and to them! – they still approved of the way he was doing his job and did not want him removed from office, even though he had probably committed a crime. Politics simply matters less and less; western publics are simply not listening to their politicians; instead they are turning to 'experts', journalists and a range of non-traditional authority figures – businesspeople of course, but also celebrities, royalty and talk show hosts, for social and political views and guidance.

Not only are politicians held in low regard, but so too are public servants. The very best examples of the public sector – the meritocrats, the highly educated achievers who run many of the civil services of the West, even those in France and in the European Commission in Brussels – are branded as 'technocrats' and seen as much less worthy than the risk-takers in the private sector. The public servants in the American military have been excepted, primarily because of the patriotism engendered by the 'war on terror'; but, in reality, even soldiering is no longer held in high regard. Somehow the crafts of administration and management in the public sector are 'bureaucratic', whereas the same hierarchical functions in the private corporate sector are largely unnoticed. In the real world the politicians and bureaucrats in the public sector often manage far fewer resources than the chief executive officers of the private sector or the major financial families.

The Growing 'Futlity' of Elections

Political institutions are also in trouble. In the globalised market democracies of Britain and the US, governmental institutions – from the British Parliament and monarchy to the US Congress and presidency – are losing their appeal with the public. No longer viewed as authoritative and serving a general interest, political institutions are seen as mere tools of the political class who inhabit them. And in the process even the institutions themselves have come to be viewed as players in a kind of market system. Britons' low view of politics and politicians was reinforced by the 2009 expenses scandal, and in the US the public's low regard for the US Congress has become a settled feature of political life, and intriguingly the elected members of the Congress regularly fall well below the respect and trust ranking of the unelected members of the Supreme Court; while British opinion polls regularly report that large numbers of Britons, particularly amongst the younger age groups, no longer believe that the monarchy and royal family have much relevance to their lives.

Elections are also in trouble. No longer 'democracy's great day', elections are, often accurately, now viewed as exercises in manipulation, their outcomes governed by public relations advisors and expensive media campaigns. From the right, mass democracy, and the politicians who operate within it, are seen as pandering to left-wing sectional interests and a direct cause of the so-called overblown, unfundable welfare state.[37] For many on the left, elections are dismissed as a middle-class preserve that have no meaning for large numbers of the excluded, particularly the growing underclass.

In Britain turnout percentage has been on a general downward curve since the war. The numbers voting in general elections fell from a high of over 80 per cent in the early 1950s to the low 70s in the 1980s and was lower still in the two general elections of the twenty-first century (59.1 per cent in 2001 and 61.4 per cent in 2005). The turnout rose a little, but was still only 65 per cent in 2010. The European Union elections usually attract significantly fewer British voters, and voting for local elections is often in the region of 20-40 per cent. (In that other 'Anglo-American' business-friendly democracy, the US, before the presidential candidacy of Barack Obama, very low turnouts in inner-city areas were part of election lore. Turnout rates in elections are generally falling. In the US, presidential election turnout percentages are normally in the low 50s. And they are in continuing decline – in the three elections of the 1960s the figure was over 60 per cent in each, but every election since 1980 has seen a turnout in the low 50s, except for 1996 when it fell as low as 49.1 per cent and in 2004 when it rose to 55.3 per cent. A typical election was the 1988 contest when 91 million people voted, but *the same number* – largely composed of inner-city blacks, Hispanics and the rural and urban poor – stayed away from the polls. In elections for Congress the figures are even lower. Even after several well-publicised registration drives the turnout amongst American blacks is still alarmingly low.)

Society Against Politics

Some argue that this crisis of confidence in government and politics is simply a result of specific, avoidable events. Events like the deception surrounding the Blair government's decision to join the US in invading Iraq in 2003 or the parliamentary expenses scandal. Others place the crisis at the feet of what, in the fashionable arguments of the 1970s, came to be known as the 'overloading' of government, or the inability of political institutions to deal with the extent and complexity of the changing demands upon them. Others suggest it is all down to the robust health of democracy – the inherent healthy questioning of authority, the probing of leaders and public figures.

But lying politicians, or complex government, or a culture of robust anti-authority, are only part of the story. The 'free market revolution' of the 1980s and 90s produced deep social changes. These years witnessed a huge increase in small businesses, many of them sole proprietorships, started up by workers laid off by big corporations. In the process many of these new small business people allied themselves with the interests and anti-politics culture of bigger businesses. The consumer and debt culture of the times naturally led to the replacement of community and citizenship values by consumer values – by a money-oriented culture over old-fashioned social responsibility. It all added up to one thing: a shift of power away from the public, or political, realm run by government to the private, consumer, realm run by business.

One of the most underpublicised social changes of the whole postwar period has been the rapid growth in the number of people who pay tax. In the 1950s tax paying used to be a concern of a 'rich' minority only. But as broader swathes of the population became subject to 'Pay As You Earn' (in Britain) and many middle class folks started paying inheritance taxes, a rich vein of populist resentment against 'government' and its taxing powers became available for tapping. President Ronald Reagan's famous electioneering sound-bite – 'Get the government off the backs of the people' – successfully exploited this sentiment. As did presidential candidate, multi-millionaire, and doyen of the low-tax regime, Steve Forbes, whose standard pitch would include the line: 'politicians say "we" can't afford a tax cut. Maybe we can't afford the politicians.'

THE CORPORATE MEDIA

This growing distaste for politics may be due to big societal changes, but it had considerable help of the still ascendant business community, not least its burgeoning corporate media arm. In the age of the internet the corporate media may no longer possess monopoly power over news and information, but through their websites as well as their television and newspapers, they can still set an agenda. It is often forgotten that for western publics the world of the public sector – the world of politics – is still filtered through privately – owned media by a business class that brings its own values and opinions to bear. Journalists, pundits and newspaper editors are employees of big business enterprises, many of them global companies. The media environment has been somewhat more diversified with the internet, but has not changed that much. Small non-corporate websites run by individuals are rather like old village meetings – good for local democracy, but rarely able to move national opinion; and bigger non-corporate websites often simply relay, through the click, news and data from bigger corporate media outlets.

Although the media class – well-paid, educated, urban and relatively sophisticated – tend to be progressive on social issues, they tend to reflect their employers' pro-business, and anti-political, views on economic issues, particularly taxation although on high salaries, they probably don't need corporate pressure for their low tax views.

Media owners are business people. The media class is thus a business class – and therefore naturally interested in profits. And profits lie with giving the new narcissistic consumer society what they demand – less 'politics' and more 'lifestyle': more coverage of sex, money, fashion and sport. This kind of new news content has served to further marginalise 'serious' politics, turning the world of public life into a 'boring' arena occupied by men in suits. And in the process traditional political concerns about economic and social justice became 'boring' too.

Big Business and The New Coalition Government

With the election of the new Conservative-led coalition government in May 2010 big business, the business class, and the business culture that went with it, was given a new lease on life. Instead of placing the blame for the great financial crash, and the recession, on the deregulated market system, Prime Minister Cameron launched a campaign against the very institution which had saved the banks and the country a year earlier – the so-called 'overblown' state ('overblown' in large part because of the need for taxpayers money to bail out the private financial sector, and 'overblown' too because of the need to enlarge the welfare state to cope with the social casualties of recession). And, as part of this strangely-timed campaign to reduce the size of the state, the new government was also embarking on a programme to cut the size of the government deficit by the deepest cuts in public expenditure seen in a lifetime.

The British government was thus seemingly placing itself firmly on the wrong side of history. The state, and its public sector, had not caused the crash – it had simply provided the life-support system which was keeping the economy, and the private sector, from imploding. Yet, in 2010 Britain was on the brink of pulling the plug on this life-support system without any guarantee at all that the patient could survive without its help.

There was a sense in which the country was at a crossroads. One road – the road to a balanced budget and a smaller state –

was about to be taken by Britain's political and financial leaders who were arguing, as Mrs. Thatcher had famously argued some three decades earlier, that 'there was no alternative'. Yet amidst the neoliberal certainties of the need for global competitiveness, market dominance and massively reduced public expenditure, there was extreme nervousness. There were real worries that the private sector could not take up the slack and become the engine of growth – and real fears about coming unemployment and social divisions. But Britain's neoliberals considered this a risk worth taking.

There was, however, also a sense that amidst all the fervour for cutting the budget, there was a turning, another road, another way, that was being missed. Advocates of this other way were largely outside of mainstream politics – and, in Britain at least, were given minimal publicity. But an alternative road was coming into vision – one pointed to by prominent figures such as the economist Paul Krugman and the economic historian Robert Skidelsky. In the US Krugman was arguing for a renewed stimulus package and a tougher attitude towards the global imbalances (and low cost imports). But in Britain too, although the neoliberal consensus remained firmly in power, there were the beginnings of a serious revolt against it.

CHAPTER SEVEN

THE OTHER ROAD?

SOCIAL DEMOCRACY, PROTECTIONISM
AND THE RETURN OF SOCIETY

THE RETURN OF SOCIETY

Adair Turner, Baron Turner of Ecchinswell, is, on the face of it, an archytypel member of the upper middle-class English financial establishment. A graduate of Cambridge University with a double first in history and economics his career includes stints with BP, Chase Manhattan Bank, Merrill Lynch Europe and the Confederation of British Industry. He is slightly different from the standard public school educated City type – a distinction that may explain his radical edge and meritocratic air – in that he is a grammar school product, married to a foreigner, and in 1981 joined the SDP. But, for all that, he seemingly remained well within consensus thinking in the City. This is why there was considerable amazement when, in late August 2009, two years after interbank lending froze and a year after the Lehmans collapse, Adair Turner, the Chairman of the Financial Services Authority (FSA), gave an interview to the September edition of *Prospect* magazine which was a searing critique of the fundamental legitimacy of the financial services industry. He argued that the City had become swollen, questioned whether it should be reduced in size, and suggested that a financial transactions tax, a 'Tobin tax' should be considered. For an establishment figure, at the very centre of the business community, it amounted to a radical departure.

Yet more radical still was his assertion that much of the City's activities were 'socially useless'. Mrs. Thatcher's 1980s dictum that 'there is no such thing as society' (only individuals), had set the tone in the corridors of power for much of the neoliberal era. So the idea that we should measure economics and finance by virtue of their social outcomes – that finance should serve 'society', and not the other way round – was a proposition that had rarely been heard in the corridors of power for decades. It was the kind of thinking had been marginalised during the ascendancy of accountants, economists and the corporate bureaucracy.

But as the recession started to bite, 'social goals' – that is employment and jobs, and issues of equality and morality – rather than rules driven by a narrow view of economics and accountancy, gradually began to enter the debate. During 2010 this new social concern has been stirred by the 'sovereign' debt crisis – the global financiers' term for government deficits – that was appearing on a global scale. These deficits were the direct result of the Wall Street/City of London collapse and the consequent global deleveraging. They had swollen dramatically as a result of the government bailouts of the banks and the rise in social spending due to the deleveraging-induced recession. Every single western nation was facing these problems, but they were particularly acute in Iceland, Ireland, Britain, some of the Club Med and Eastern European countries.

These deficits had many politicians reaching, often competitively, for the axe – in the fanciful belief that cuts in public expenditure would help reduce the deficit – but the inevitable rise of unemployment and social distress was facing resistance. Previous budget deficits, and the cuts and austerity that had flowed from them, could, with some justification, be put down to standard 'profligacy' by governments. But this time the widely-agreed cause was very different. This time it was down to a different kind of 'profligacy' – that of the banks and the global private financial services sector. In other words, for the first time since the early 1980s, the political left could make a case – one that could be heard – that the usual culprits, the trade unions and big government, had not caused the economic crisis; public spending was the saviour rather than the sinner. This point was not just the argument from the left for German Chancellor Angela Merkel had, in a TV interview on 6th May 2010, stunned many by arguing that the root cause of the global crisis was not state 'profligacy', but rather the banks. The main need was now to 'confront the markets' and the speculators. She was following other mainstream European leaders like President Sarkozy of France who had launched into a full-blooded attack on Wall-Street 'Anglo-Saxon' financial capitalism at the 2010 Davos conference and Spanish Prime Minister Zappatero who had argued that the crisis was caused by global capital in Wall Street and was being paid for by hard-pressed governments trying to protect their welfare societies.[1] The mood was certainly changing (though not in Britain).

PROTECTIONISM: PROTECTING PEOPLE

During 2010 the full effects of the financial crisis were also demanding a serious review of the value of economic globalisation and its key underpinning, 'free trade'. Since 1945 Britain had witnessed a near consensus on 'free-trade'; and as 'free trade' reached the status of a shibboleth, its alternative, 'protectionism', become virtually a term of abuse. Most every western politician (outside of France) would regularly warn about the dangers of 'lapsing back into 'protectionism'. Yet before the Second World War 'protectionism' had many supporters at the highest level in British politics (Joseph Chamberlain's 'imperial preference' was considered by many to be a serious strategic option for Britain in the early twentieth-century); and the issue had divided British politics and caused splits in major parties.

Yet, kept in the attic for decades, by the early years of the twenty-first century 'protectionism' was out, and was growing – for the financial crisis had brought forward a whole series of protectionist measures. The most obvious act of 'protectionism' was the great bank bailout. Free-traders had always denounced: 'government interference in the level playing field of the global market' when governments put money into their economies. In this case, governments were pouring billions into the banks to save them. It was 'state aid' with a vengeance. And the most generous were those two great advocates of 'free trade' – Britain and the US. British Prime Minister Gordon Brown's bailout of the City of London, and US President George W. Bush's support for Wall Street, followed by his successor's stimulus package and rescue of the US car industry around Detroit, were the greatest acts of protectionism seen since World War Two.

Of course, whether 'protectionist' or not, these emergency intrusions of the state into the global market saved western societies from severe damage. The West's leaders were denounced at the time by market fundamentalists in the Republican and Tory parties. Yet, during the bank crisis Gordon Brown, George W. Bush and Barack Obama had been looking into the pit. Bush's Treasury Secretary, Hank Paulson, who masterminded the historic events, subsequently reported that 'the intervention we undertook I would have found abhorrent at any other time', but 'as first responders to an unprecedented crisis that threatened the destruction of the modern financial system, we had very little choice'. He also reported that during the bailout he had been 'really scared' and told his wife that he was relying on prayer, 'placing my trust in a higher power'.[2] These leaders viewed the crisis as nothing less than a threat to western civilisation, one as serious as that posed by a prospective massive terrorist attack. (Indeed, intriguingly, Hank Paulson in the quote above used the terrorist crisis term 'first responder'). And with so much at stake it is worth asking: if the state was not going to protect the people and the social fabric, the question was: who was? And who could?

Seen across the economic spectrum as the 'saviour' during the banking collapse, government (and the state) was in favour for the first time since the 1980s. This new atmosphere provides an opportunity to take a new look at the state, and to remove the fear that has been engendered by years of successful neoliberal campaigning. It is an opportunity to see the role of the state (and politics) in a more congenial light, and in a more rounded way: to see it, that is, as having played a positive role in British history and in the development of both British liberal democracy and British capitalism.

THE RETURN OF THE STATE

Certainly from ancient times when humankind began to organise itself into society, politics has existed in some form or another. In the days of the Greek polis Aristotle depicted politics, not economics, as 'the master art', concerned with the allocation of resources and much more besides. The ancients seemed to possess a clear understanding of the limits of economics ('the dismal science'). In the middle ages, too, economics was subordinated to a host of social goals, such as the idea of a socially 'just price' or protectionist and producer interests (often called guilds). In medieval local communities the church often held sway over economics, and in Catholic Europe, in an approach reaching down to today's Christian democracy very definite ideas about the economy – almost amounting to a Christian code of economic policy – were propagated.

This subordination of economics to politics was inevitable in a world of traditional communities where non-economic loyalties took precedence, where community goals were seen as transcending individual economic advancement. People were loyal to their communities in a way that is difficult to understand today These communities were not instrumental or contractual, establishing obligations in return for services. Rather they were seen as living organisms which, existing long before the individual was born and surviving long after he or she had gone, required not only loyalty but also obedience.

The sheer religiosity of these traditional medieval communities ensured the supremacy of politics over economics. Spirituality took precedence over the material world; and the debate over religion (what today we might call ideology), much of it with a highly political content, overshadowed people's vague understanding of economics.

In Europe during the seventeenth and eighteenth centuries, as local markets expanded into national ones, the emerging nation-states slowly took over the political functions of the localities and the church, and began to impose their own regulations and taxes. If anything, this new world of nation-states led to a strengthening of politics.

A transcendent sense of community remained, but was given form and life by the emergence of a new and larger political unit, the nation-state. These nations, and their states, became the primary focus for loyalty – often even competing with and overcoming the family unit. Analysts have suggested that a sense of identity 'is inseparable from an awareness of ourselves as members of a particular family or class or community or people or nation, as bearers of a specific history, as citizens of a particular republic; and *we look to the political realm* as a way in which we can develop and refine our sense of ourselves'.[3] We tend to forget the strength of this identification with the political realm, the political community, represented as it has been over the last three hundred years or so by the nation-state. Alan Milward suggests that the ultimate basis for the survival of the nation-state is 'the same as it always was, allegiance'.[4] During the twentieth century millions of people have displayed their allegiance to the political idea of nation by making very serious sacrifices, including a willingness to make the ultimate one.

Of course the *genuine* level or intensity of political allegiance, or loyalty, is very difficult to measure. The nation-state also had ultimate legal authority over the lives of its people. It could (still can) fine, tax, imprison and even take life. There was no higher legal appeal, and most people were powerless to leave its boundaries. In such circumstances a degree of political loyalty or allegiance was hardly surprising, perhaps more as much a measure of *force majeure* than of genuine feeling. Linda Colley has attempted to measure this political loyalty by the yardstick of people's willingness to serve in the armed forces.[5]

The State as a Liberal Force

Even though the global economic crisis has led to a serious review of the role of government in the economy – seen increasingly as an economic stabiliser and indeed as an enabler of business – many of Britain's business leaders and business-led opinion formers have remained very hostile to state and government. The public sector is still seen as the mechanism for redistributing income and wealth (away from existing holders) through increasing taxes and 'crowding out' private investment. And, intriguingly, these business forces have often found common cause with public sector social democratic reformers who, for very different reasons, were also suspicious of the British state, mainly for its unaccountable, centralised power.

And in the process, in Britain at least (and certainly in the USA) the state has come to be seen as a reactionary, conservative force – an essentially illiberal phenomenon, set against the individual's rights and freedoms.

In the real world the 'sovereign individual', although sometimes, undeniably, reduced or even threatened by the state, can also be protected by it. Indeed the state may be the sovereign individual's only ultimate protector. After all the state, the polity, is the only body that can guarantee the rights of citizens and their space, not only against private interests, including big corporations, but even against itself and its own subdivisions of government. In fact this notion of the state protecting the individual against the state is at the very heart of the American constitutional idea drawn up by the men of Philadelphia. The state would be split up – separation of powers – in order to protect the individual from any one part of it; and the state through its bill of rights, would protect minorities from majorities using government to oppress them.

This work of liberty is done by the law – by the state's law. That erudite political thinker, the late Maurice Cranston, has argued that the rule of law is utterly central to ensuring the liberty of the individual.[6] It is a stark fact that the more zealous marketeers sometimes overlook the fact that the state remains the only possible mechanism not only for creating law, but also for enforcing the rule of law. Thus without the state – even with a severely weakened state, as in post-cold war Russia, a society of mafias and gangs – society would be lawless. And lawlessness poses a much more serious threat to the individual – to his or her property, even life – than do the oft-cited 'excesses' of government, such as bureaucracy or tax-gathering. The rule of law is arguably the state's most profound gift to civilisation.

There is now little doubt that what William Greider called the 'manic logic' of new global capitalism seriously threatens the reign and rule of law, or at least as we have known it. Supporters of business continue to proclaim the importance of law, about the responsibility of businesses to exist 'within the law'. Yet this obeisance to the law by businesses can often be disingenuous. The fact is that many big corporations see the law as their primary threat, as they make a point of escaping, or threatening to escape, from those laws they do not like, and relocating, or threatening to relocate, to more conducive legal environments. It is a stark reality, but in this sense, for corporations, the rule of law no longer exits. In the ideal world of global capitalism the long arm of the law will not always reach. There will be no extradition treaties for mobile capital or for corporations in pursuit of lower social costs.

As well as securing the law, there is another powerful argument for the state as protector of the individual and of individual freedom. Historically, a strong case can be made that the freedom and space of the individual has best been protected, even enhanced, where there has been a balance between public and private, state and market, where the public sector can cooperate with and compete with an equally strong private sector. The pluralism inherent in such a balance can at least secure some autonomy for the domestic citizen.

279

Obviously for supporters of individual freedom it is the character of the state, rather than its existence, that matters. Yet in the new global order the democratic state – the state that enforces the law properly and fairly, even the state that remains in balance with the private sector – has also become the enemy, to be circumvented if possible, defeated if necessary.

State, Peace and Politics

The freedom of the individual can only exist if conflicts can be resolved sensibly and peaceably. The political world, rather than the economic world, was always considered the primary mechanism for such acceptable conflict resolution. After all, at the heart of the idea of the modern study of politics is both the recognition of conflict and difference and disagreement, and also the processes whereby people resolve, or do not resolve, conflicts.

Thus according to some schools of thought there is no politics in agreement, or in forced agreement. The political philosopher Kenneth Minogue argued that 'despots don't belong' in the definition of politics.[7] As Maurice Duverger puts it, the 'two-faced god Janus is the true image which…expresses the most profound political truth' of group conflict and its resolution based upon discussion and compromise.[8] Politics only comes into operation once a single power centre – crown, dictator, party (as in the communist system) – is removed or fades away. In contrast, of course, a market can exist under a dictatorship, or even, as we are still seeing in communist China, a one-party state.

The skills of the politician are democratic skills, so much so that today the much maligned skills of 'politics' – the ability to read public mood, the sense of what is possible and what is not, the ability to compromise between interests, the ability to articulate goals and values – are essential in mastering the arts of democracy. In contrast, and it is a crucial distinction, the skills of the business person – organisation, management, risk-taking – are leadership skills, aimed at helping forward an individual unit or company They are certainly creative, but they are not particularly democratic. They are aimed at producing a product or a profit, not at securing certain values or at resolving conflict.

However, regardless of this long history of politics and law as conflict resolvers, global marketeers still see the 'market' as a much better way of resolving conflict. They correctly point to the history of politics as being the history of the nation-state (as much as the history of law), and to how this self-same nation-state was the source of the great and deadly conflicts of the past.

In contrast with this sorry history of conflict and war, they suggest that the new world market they supported would usher in, on a global scale, an epoch of peace (and that the global market will ensure peace not simply because it is a market, but because it is global). This argument, a powerful one, rests on the proposition that it was the market, not politics, that created one global system, and one global system is inherently more stable and peaceable than one with subdivisions – nations – that cause emnities and conflict.

However 'one world' economically does not mean one world politically. And intriguingly globalisers who push for and celebrate a world market do not demand a 'world government' as well. The dynamic of global capitalism seeks no balance between public and private on a global basis, and resists – largely for tax reasons – world government. So in the real global economy, economic inequalities and resentments can be expected to grow; and these inequalities could spawn serious rebellions and violence.

As George Soros argues: 'I can already discern the makings of the final crisis [of global capitalism]. It will be political in character. Indigenous political movements are likely to arise that will seek to expropriate multinational companies and recapture the "national" wealth. Some of them will succeed in the manner of the Boxer rebellion or the Zapata revolution.'[9] There is no reason to believe that whole nations will not opt out of the global economic system, causing conflict with their neighbours, and ultimately violence. Could Malaysia, which in 1998-9 was resisting the imperatives of global capitalism from a very, very small base, be a prototype?

And all this in an environment where there is no democratic world government to resolve these conflicts through the exercise of law. The 'one world' of global capitalism may become a very unsafe place indeed. And crucially without world government, without a global political dimension, those economic conflicts that are resolved will not be settled as they broadly are under political regimes, in favour of majorities or on the basis of rights upheld by the law. Rather they will be resolved in true market fashion, in favour of those with economic power, with that rawest of measurements: most money, most resources. Again, unavoidably, those who control the market, the super-rich with their super capital, will inevitably win.

The State as a Force For Democracy

As well as securing the rights and freedom of the individual, governments – proper, democratic governments – should ensure that 'the people', rather than elites, rule. Supporters of global capitalism, however, dispute the idea that the state (and the politics it organises and protects) can ensure popular sovereignty. They suggest that only through the market mechanism can true popular sovereignty – the idea that people, rather than elites, rule – become a reality. This, as we have seen, is the notion of the 'people's capitalism' of Margaret Thatcher and Ronald Reagan. In its essentials it argued that politics and government limit, rather than enable, access to power.

This question of access is at the heart of this criticism of politics. Arthur Seldon took the lead in arguing forcefully that the sizeable government and state created during the post-1945 era produced a class of 'political people' who manipulated this state system in order to achieve an advantage for themselves. This idea of 'political people' could also be extended more widely to many in the middle classes, and was most evident in health and education, where the 'political people', the well-connected people, through their social status (which in the postwar period was still very, very important in European countries such as France and Britain) or contacts in the system gained what amounted to preferential treatment within the state system.

This populist appeal – that in the state and public sector, special elite groups gained at the expense of 'ordinary people'– subtly, or not so subtly, undercut the political left as the protector of the weak and underprivileged, portraying socialists not as caring democrats but rather as 'top people', uncaring mandarins. This was a more effective rerun of a theme from the early 1970s when the political and intellectual left were depicted as phonies: in the US as 'limousine liberals' and in Britain as 'Hampstead do-gooders'.

This right-wing populism was effective because it had some truth to it. There is a strong argument that the middle classes gained disproportionately from the welfare state, and that the welfare system was open to manipulation by the articulate and well-connected. Also, the British social democratic state, as it developed in the 1950s, 1960s and 1970s, did indeed become both bureaucratised – producing insensitive and bossy elites – and politicised, creating political classes who saw both the state and the world of politics as exclusive preserves for their own benefit. And in the process government did indeed cease to operate as a neutral referee between private interests or as a well-organised welfare system, but instead became 'an interest', rather like a 'special interest' or a 'corporate interest'. And many of those who worked for government, who served the state, no longer saw their occupation as a special vocation – a proud vocation uniquely allowing the office holder 'to do the people's work'.

The undeniable fact is however, that all the charges of state bureaucracy, of special interests and of unfair advantages could just as easily have been made about the market-based system. Corporations produced their own bureaucracy and organisational rigidities, inefficiencies often successfully hidden from shareholders by managers. 'Who you know', rather than 'what you know' – 'networking' – worked just as powerfully in the private sector. Large businesses thrived on 'connections'. Unsavoury (even outright corrupt) connections between large private corporations and the state (such as the US Congress and executive departments such as the Pentagon) were the routine meat and drink of the lobbying system. Job appointments were less regulated than in the public sector, with fewer rules about interviewing and discrimination. And amongst small businesses, nepotism – almost by definition – has always been an acceptable form of business recruitment.

Participation

As well as achieving popular sovereignty, claims were also made that market capitalism resulted in another crucial democratic outcome: a high and wide rate of participation, higher and wider than that offered by *political* democracy. Arthur Seldon suggested that modern capitalism, by minimising the writ of politics and maximising the writ of the market, 'creates a more effective form of democracy' by enabling 'all the people, the common people as well as the political people, to decide their lives'.[10] He then posited what he called 'the central question': 'is it easier for the political process to include all the heads or for the market process to endow all the people with money?' He of course came down in favour of the latter being more inclusive.

There was however a misreading of 'political democracy' here. Modern democratic politics, was never just about 'counting heads' or participation. It was certainly about allowing those who wanted to participate to do so, *and to do so as of right.* (You had the right to vote because you were a human being, whereas you participated in market democracy because you were endowed with money.) But it was more than that. Under the democracy of the state, access and participation were to be secured through rights, not just votes. And rights (as I argue later in this chapter) can allow 'the common people' access to the governmental system and the decision-making forums of society just as effectively, in fact more effectively than voting every few years.

Some pro-business intellectuals believe that the private capitalist sector can help participation through means other than the 'democracy of the market' – for instance by encouraging participation through companies themselves. Company workforces already take part in company decision-making in small ways, but Charles Handy, amongst others, has suggested that a restructuring of the corporation could allow for a real advance in corporate democracy. He suggests that the modern corporation is 'inadequate for modern times', that 'a public corporation has now to be regarded as a community, not a piece of property', and that we need a 'citizen corporation' in which 'the core members of that community are more properly regarded as citizens rather than employees or "human resources", citizens with responsibilities as well as rights'.[11]

The idea is that in these new 'citizen corporations' the private ownership of property will remain, as will the market, but that within the privately-owned unit a new sharing of power and decision-making should take place. A variant of this is, of course, the existing cooperatives. In the cooperative movement the key idea is that the market mechanism is retained as a means of providing most goods and services, while the ownership of capital is socialised...all productive enterprises are constituted as workers' cooperatives, leasing their operating capital from an outside investment agency. Each enterprise makes its own decisions about products, prices, etc...net profits form a pool out of which incomes are paid...Each enterprise is democratically controlled by those who work for it.[12]

One problem with this private sector model of participation is that, even if it was expanded to include public sector enterprises, the new-style market democracy it advocates takes no account of the millions and millions who have no connection with companies whatsoever – students, the elderly the unemployed. *Political* democracy, on the other hand, can include everyone. Market democracy – particularly in the global market – limits decision-making to economic and economic-related issues, whereas political democracy encourages participation in a range of non-economic issues, from international policy to cultural and even social and sexual issues.

Another problem with market democracy is the huge inequality in participation. Certainly everyone who has access to the market can participate in it, but unlike political democracy, where participation is at least theoretically equal (one person has one vote, everyone has the same rights), the extent of market participation depends on the amount of resources you can bring to the market. Put crudely – for it *is* somewhat crude – big bucks mean greater participation. And under global capitalism, where capital is even more important *vis-à-vis* labour (and the state), then this inequality of participation is even more marked.

The criticism by market supporters of low participation rates in political democracy are powerfully made. However politics is open to reform. In one sense the history of government is the history of adjustment and adaptation to wider and wider participation and access, in other words to democracy. The Greek idea of the polis may have existed alongside slavery, but Greek politics gave us the word and the idea – the gripping, powerful idea of 'democracy'. Democracy remains a political word with a political meaning. The political institutions of the medieval world – kingship and the like – certainly excluded the majority of people and entrenched serfdom, yet the English Parliament was formed in this period. Although the great political/constitutional document of American independence was written in Philadelphia by English landowners, who excluded women and happily ignored slavery, it was malleable enough to become the most celebrated and mature example of democratic constitutionalism and arguably it still is the greatest single written institutional expression of the democratic idea.

Not only is it possible to reform government and the state, to continue to adapt it to the growing modern need for ever-increasing participation and access, but reforming government in order to achieve this task is now relatively easy because of modern techniques and changing technology. The widespread use of information technology – television, computers, internet and the like – makes a surfeit of political participation now practically possible. We can participate – discuss, vote – from home. The citizen is now able to vote – monthly, weekly, daily, even hourly – both on single issues and for representatives. It is now technically possible to arrange a fairly competent referendum every day of the week. (So rather than political democracy limiting access or participation, the modern-day problem may be democratic fatigue.)

Anthony Giddens, in his theoretical book on social democracy, *The Third Way*, sees the possibilities of renewing rather than shrinking the state. 'What is necessary', he suggests, 'is to reconstruct [the state] – to go beyond those on the right who say "government is the enemy" and those on the left who say "government is the answer".' And he outlines specific strategies that the modern state should employ in order to renew itself: devolution, the further democratisation of democratic institutions, renewal of the public sphere through transparency, administrative efficiency, mechanisms for direct democracy, and government as risk manager (by which he means, in part, regulating scientific and technological change).[13]

Minorities

Market theorists and propagandists sometimes argue that 'political democracy' is potentially authoritarian, and therefore careless of the rights of minorities. In this mindset 'the state' is – if not exactly the door to communism or fascism – incipiently authoritarian, certainly compared with 'the market', which is viewed as inherently libertarian. Even the relatively mature democratic states – say the US or Britain – although not in themselves necessarily oppressive, have a very definite potential to be so. Their problem is majorities! Their 'working method of making decisions by majorities, or counting heads, and ignoring many heads merely because they are less numerous, is a childish and uncivilised way of deciding the use of resources'. In contrast market democracy, by 'counting pennies not heads', provides some power for 'all heads, including those of minorities and…independent and idiosyncratic individuals'.[14]

This idea that minorities and 'idiosyncratic individuals' are protected by money, even lots and lots of it, is fanciful. Stable mass prosperity, whereby majorities feel secure and unthreatened, is probably the most effective protection for minorities. But in times of economic trouble the market, by its propensity for increasing inequalities, may make life *worse* for minorities because of the creation of increasing social tensions in which minority groups become vulnerable. And it is in these difficult times for minorities that politics – in the form of an entrenched democratic political culture – and the state – in the form of a written constitution and, crucially, the rule of law is the best guarantor of minority rights. Whatever the causes of the two great holocausts – the slaughter of the Armenians in Turkey and the Jews in Germany – it was the lack of a political safety net – of strong democratic institutions, of a democratic political culture – not the lack of markets, that led economic failure and social tensions to break out into slaughter.

In a global economy in which no state is strong enough to create this political safety net, minorities may find themselves with less and less protection.

Rights

The battle for individual rights has been the very stuff of the history of western civilisation. It has exercised the minds of the great liberal thinkers from John Locke to John Stuart Mill, and great polemicists such as Tom Paine and Thomas Jefferson; and it has enlivened the pages of great political documents from the Magna Carta through to *The Rights of Man* and the American Declaration of Independence, right up to the present day and the UN and EU Declarations. These traditional 'rights' – such as freedom of speech, assembly and petition, and worship – are now joined by social rights such as the that of privacy, reproductive choice and non-discrimination based upon equality. Even economic rights, to jobs and economic security, are now, more controversially, on the agenda. Rights are so much a part of the fabric of western life, even a measure of civilised living, that some believe the culture of rights has led to the disregard for responsibilities.

Rights are essentially political, articulated by politicians and political writers. They are written down in political documents. And political, constitutional and legal systems enforce and encourage them.

It is universally accepted that the state – the political authority – is the only mechanism that can entrench rights. This is so because it is the only acceptable mechanism for law – making and governing the physical forces of coercion that lie behind the law – the police, the military in 'aid of the civil power'. No one, except extreme libertarians and anarchists, suggests that the much-vaunted market – or market players – should actually make laws (although in the real world large agglomerations of private capital can control legislatures or ignore laws) or take over the role of the courts and the police (although private security services sometimes blur the distinction between state law and private rules).

The fact is that the market – and certainly the global market – cannot on its own either create or protect rights. Nor can (or should) the principal inhabitants of the market place – the large corporations! Ultimately we need to face the fact that business people are not in business to protect rights (or, more generally, to make the world a better place!) Regardless of the protestations of the business ethics industry, most honest business people will admit the truth of this. And in a world in which corporations have their way, having outmanoeuvred the state, then the future for any realistic regime of rights looks increasingly bleak.

As the claims for rights come to be extended beyond political rights to economic rights, then the very idea of rights clearly comes into direct conflict with modern market democracy and global capitalism. When, for instance, the 'right to employment' is claimed, this is obviously denied by supporters of the global markets, and even by market democrats who see it as threatening the smooth working of market capitalism, particularly the ability of employers to hire and fire at will.

Pluralism

For many political theorists, pluralism is the lifeblood of democracy and the democratic way of life. Plural power centres offer protection against the dangers of centralisation inherent in a single authority, and give to the individual freedom of space and maneuverability.

Pluralism is modern capitalism's strongest argument. Whatever can be said against the global market it does not tend to centralise power – at least not during the early stage it is still in. The global marketplace is simply too big and too diffuse to allow such centralisation. So far, whatever its other democratic shortcomings, modern global capitalism remains a veritable cornucopia of pluralism: almost a bustling anarchy, with many, many decision-making centres. The sheer number of companies and units of capital competing around the world ensures such pluralism. And the new mobile capital of the global economic order also ensures political pluralism because it acts to break up political units so that it can divide and rule.

Of course modern global capitalism is witnessing an increasing number of mergers between corporations. Giant and highly centralised super-corporations are beginning to dominate the various sectors of the global economy The huge mergers of the 1990s – many of which, such as those between

British Petroleum and Amoco, and Deutsche Bank and Bankers Trust, were truly transnational – all point to a worrying future of great agglomerations of economic power. Even so, there is still little prospect of that creature of the imagination, 'one great corporation', dominating the world.

On the other hand the political system, the interstate or international relations system that globalism has largely replaced, tended to concentrate power in far fewer locations. And in the Cold War's nuclear age some of these political power centres – individuals such as the president of the United States and the general-secretary of the Soviet Union, and their respective inner-sanctum colleagues – accumulated so much power that, unlike even the biggest corporation, they held the awesome power of life or death over millions. That the state can possess such an illiberal, centralising potential that may not, in quite the same sense, be present in the market is recognised. Even socialists now accept that in state-dominated economies there is a pluralist deficit. As Christopher Pierson has written:

> What has seemed to many commentators to be fatally damaging to this socialist argument is the continuing failure to generate a satisfactory model for the democratic control of economic life. This objection seems even more compelling now in the light of the recent experience of the two most prominent and quite divergent forms which 'real socialism' took in the twentieth century – the Soviet model and western social democracy.[15]

Of course one of the reasons why democrats and liberals support the idea of pluralism is that, by preventing the growth of any power centre reaching the point where it can threaten the individual, such pluralism enhances individual rights. Capitalist economic pluralism, however, does not serve this function. It certainly provides many economic decision centres, and this type of pluralism certainly helps consumer choice. But extending consumer choice, important though it may be, is not the same as protecting political rights such as freedom of speech, assembly and worship – or indeed economic rights such as a job! Political rights are protected by law and the state, and no matter how diffuse economic power may be under global capitalism, if the state is weakened, so is the ability to protect rights. And also, we should not forget that no matter the number of economic decision-makers in the market, not one of them – not one – has, *in their economic role*, any fundamental interest or motivation in protecting human rights.

Through the mists and subtleties of the great debate about globalisation and democracy there remains one very worrying political truth. Whatever the politics and values of the new world we are heading into, they will not be democratic – at least as we have known and understood the word. The kind of liberal-democratic political systems that grew from and developed out of the political upheavals of the late eighteenth century in France and North America – what we now call liberal-democracy – were coexistent with nation-states, and are likely to die alongside them.

So, as the nation-state withers on the vine under the pressures of globalising capital, so does democracy. It is a huge problem.

BUSINESS AND STATE TOGETHER: A HISTORY

Even though the state has been the mechanism for most all the democratic advances in Britain, as we have seen in earlier chapters the Thatcher/Reagan neoliberal revolution turned history on its head and ushered into the British zeitgeist a new antipathy to the state and the public realm. And the new Cameron government in 2010, coming into office in the aftermath of the great private capital financial crash, instead of reversing this trend, has, at least in the short-run, continued it. The state became the enemy, not the enabler. This new atmosphere continues to allow the ascendant business forces unleashed during the 1980s to develop an unremitting hostility to the public sector, so much so that the political right could start to contemplate a strategy which would dismantle the post-1945 mixed economy and to create in its place a 'minimalist' state.

Business leaders, and their supportive politicians, have used their power within the corporate media – in Britain, principally through Sky TV and the country's leading newspapers – to demean and disdain the public sector, and even the democratic polity itself, on a constant basis. As I outlined in the last chapter a perfect example occurred when, in early 2009, *The Daily Telegraph* launched its highly successful campaign against MPs' expenses – even though the abuses involved small amounts of money compared to the real scandals in the private banking sector.

However, this extreme hostility to the state is relatively new. Historically, business, particularly big business, has tended to work with, rather than against, the state and the public sector. Certainly, as the state has grown in size and scope, the business community has, until recently, always seemed to recognise the ultimate sovereignty and supremacy of the political realm. Even during the high point of the unfettered market relations of the nineteenth century, politics remained in charge, managing to constrain the raw economic power of Victorian capitalism. Trade and commerce may have blossomed, and increasingly broken free of borders, but in those Victorian times – in the leading capitalist nations, Britain, the United States and Germany – political sovereignty was unquestioned. The Victorian nation-state was not to be trifled with, or at least not in the way in which global capital treats the contemporary nation-state.

Of course this was the age of imperialism in which the nation-states (and their ruling groups) directly and politically controlled vast territories and peoples. The fundamental dynamic here was political – contests between peoples and civilisations, conquests, and pre-democratic values such as racial superiority and paternalist political views such as elite governance. These empires were geopolitical systems, in which trade might not always exactly 'follow the flag' but was always securely wrapped in it. Commerce played a crucial but ultimately secondary role to the political dynamic of empire, being run from London, Paris, Amsterdam, Madrid and Lisbon. And it was politics – through imperial expansion of the European nation-states – that fuelled the globalisation of this Victorian era whereas today's globalisation is the product of economics, of companies and capital, not nation-states.

In Britain in the Victorian era, politics – in the form of an expanding political community based on an emerging, middle-class, male democracy – established ascendancy over the burgeoning capitalism of the era. Victorian capital may indeed have been confident, and profitable; but in an era of strong political loyalties, and, unlike today, rooted in its own country, Victorian capital was ultimately subservient to politics, to the Victorian state, in a sense in which it is not in the global economy. The political community through the state, could improve labour conditions, take the first tentative steps towards a welfare state, and increase public expenditure and taxes without provoking capital flight.

The great Victorian debate was not about whether society or politics existed, or should exist, but rather about how big the state should become – about how much regulation the economy should include. Even the great free-market thinkers of the Victorian era saw politics as sovereign. They may have seen the means towards achieving the free society as largely economic, but their ends were usually political.

In an interesting twist, many of these same 'free market' Victorians were political radicals whose overriding concern was not economics, but political and social change. For them the state was wrongly ordered and should be reformed, not abolished. And, unlike today's supporters of the 'free market', these Victorians believed in securing rights for the broad mass of middle-class people, and saw the state – in the form of the law – as a crucial mechanism. For them the central obstacle was social: the power of the aristocracy and landed interests (reflected in the monarchy, the House of Lords and the limited franchise for the House of Commons). And it was the long-standing political ideology of freedom – of freeborn Englishmen – which fired the minds of nineteenth-century radicals. Certainly Herbert Spencer and Auberon Herbert, and before them Tom Paine, were supporters of minimal government, for they saw the state controlled by a corrupt aristocracy, and sought a greater space for business and the market which would promote a less paternalist, less objectionable, more middle class, society, with better, more democratic values. But the aim was social and political, not economic. What these anti-aristocratic businessmen would think of today's early twenty-first century big business class, with its entrenched and inherited power, is a fascinating speculation.

Even during the so-called 'gilded age' of American capitalism in the late nineteenth century, capital was political and social – that is, bounded by the idea of limits placed upon its reach and power by the needs of a wider community. Max Weber in *The Protestant Ethic and the Spirit of Capitalism*, and the Christian Socialist R. H. Tawney in *Religion and the Rise of Capitalism* saw a direct link between religiously inspired ethics and capital, 'a code of Protestant conviction which said that gaining wealth was connected to virtue but was also a trust' [8] There was wide acceptance of the idea that making money (profits) was morally acceptable as long as there was an ultimate social goal. In the US the idea that capital has an ultimate social responsibility was given practical form in the great philanthropic trusts and foundations of the Rockefellers, the Mellons, the Carnegies and their like. These moguls were certainly not keen on state interference in the making of capital, which was often a grubby and ruthless business, but once the pile was made the idea of wider social responsibility (often in the form of charity) took over.

As an historian of the 'robber baron' period has argued:

> In short order the railroad presidents, the copper barons, the big dry-goods merchants and the steel masters became Senators, ruling in the highest councils of the national government, and sometimes scattered twenty dollar gold pieces to newsboys of Washington. But they also became in greater number lay leaders of churches, trustees of universities, partners or owners of newspapers...and figures of fashionable, cultured society.[16]

As one commentator of the time suggested, these robber barons with a conscience, and with a 'becoming gravity', offered themselves as guides 'to literature and art, church and state, science and education, law and morals – the standard container of the civic virtue'.[17]

Business and the Twentieth-Century Nation

The supremacy of politics over economics in the twentieth century was exemplified by the ideology of the rapidly expanding corporate world. These new corporations, which over the century had replaced the traditional family firm, were large, multi-unit operations. They represented a new managerial capitalism where month by month, year by year, decisions were increasingly taken by a race of professionally and technically competent managers. As Pulitzer Prize winning management theorist Alfred Chandler has argued, these modern big businesses were rather like independent political units, and 'took the place of market mechanisms in coordinating the activities of the economy and allocating its resources'.[18]

By controlling the market rather than competing within it, these big new corporations increasingly acted politically. As Werner Sombart argued during the 1930s, they began to take on a life of their own, the emerging managerial class having as much political and social interest in the land as any trade unionist or civil servant. They sought, and often obtained, influence over legislation by financing congressmen and senators. And, crucially, the new breed of career managers and corporate bureaucrats 'preferred policies that favoured long-term stability and growth of their enterprises to those that maximised current profits'.[19]

Although often driven by profitability, the new culture of the big, multi-unit, largely-American, corporation still considered the company to be part of the wider political community with its political and social obligations. One such political obligation was obeying the law. Of course pre-global capitalist corporations used their muscle to attempt to bend legislatures to their will and sway laws in their interests, but once political decisions had been made, they carried on business as part of the wider nation-state.

Although today's global corporations all declare their adherence to the laws of the lands in which they operate, their ability to relocate in territories where laws are more amenable means that their protestations are an empty boast.

Most of the pre-global companies operating in the Victorian and Edwardian eras saw themselves as political and social communities rather than simply profit-making organisations. The workforce was led to believe that the company was a community, almost a family (Henry Ford even became a kind of agony uncle); and a 'community of feeling' was promoted through job security, pensions and health benefits – although this was often in order to forestall trade union activity. This approach amounted to a form of micro-welfare capitalism. Elton Mayo, the founding father of the human relations school of management, publicised the corporate welfare practices of AT&T's Hawthorne Works in the late 1920s and early 1930s. Management theorist John Sheldrake has argued that 'the package of benefits at the Hawthorne Works was, by contemporary international standards, impressive and included a pension scheme, sickness and disability benefits, a share purchase plan, a system of worker representation, a medical department and hospital'.[20]

In Britain the same kind of community attitude could be seen in the mid-Victorian mill towns where, according to F. M. L. Thompson in *The Rise of Respectable Society*, 'life centred on the mill, not simply because it was the source of work and wages but because it formed a distinct community and attracted specific loyalties'.[21] Indeed the cotton textile industry became the focus of paternalistic activity – what would later be termed 'welfare capitalism'. From the middle of the century it became increasingly common for big employers to provide reading and newspaper rooms at the mills. By the 1890s works sports grounds were common, as were brass bands.

A growing interest in the idea of scientific management demanded the recognition of a mutuality between managers and workers. F. W. Taylor's work on management, which advocated such a mutuality, attracted a considerable following in the US, Japan and Germany as did the ideas of his disciple, Henry Gantt.[22]

The idea of businesses as communities – of a social or political leavening of the raw economic commercialism of the corporation – did not normally go as far as seeking to involve the 'community of workers' in commercial decisions. After all, this kind of capitalism was paternalistic, not democratic. The corporation was for the workers, but not of them. Even so, after the Second World War 'co-determination', in which employees were allowed some kind of general input into commercial strategy through reserved positions on the governing boards, became a feature of West German corporations. Intriguingly, it was an idea encouraged by the victorious allies who would not have given house room to the notion in their own countries! What stopped worker participation in its tracks in the Anglo-American world was the, often visceral, opposition of some business leaders. But the trade unions were also against it – seeing their function as adversarial negotiators, not mutual builders.

Businessmen before the period of globalisation were themselves ruthless, and made huge fortunes. Many of them had been dubbed the 'robber barons' and – by Teddy Roosevelt – the 'malefactors of great wealth'. Yet these tough-minded capitalists tended to see business as having some social function beyond the factory gates: business was part of a wider community with concomitant responsibilities. The tone was set by John D. Rockefeller, of whom a serious critic conceded that his 'prodigious investments in public charities which, begun in 1890, were conducted upon a scale befitting the man's princely power, and most certainly fitted to scale Heaven's walls'.[23] And long after the age of these robber barons, the American companies of the twentieth century continued to invest in local communities – in the townships and villages in which they operated, and expected to continue to operate. All manner of local cultural services and amenities, including symphony orchestras and opera companies, received corporate support.

Of course this political and social dimension of business made good business sense. A contented workforce could be expected to work more efficiently and thus produce more profits, and, crucially, would be less likely to demand trade union representation. And local community activity was good for public relations over the long-term.

For all their self-interest, pre-global capitalist businesses saw profitability and politics as linked. The interest of the shareholder was not utterly paramount. The aim of the corporate game was certainly to make profits, but power, prestige, acceptability and recognition were, along with money, powerful business motives. And the path to business success did not always involve lower and lower social costs.

Interwar Co-operation

Of course, business concern for the wider political community was enhanced by the deepening relationship between the state and the corporations. The rapid growth in government before, during and after the Second World War opened up for the private sector, big and small, a veritable cornucopia of government contracts – particularly in the defence industry. And as the state grew after 1945, politically-driven procurement policy became even more important than operating in the market. In such an environment, big business increasingly saw itself, or said it did, as contributing to national (political) goals, not just chasing profits. Business and state – and sometimes trade unions – worked together in an 'every one a winner' symbiotic relationship. A new ideology of cooperation, or corporatism, came into fashion.

The concept of cooperation between business, unions and state, much derided by today's supporters of the 'Anglo-Saxon' capitalist model, had been floated officially in Britain during the Mond-Turner talks in 1928-9, and big business organisations (such as the Business Round Table in the US and the CBI in Britain), sensing it would be more profitable, immediately warmed to the idea. In the US the business world was divided, but some of the CEOs from the biggest corporations opted for agreements with the unions and the New Deal administration.[24] In the political world, many big-business supporters of the moderate wing of the Republican Party and 'One Nation' Tories in Britain propounded these corporatist views well into the 1970s. In continental Europe proponents of the social market continued to stress the advantages of cooperation between what they called 'the social partners' of capital and labour; the state and big business continued to work together on long-term, strategic plans for investments and markets.

Business, Democracy and War

Despite the evidence for the corporation as part of its society, there is an argument that, even in the Victorian age, the dynamic of a restless, borderless, burgeoning capitalism was underway – and that national governments were slowly losing their autonomy and authority. (Some theorists have even suggested that the late Victorian economy was more globalised than today.)[25] It would have been rash to predict that what lay ahead was a new age of nationalism. Yet, just such a new age was indeed about to dawn, and with it the continuing ability of the nation-state (and therefore of politics) to constrain the power of economics, business and the market, and to keep capitalism civilised.

This resurgence of the nation-state was the product of two extraordinary new phenomena – mass democracy and mass war.

By the second decade of the twentieth century mass democracy was well advanced in the industrialised countries. The franchise was becoming a majority affair and the middle classes were increasingly involved in their societies. The idea of popular sovereignty – that the people owned their government – was growing: strongly in the US, moderately in some continental European countries and somewhat less in Britain. And, crucially, the nation-state became the forum – the only possible forum – for the expression of these democratic instincts and aspirations. It gave the nation a huge shot of legitimacy.

But it was war, more than democracy, that revived the twentieth century nation-state. The sheer nationalistic fervour of 1914-18, when millions volunteered to fight (and die), remains inexplicable for many. But it existed. It produced a huge emotional commitment to the nation-state, not only during the war, but afterwards too, resting on the legions of heroes who it was claimed gave their lives for the nation, for king and country And war benefited the craft and calling of politics too. The Second World War leaders (Churchill, Roosevelt, De Gaulle) were politicians, and their mythic status gave authority and credibility not only to the political class but, more broadly, to the state. Business and businessmen were marginalised by war, were thought to play little part in the great military clashes and political crusades, except perhaps as shadowy and sinister armaments manufacturers. The state, not the market, won wars.

The Second World War, unlike its predecessor, was a 'good war' and produced little subsequent pacifist and internationalist sentiment. A major media industry – primarily Hollywood, but television and the literary world as well – hugely reinforced national sentiment in many of the victorious countries. Patriotic themes and negative images of defeated foreigners ('Huns', 'Japs') conspired to enhance postwar nationalism. The war against Hitler was conducted by an alliance, but each nation separately was able to claim an heroic role.

The nation – with its centralised state and its politicians – not only 'won the war', but also in its aftermath appeared to produce the economic goods. The state, like the nation, emerged from the Second World War rather well. It had mobilised resources in a righteous cause, and it had been victorious. In the postwar decades it constructed a popular welfare state which brought education and healthcare to those who had been unable to afford it. The state still had negative aspects – it was seen as inefficient and ridden with bureaucracy – but as the majority of the population still did not pay a large amount of their income in taxes, it was not yet a dark force.

As a social democrat theorist Anthony Crosland wrote at the height of the postwar boom in the 1950s: 'Whatever the modes of economic production, economic power will, in fact, belong to the owners of political power' – in effect the owners of the nation-state. He believed that this political world would last, that 'political authority has emerged as the final arbiter of economic life', and that 'the brief, and historically exceptional, era of unfettered market relations is over'.[26]

Yet in the 1950s this enhanced credibility of government and state went hand in hand with the revival of the private sector and its enormous productive capacity. The capitalism of the 1950s and 1960s, the high point of social democracy, operated in the context of an extraordinarily productive balance between economics (and the market) and politics (the state and government) that lasted until well into the 1980s.

During these decades business still deferred to national leaderships, to government and politics. Part of the reason for this was the inherited 'authority' in the idea of the nation, and in politics and the political world. The emerging big businesses, however, also found the nationally based, social democratic, 'mixed economy' conducive to its needs. The nation-state was providing a healthy infrastructure for the private sector and was subsidising business in numerous ways. This was the age in which a Conservative prime minister (Edward Heath) and a Republican President (Richard Nixon) introduced wage and price controls; in which big business supported the election of a big-spending, 'Great Society' president (and turned its back on Reaganite Barry Goldwater); in which industrial policy or national planning was not anathema to business in Britain. It was an age in which business believed that trade unions had to be taken seriously, indeed often appeased. And as I shall argue later, the welfare state – existing in an age when, in Europe certainly, socialism and communism were on the political agenda – was seen by many business leaders as a force for social stability.

The Cold War, Business and Politics

The Cold War began in the late 1940s, the same period in which huge amounts of western public and private capital were beginning to be invested around the world and later pump-primed the era of global capital. Paradoxically, it was the Cold War that staunched the process of early 'globalisation'. For the intensity of the East-West conflict locked the 'emerging markets' of Eastern Europe, the Soviet Union and above all China, out of the world economy for almost five decades. The Cold War also breathed life into the nation-state, and gave it a centrality that for fifty years would keep it from being overwhelmed by global capital, global business and the global market. J. G. Ikenberry goes further. He sees the Cold War as a 'long era of global struggle' that not only strengthened nations, nation-states and national governments but also 'centralised' them.[27]

Thus did the Cold War keep western politics ascendant over western business. 'The business of America' could no longer be about business alone. It had better also be about freedom. Government and business not only worked together to get the Marshall Plan off the ground, but saw the ambitious plan as 'a simple necessity, a down payment on the American century' Amongst the politicians Truman and many of his Democrats were not enamoured with business – the feeling was mutual – but they understood the need to co-operate. And, later, as a key aspect of the Cold War, American policy in the Middle East, also brought cooperation between business and government. Daniel Yergin has suggested that US relations with the Saudi royal family and the Middle East was 'the point at which foreign policy, national security and corporate interests would all converge.'[28]

In the Cold War anticommunism – the great cause of the West – became a focus of loyalty. The business world, with its anticommunist instincts, naturally supported the cause, and corporations, even the largest and most powerful of them, remained subordinate to the broader political, ideological and indeed cultural struggle.

Of course during the Cold War decades, particularly in the 1970s during the period of detente, business began doing what it inevitably does: breaking free from politics in search of profits. And even in these years of East-West tension, particularly in the later period, there was a decided increase in economic relations between western corporate capitalism and the communist bloc. Western companies were pioneering the economics of 'globalisation': in particular they were increasingly taking advantage of the Eastern Bloc's low-paid, strike-free labour. An intricate process of buy-back agreements – dubbed 'Vodka-Cola' in which 'you bottle our Coke and we'll buy your Vodka'

– were developed in order to bypass the non-convertibility of communist bloc currencies.[29]

The advantages of western capitalist access to the low-cost, union-free command economies of the Eastern Bloc were recognised early on by such prominent business figures as Armand Hammer of Occidental Petroleum and Cleveland billionaire Cyrus Eaton. Many European business leaders also benefited from dealing with Eastern Europe and encouraged the West German policy of Ostpolitik between the Federal Republic of Germany and the Communist Bloc.

Even so, during the rule of the communist parties (in the period up to 1989) trade and capital flows were minimal, certainly compared with the opening of the floodgates following the collapse of the Berlin Wall and the dissolution of the Warsaw Pact. The requirements of politics – international geopolitics – took precedence over business. In the US Congress politicians – as part of a major act of political interference with free trade – were able to pass into legislation 'national security' measures whereby whole sectors of western industry and commerce, particularly those connected to the defence industry, were denied trading rights with communist countries. These national security laws of the West, primarily aimed at denying technology transfers from West to East, were of course never fully complied with, but during the Cold War most businesses continued to place loyalty to the western political community ahead of profits.[30]

Of course this restraint of the western business class was also to do with self-interest, as corporations that skirted the legal rules and traded with the Eastern Bloc might find it difficult to secure highly lucrative defence contracts from the Pentagon. Also, because of strict western legal restrictions, the Soviet Union was unable to use its large reserves of gold as a means of financing the purchase of western technology. And capital injections into the Eastern Bloc were risky because of the inconvertibility of the communist currencies and the limits to simple barter deals in return for massive transfers of capital and services.

There was immense political and social pressure on companies not to trade with the East, pressure made all the more powerful by the anti East-West trade alliance in the US of Republicans and cold war liberals. Business leaders did not want to fall foul of Reaganite Republican sentiment or be attacked by neoconservatives. *Vodka-Cola*, the title of an influential book published during the period of detente, was a term of abuse amongst those in the resurgent conservative and neoconservative movement in the late 1970s and early 1980s and Armand Hammer became a hate figure amongst Republican and Democrat cold warriors for some time. In the great cause of 'making the world safe for democracy' business was expected, even by the most pro-business elements in the political class, to toe the line.

Many western business elites, and their political allies, not only saw themselves as part of a broader political cause opposed to the Soviet Union and communism, but they also believed, certainly in the early years of the Cold War, that the West needed to be defended at home, within the domestic societies, against the spread of communist ideas. The Soviet Union, its Communist Party and its ideological and propaganda apparatus around the world, was taken extremely seriously as a threat. Its ability to attract western converts by offering an 'alternative model' of society was not underrated.

A wide range of business people – including the 'super-rich' of the time – regarded social democracy as the best antidote to communism. A sizeable state sector, a welfare system and above all full employment (guaranteed if need be by deficit financing, some subsidies, higher taxes and even a little inflation) would ensure sufficient social stability for alternative models of society (particularly socialism and communism) to have little allure for western peoples. For the same reasons, some of the richest people in the western world promoted the politics and culture of social democracy amongst western intellectual elites in the universities, the media and politics. And of course a sizeable state – the public sector no less – was needed to organise the military opposition to the Soviet Union and communism.

POST-CRASH BRITISH BUSINESS

The story of the 1980s and 1990s, and of the New Labour years that followed, is the story of the humbling of the state in the West – of the reordering of the erstwhile balance between state and business decisively in favour of business. The state was not only purposely down-sized through privatisation but, more importantly, it was completely refashioned to meet the requirements of business – a relatively low business and inheritance tax regime, all the 'handmaiden state' functions (such as infrastructure, subsidies, contracts, outsourcing), and little interference in open borders for trade (and, increasingly, for labour migrants).

But the greatest achievement of western big business in this 'gilded era' was to add China with its millions and millions of low cost workers to its labour and cost pool. This addition of China was the heart and soul of the famed 'global economy'. It not only lowered costs and bumped up profits but, crucially, it created a low inflation environment throughout the western world which from the late 1990s onwards would allow another huge burst in debt and credit – a debt bubble that would fuel the consumer-driven economy, the pride of the Greenspan/ Clinton/Bush/Blair era.

In November 2001, when China formally joined the World Trade Organisation (WTO) this new relationship was sealed.

CHAPTER EIGHT

CAN BRITAIN MAKE IT?

'LITTLE ENGLAND' IN A DANGEROUS WORLD

2010: NEW GOVERNMENT: SAME IDEAS?

In May 2010 as Britain's crisis deepened the new coalition government under Prime Minister David Cameron had, like the wider political and financial elite – no serious new thinking to offer. The new government, like so many before it, started its tenure by blaming the old regime. However, it found no fault with the fundamentals of the financial and economic system; and it proclaimed, in true neoliberal fashion, that it was the government deficit – not unemployment or social cohesion – that was the overriding problem facing the country. The new Liberal Democrat Deputy Prime Minister, Nick Clegg, had talked during the election campaign of the need for 'savage' cuts.

From this neoliberal perspective Britain's deficit was indeed a huge and dangerous problem. And by the time of the general election of 2010 it was clear that Britain was one of the worst cases. The budget deficit was higher than all of its major European neighbours – in late 2009 it was standing, and rising, at 12.6 per cent of GDP (in normal times 3 per cent was the preferred limit in the EU); and in late March 2009 the total British 'national' debt stood at 55 per cent of GDP and was rising quite sharply.[1] The Labour government had not only financed the rescue of the hugely overextended banking system but, as the recession bit and unemployment grew, was sustaining a growing welfare budget. These debt and deficit figures were placing great strains on sterling, and there was a widespread fear of a serious run on the pound. Prime Minister Gordon Brown and Treasury Minister Alistair Darling had been caught between Scylla and Charybdis, increasing public expenditure (private investment and consumption were anaemic) in order to engender growth and employment, while at the same time retaining some measure of fiscal responsibility in order to defend sterling in the speculative markets. It was a high wire act; only sustained by the promise to cut the deficit in half from 2011. The Conservative policy was to cut the deficit sooner and more deeply.

The only debate was thus over timing – how quickly to set about cutting (or raising taxes). There was, however, a growing body of opinion arguing that the sheer size of these projected and demanded, cuts, if introduced too soon, would likely lead to a further downturn (and perhaps too to a currency crisis – caused by the prospect of a downward spiral of low growth and low tax receipts leading back to high deficits, and doubtless further demands for further cuts). George Magnus, a senior economics advisor at the UBS bank, proclaimed that any premature cut could provoke a 'savage' reaction in currency markets and would 'endanger the recovery of the banking sector and the UK labour market – a view publicly supported by Britain's leading Keynesian economist Professor Robert Skidelsky and other leading economic thinkers.[2] Britain's economy was so low in the water that a currency crisis was being confidently predicted on all sides of the debate.

Yet the new coalition Conservative-Liberal government took little notice of these warnings, and within two weeks of taking office embarked upon over £6 billion in savings, threatening too to cut even more within weeks. With 'savage' cuts on the agenda the desperate prospect for Britain's future was high levels of unemployment likely to last for many years – as was a hardening of wealth and income divisions, a further growth of the dependency (welfare) culture, and greater national, ethnic and religious divisions, particularly growing tension between the indigenous population and the Islamic people. There was a further problem – that these existing sharp social divisions in Britain had only been held together by a growing and booming economy. So, lose the dynamism and hope of boom times, and the tearing, indeed rupture, of Britain's social fabric was becoming a distinct possibility. It was so serious that, should unemployment indeed rise significantly, say to 1930s proportions, then the question would arise: Could Britain survive as a liberal-democratic, civilised advanced society?

As the new coalition government bedded in, it was clear that the same British financial and political elites, in all parties, who had supported the old deregulated City-dominant financial system were still running the show – and still had no answers. There had been no revolution in thinking at the top – whether in government, in the opposition, in the Bank of England or amongst the opinion-forming London-based journalist class. The dominant narrative presented to the people was a simple one: the financial system had been 'saved' and the country was on the road to 'recovery'. The recovery would be difficult, and some tough budget-cutting times lay ahead, but there was no need to change the fundamental structures of the financial capitalist system or of the global system it within which it operated. The patient would return to full strength soon, as soon as the private sector revived, and the life-support machine of the state could be removed. In other words the main western leaderships were attempting to refloat the whole global economy without changing its essentials. A minority, mainly market economists and right-wing journalists, disagreed. They wanted a neoliberal solution to the neoliberal-caused crisis. They saw the crisis as an opportunity to allow the market to 'correct itself' by allowing the banks to fail, by cutting the public sector more ruthlessly and by deregulating rather than re-regulating.

It was an environment in which radical new thinking was largely absent. In 2010, at least, few leaders of opinion in Britain were even faintly echoing the view of the American economist Paul Krugman that a big new 'Keynesian Plus' stimulus was needed. And absolutely no mainstream voice was suggesting a radical overhaul of the entire financial capitalist system.

It was obvious that in Britain at least this crisis was not going to be used as the opportunity for making major structural changes in the economic system. Obama's chief of staff, Rahm Emmanuel, may well have declaimed that we should 'never let a good crisis go to waste' – in Britain it was 'as you were'. There was much anger at bankers and the size of banks (with proposals to split them up), there was also increasing talk about inequality and bonuses, but there was no serious or systematic critique of the fundamentals of the economic system that had caused the crisis. There was no sense that the financial capitalist system itself needed overhauling. In other words: Anglo-Saxon capitalism has failed, long live Anglo-Saxon capitalism!

NEW POLICIES?

Although political leaders in the West talked repeatedly about 'never letting this [the banking crash] happen again', in Britain, as in the other G20 countries, there were few really radical policy proposals – ideas that would seriously reshape the old failed system, or indeed replace it, ideas that would at least signal a new direction.

For instance, there were no suggestions that the structure of the western firm needed revisiting – no proposals for the corporate shareholder model to be replaced by a stakeholder model (an earlier idea of the Blair years).

There were no proposals for a more progressive taxation system that would end and reverse the deepening inequalities and make the super-rich pay a fair share of tax – no proposals for a tax on wealth, a land tax, a steeper inheritance tax (anything over the average house price) or a rise in taxes on incomes, wealth and corporations. The British government had introduced a tax on bonuses, but this, like so many other measures affecting banks, was temporary in nature; and, although a 'Tobin tax' – a tax on financial transactions – was mooted by Prime Minister Gordon Brown it was sidelined pending international (G20) agreement.

There were no realistic proposals to rebalance the lopsided (pro-service sector) British economy – with a serious industrial policy (in or outside EU) to protect against the ravages and vagaries of the global market. There were no proposals to rebalance the economy away from the dominance of the private sector – for instance by abandoning the Private Finance Initiative (the PFI) or returning to public ownership (of any kind) some of the utility sectors, particularly energy, transportation (rail and bus) and water. Nor were there any pledges made about limiting future outsourcing.

There was little talk either about the need to reshape economic globalisation, about how to limit the damaging impacts of globalisation, or about how Britain was going to relate to the new protectionist-oriented multipolar world that was emerging and how it might work with fellow Europeans to limit the impact of global finance. There was an implicit rejection of Britain working with a European Monetary Fund or joining the eurozone, as both major parties set themselves against further 'federal' moves. It seemed that British grand economic strategy amounted to a firm determination that the country would face the coming dire economic and financial environment in 'splendid isolation'. In other words, the geo-political outlook of Britain's elite would hardly have changed since the last big crisis in 1940.

A NEW VISION?

This lack of policy was because at the top of British politics and society there was a lacuna of vision. The global market system had failed, spectacularly so, but the politicians and commentators were still operating under its rules, rather like a worm still wriggling long after it was effectively decapitated. What was needed was a whole new political and economic direction, a new political economy. Some commentators, precious few, were reaching towards such a genuinely new vision – and were prepared to think well beyond the conventional categories. Two such radical thinkers were the social democratic theorist David Marquand and the economic historian Robert Skidelsky. Marquand went as far as calling for a new system that was economically 'socialist' and politically 'republican'; and Robert Skidelsky sought a super-Keynesian system based upon a 'macro-economic stimulus'.[3] Yet, whatever label is used, be it 'socialist' or 'Keynesian' – or, my own preference, 'protectionist'

– any new way forward will need to start with a fundamental rejection of the previous neoliberal order.

In any such new economic system fit for the post-neoliberal world the key ingredient will be sustainability. The old market system is wild and frighteningly unpredictable, possessed of great ups and great downs while social democratic economics offers more stability. Even following the hung parliament of 2010 however, Britain's elites were still averse to any return to the social-democracy of the 1950s and 1960s. They were still seared by the experience of the 1970s when the social democratic model appeared incapable of delivering prosperity as it imploded during the 1978-9 'winter of discontent'. Critics of British social democracy however did not see the events of 1978-9 as a peculiarly British implosion, caused by peculiarly British labour problems (peculiarly British trade unions, and peculiarly British management failures) and a peculiarly British unmodernised (essentially post-'imperial') economy and society. Yet, while Britain floundered, social democracy survived and flourished on the continent, in both Germany and France, whose more 'social' market economies and welfare societies sheltered them from the full force of the 'Anglo-Saxon' global market.

A new direction in Britain's political economy would inevitably begin to align the economy with those of the leading continental countries. Like the continental powers, it would need to place permanent limits on the 'madness' of the global market, particularly on the casino financial markets, and it could only do so by stronger regulation of the market and the private sector. It would recognise the undeniable fact that only the state can effectively act as a balancing force against the power of the market.

As well as sustainability a renewed social democracy would stress the importance of the principle of equality, not only politically (in terms of rights) but economically too. In practice this would not mean rigid equalities of income and wealth, but rather the adoption of policies that encourage equality of opportunity and a socially mobile society – and, specifically, would discourage the entrenching of a privileged class. A social democratic political economy would continue to encourage a large profit-making private sector; but as such a sector would consistently create glaring inequalities, these would need to be limited by a consistent redistribution of both income and wealth. Again, this is a goal that can only be achieved by a state big enough to limit market power.

In order to work, and to gain acceptance, all this entails a new view of the state, and of the role of government. As I outlined in earlier chapters social-democratic theory sees the state as being able to play a positive role as an enabler, as widening opportunities, not narrowing them; it also sees the state as the only effective protector of liberties (rights, and the rule of law) and not as oppressor. And in economic terms it sees the state – and the private sector – as essentially neutral. Social democratic theorists, in contrast to market theorists, believe that neither state nor private ownership has a moral content and should not be judged on that basis, but rather by how well they function in any given circumstance. And, as with ownership, so with investment, expenditure and credit. For social democrats there is no moral distinction between private credit (essentially private banks) and public credit (essentially government deficits). Public credit may be less prone to wild swings, and may be needed to supplement private credit when it implodes (as in the spectacular Wall Street/City collapse), but as between public and private there are no inherent moral judgements to be made. In 2010, with private credit and finance drying up in the global deleveraging, for social democrats the growth of public credit and government expenditure became utterly imperative. Also, for social democrats the fiscal deficit was only one of the two important deficits – for as Peter Orszag, the Budget Director in the Obama White House, pointed out in February 2010, there exists the 'other deficit' – the GDP deficit. This is the difference between what the economy can produce and what it does produce – in other words the spare capacity caused by massive unemployment of labour and resources.

Finally, and crucially, if the state is to have a bigger role then a social-democratic approach will insist upon its democratisation. Intriguingly, there was something of a consensus in early twentieth-century Britain between market supporters and social democrats about the nature of the British state and constitution: that Britain had both a transparency deficit and an accountability deficit. And that Britain's highly centralised and historically secretive state system, bolstered by a 'ancien regime' (with an unelected House of Lords, a secretive Privy Council, and undemocratic royal prerogative powers) was no way to run a modern polity or deal with these twin deficits. So, for social democrats at least, alongside 'the return of the state' it was imperative that this state should undergo some serious surgical constitutional reform. Such a radical agenda – in its own way as radical as the 1688 template the British were still living under – would necessarily include a written document, federal institutions, checks and balances, and a separation of powers (including a separation of church and state) and entrenched rights.

BRITAIN ALONE IN A PROTECTIONIST WORLD
The Collapse of Globalisation

In 2010 Britain faced a double crisis: an era of austerity because of its unbalanced, overly credit-based economy and massive public expenditure cuts (whichever party won the imminent general election). But, unlike previous economic crises, it was also facing the need to adjust to a rapidly changing world order – nothing less than the collapse of economic globalism, or 'globalisation'. This collapse had been long in the making. By the late 1990s the growing imbalances of trade between Asia and the West were becoming unsustainable as they systematically destroyed both the employment base and its balanced economies; early in the new century the resultant global financial imbalances (primarily between China and the USA) were reaching critical proportions. The evil day was put off by a few years by a seriously irresponsible explosion of credit in the West which included Britain. The banking and credit crash was in essence the crash of globalisation. And as the various states around the world moved in to shore up the banks these essentially protectionist moves further collapsed the globalist model.

The 'rules' of global markets, both formal and informal, were increasingly broken, for as recession, depression and massive unemployment threatened, then states acted unilaterally, and asked questions afterwards. The bank bailouts and quasi-nationalisations broke the rules; so too did the stimulus packages, so too did the often unilateral moves to regulate financial markets. As Daniel Price, an assistant to President George W. Bush for international economic affairs, said in September 2009: 'Regulatory reform measures that, if unchecked, will foster a disintegration of the global economy and re-raise the very barriers to cross-border trade and investment that the world has spent the past 60 years dismantling.'[4]

At its most intense in France, the growth of protectionist sentiment could be seen during the 2005 referendum on the European constitutional treaty when French popular opposition to the neoliberal globalist agenda of the European Commission led to the victory of the 'no' campaign. Even in the USA protectionist sentiment was on a rising curve. The refusal of the politburo in China to raise its currency against the dollar (and therefore to ease its exports to the US) was a constant source of tension, and a bi-partisan alliance in the US Senate, led by Senators Chuck Schumer and Lindsay Graham, was constantly threatening China with sizeable tariffs should it continue its currency policy regime. Also, the issue of 'outsourcing jobs' that was a key feature of the successive Democratic presidential campaigns of John Kerry and later Barack Obama; and the US public was increasingly supportive of protectionist intervention in the 'global' market.

Britain and The New Protectionism

The signs were there for all to see, but Britain's elites remained in denial that anything was fundamentally wrong with the global economy and global finance. Indeed the New Labour administration of Tony Blair not only pursued a globalist policy but also became a cheerleader and proselytiser for globalisation. His argument was that there was no alternative to accepting its rules, and that British economic strategy should be based, not on attempting (with its neighbours) to shape the global system, but rather to equip the people with skills so that they could compete (with Asians) in the world economy.

So Britain remained, under both Conservatives and New Labour, the most open of all the G8 countries to the global economy. The country, more than any other major western nation, threw its lot in with, and thus placed its fate in the hands of, the globalisers. Indeed it extended its reach – both financially – through the City of London's world-wide operation – and through its interventionist foreign and military policy (as it became the chief ally of the American empire in Iraq and

Afghanistan). And, largely because of the global impulses of its elites, Britain remained outside an integrating Europe and the eurozone (though still, awkwardly, within the EU).

During the boom years of the 90s onwards 'globalisation' seemingly served Britain well – for although global market forces eroded the country's 'uncompetitive' industrial sector they also engineered a quite dramatic switchover to the booming service sector – primarily financial services. Yet, many realised that should globalisation fail, Britain would be disproportionately hurt. Even so, throughout the 1990s and on into the new century Britain's elites remained in thrall to global markets (and their alluring limitless possibilities, for profits). They remained in denial about the inherent weaknesses of the global economy right up until the global crisis hit the City of London in 2007-8 and beyond. And they could not see that the great banking crash was also a national train wreck in which everything that Britain's financial, and financialised, elites stood for was up-ended – virtually overnight.

Jobs, Jobs, Jobs

Of course, following the crash Britain's zeitgeist slowly began to change: some, small, voices began to systematically critique the global capitalist system and even proffer an alternative – a 'protectionist' strategy for the country which would put jobs first, centre its economic policy on employment and growth, and resist the siren demands of the global economy to become ever more 'competitive'. In March 2010 *Guardian* economics editor, Larry Elliott, argued that such a strategy, with its echoes of the Labour left's 'Alternative Economic Strategy' of the 1970s, had some merit, though it would not likely be tried, at least not for some time. He quoted from a London University (SOAS research paper) which argued that such a strategy would involve 'devaluation followed by cessation of payments and restructuring of debt. Banks would have to be nationalised and public control extended over utilities, transport, energy and telecommunications. There would be industrial policy, including strategies to improve productivity. Infrastructure and environmentally sensitive investment, and support equitable growth. This option requires a decisive shift in the balance of political power in favour of labour.'[5] It would also require a decisive shift away from the three decades-long strategy of accommodating to 'economic globalisation' and towards forms of protectionism.

As the recession began to bite 'protectionist' sentiments, if not policies, were breaking cover, mainly on the British left – not just amongst left-leaning academics and journalists, but also amongst trade unionists and lower income 'working people'. 'Protecting jobs' was becoming a number one political issue. Indeed, before the crash, on the eve of becoming Prime Minister in 2007 Gordon Brown had argued that 'It is time to train British workers for the British jobs that will be available over the coming few years and to make sure that people who are inactive and unemployed are able to take the new jobs on offer in our country'. This 'British jobs for British workers' approach was subsequently, following a strike at the Lindsay oil refinery in North Lincolnshire about UK construction jobs being awarded to European workers, caught up in charges about racism and xenophobia, and was attacked by columnists from all sides of the spectrum. But Brown stood by his remarks: he said 'I don't see any reason to regret [my statement]' and 'I understand people's worries about their jobs'.[6]

By the time of the 2010 election 'protectionism' was no longer likely to frighten. The 2007-8 bank and credit crash had raised fears about unemployment to the top of the domestic agenda with real concerns about whether global market capitalism could any longer deliver on the promises made for it by all governments from Thatcher onwards. Global markets, by encouraging 'competitiveness' and a constant 'race to the bottom' on costs, were seen as driving down western wage levels and employment prospects. 'Competing' with Rising Asia was becoming an impossibility. Previously this employment and wage crisis that was facing millions had been smoothed over by abundant, cheap, credit. But that prop was now being removed. So, with living standards under serious threat, the idea of 'protecting' people – rather than making them ever more 'competitive' in the global economy – seemed increasingly attractive. 'Protectionism' – industrial policy for long-term jobs, trade protection against unfair competition, and 'social protection' when unemployed – was no longer 'unthinkable', and much more acceptable in the British political discourse.

Is Britain Big Enough?

Yet there remained one overwhelming problem with any 'protectionist' strategy for Britain – the country's size and economic imbalance. Only large, continent-states or blocs, could embark upon a workable neo-protectionist economic strategy as they were potentially self-sufficient. The USA, the EU and the eurozone were such economies. They may indeed have benefited from the global trade upturn during the boom times, but they were also big enough to withstand a serious trade downturn (with only about a 10-12 per cent of GDP exposure to foreign trade). And these continent-states also possessed a relatively healthy balance between manufacturing and services, between industrial and agricultural, and between the real economy and the financial.

By contrast, Britain, a medium-sized European state, with a skewed and imbalanced economy and far higher global trade exposure, was not nearly self-sufficient. On its own it was simply too small and too vulnerable in an increasingly protectionist world. It had placed itself in grave danger as it could hardly afford to bail out its overextended banking system during the crisis of late 2008.

How big then is the British economy two and a half decades into the Thatcher era revolution? Britain's good growth rates have helped her grow from her relative position in the early 1980s when she was tying with Italy for third place in the EU. By 2006 the UK economy amounted to $2,201,473 million or 4.9 per cent of the global GDP. It ranked fifth in the world (behind the US, Japan, Germany and Mainland China), and was roughly the same size as France and just ahead of Italy. And it was only one sixth the size of the total EU economy, and also of the total US economy.

These figures tell the story of a Britain that during the 1980s and 1990s had stabilised its shaky situation. But, in truth, it did little more than that. For by the end of the decade of the 90s British national income was almost exactly equal to that of France and only about 20 per cent higher than that of Italy. (Figures show: UK 1403, France 1453, Germany 2103, Italy 1162. These are exchange-rate sensitive, and could easily change by 10-20 per cent. They also show growth rates for UK (1965-99) coming in behind France, Belgium, Italy and most of the EU 15 nations; figures for Germany are unavailable because of the eastern states addition.) By 2009 Britain's position had worsened. The country's GDP, $2,183,607 million, was behind France (at $2,675,251 million) and Germany (at $3,352,742 million) – with the EU total standing at $16,447,259 million, the US at $14,256,059 million and China at $4,908,982 million.[7]

Taking the longer view – that of the whole postwar period – Professor Bernard Alford, at the end of his exhaustive work on

Britain's recent economic history, came to a clear conclusion: 'the thrust of our analysis' he wrote in 1996 'is that there are few signs that Britain has reversed the condition of relative economic decline that has been endemic to its development since the late nineteenth-century.' He adds, though that the status of nations is often a matter of perception, 'but that perception is so easily clouded by delusion'. In the decade since Alford's report, very little has changed that would alter his assessment.[8]

Yet, no matter its status and size, is the British economy strong enough? Is it able to withstand pressures from the global economy, from downturns and shocks? And here there is a problem – for Britain, no matter its good growth rates, remains a very vulnerable economy, much more so than many other advanced economies. One vulnerability is that the country remains highly dependent on the continuing robust health of the global economy. Britain's economic growth rates have largely been sustained by global growth which in turn has been sustained by the low inflation era caused by China's low costs. This virtuous low inflation cycle has allowed Britain to pursue low interest rates and a massive increase in private debt levels (based on a housing boom). This whole economic structure is heavily trade dependent, more so than many of its competitors, and in any downturn would be hurt disproportionately.

And by the second decade of the new century it was becoming clear that in this coming age of protectionism Britain needed, for its own survival, to be part of a bigger integrated economy; and that could only mean the EU.

The 'World Role' Obsession
This, of course, raised the thorny subject of Britain's proper role in the world and the vital linkage between this role and the domestic economy. After seven plus decades of maintaining

at all costs a 'global role', of 'punching above our weight', and three decades of grandiose financial overextension within the booming global economy, the country was vastly overstretched. It had huge 'universal' banks which reached into every corner of the world. Its limited military had taken part – the major European part – in actions from Iraq to Afghanistan (where in early 2010 British troops were dying almost daily) and its defence budget was the largest (in percentage of GDP terms) of all the USA's NATO allies. As of 2010 the country's political parties were still committed to the hugely expensive Trident nuclear system, and to continuing with its next generation. The elites who ran the Foreign Office and the Ministry of Defence, many of them drawn more widely than the traditional public schools, still retained the culture of empire and 'greatness', as did Britain's top politicians. And few, now that the boom was over, were arguing that Britain needed to face a future in which the country 'punched within its weight'. They were still resisting an adjustment to a more realistic and modest approach.

But could it so adjust? Such an adjustment would demand much more than economic changes, but also great institutional, political and psychological changes too. The country still possessed a pompous 'ancien regime' that fitted an imperial era – a lavish, imperial-style monarchy, a still unelected House of Lords, and strange secretive institutions like the Privy Council. Politically, this imperial legacy exhibited itself in a continuing fear of losing 'sovereignty' and of becoming a normal European power. In sum, even as late as 2010, and the collapse of Anglo-American financial capitalism, our elites, our institutions, and our very collective DNA, were all far too grand to allow us to abandon our 'global role' in favour of becoming a mere regional power, like Germany or even France. This national hubris had been perfectly illustrated by the overextended City of London.

Can The City of London Adjust?

Britain's financial services industry had done extremely well in the post-cold war global economy. In 2003 Britain's trade surplus in financial services was reported to be 'more than double that of any other country'.[9] In July 2004, researchers at the University of Sheffield analysed the British economy as an atlas, demonstrating that Britain was becoming dominated by London (or, rather, the City of London), and that to the north and west there was 'an archipelago of the provinces – city islands that appear to be slowly sinking demographically, socially and economically.'[10] It was an analysis which led a *Guardian* leader to argue that the 'City wields more power than ever' and that 'Britain has become a huge hedge fund making big bets on the markets', asserting presciently that 'one day the luck will run out.'[11] In his powerful 2006 study of Britain's elites, Hywel Williams reckoned that 'The City, in combination with New York now controls 90 per cent of the world's wholesale financial activity.' And he recorded that at the end of 2003 310,000 people were employed in the City (and nearly 150,000 in financial services).[12] But what goes up also comes down – and by 2008 and the beginning of the financial meltdown London's financial district was already laying off large numbers of city workers.

Yet, two questions stand out: can 'the City' and its allied commerce continue to carry on its shoulders a country of 60 million people? Or, looking at it inversely, can 60 million people succeed in bailing out such a mammoth operation as the City when it fails? And, what happens when China and India start seriously competing in financial services as well as in manufacturing? The mere posing of these questions serves to show the vulnerability of a national economy which includes such an erstwhile uniquely successful sector.

Whether 'the City' can or cannot continue to carry the country, its leading players will certainly remain highly influential, if not dominant, in determining Britain's foreign economic policy and alignment – more so even than the media moguls. And within 'the City' elite there was considerable support for a 'go it alone' policy, for standing offshore (of the continent) and seeing the global economy as our market. We might have been small, but we were profitable. This was the 'tiger option' – after the smallish Asian 'tiger' economies that were doing so well in the global market before the Asian financial crash. And as financial services prospered in the Blair era, then many in the square mile turned their thinking towards 'the world' and increasingly away from Europe and the EU.

This dominant view not only saw London's financial services as a global player working in a global market – very much a 'tiger' – but went further, seeing London as the world's most successful 'tiger' in the global financial jungle. And by 2007, on the eve of the global financial meltdown, all the talk was of London overtaking New York as the world's leading financial centre. By comparison, in this hubristic atmosphere, tying 'the City' down in Europe – even should 'the City' become the EU's primary financial centre (similar to 'New York' in North America) – was dismissed as too restrictive a vision. In a December 2006 after-dinner speech to London financiers, the EU's financial services action plan ('MiFID') was introduced by Charlie McCreevy, the internal market commissioner, and was given a less than enthusiastic reception – much less so than that accorded to the American comedienne Ruby Wax, who, bizarrely, but perhaps aptly, followed him with top billing. A *Financial Times* report by Gideon Rachman at the time suggested that 'as the biggest financial centre in Europe ['the City'] would do well in a huge liberalised [European Union] market'.[13] However, the EU remains too regulated for City tastes; as does even Wall Street following the Sarbanes-Oxley Act passed in the aftermath of the Enron scandal (a tough US regulatory regime providing a huge – though probably temporary – boost for 'the City').

The successful and profitable world of British finance created, though, another vulnerability to the British economy – that of the debt culture. For it was the dynamic and innovative credit systems and culture of 'the City' that helped, together with a willing Westminster political class, to create the country's mountainous dimension of private debt. A report commissioned by the Conservative party in 2005 reported that 'personal debt levels of more than £1 trillion mean that about 15 million people are exposed to external shocks such as a sharp rise in the price of oil' and went on to call the debt issue a 'time bomb'. These debt levels had been fuelled by the 'wealth effect' of rising house prices.[14]

These vulnerabilities in the British economy – the reverse side of its successes – make Britain's 'tiger option' a huge gamble. Britain is more exposed to the global forces than any other major western country (including the US). And should the country leave the EU, then everything will depend upon a continuingly robust global economy – and one in which competition in the service sector from China and India remains weak.

Britain's 'successful' economy – no matter its vulnerable and exposed global position – will likely continue to convince a powerful faction of opinion formers that the country can, with confidence, 'go it alone'. After all, the 'tiger option' will continue to appeal to more than just the profit makers; it will have an abiding resonance with the popular instincts of English exceptionalism – of a uniquely entrepreneurial people surviving and prospering alone on the global 'open seas'. This appeal combines short-term profits and nationalist romance – the two impulses that built the empire and will be difficult to combat.

Yet the romance of the 'island story' will come face to face with the realities of the great deleveraging, and with the lower living standards inevitably involved. Britain comes out of its neoliberal era a more unequal society than it was at the beginning. It has, though, succeeded in building up something of an American-style 'middle class' – increasingly travelled, self-confident and with considerable expectations – based upon a mountain of debt. As they are marched down the mountain this middle class will inevitably fracture, creating a growing pool of 'losers'. For a time, Britain's welfare mechanisms will help to cushion the blows; but sooner or later, the increased pressure on the welfare services will need to be funded by higher taxes (which will be resisted by the remaining middle class and the super-rich) or, alternatively, by government deficits and inflation. Both of these courses of action will increase the uncompetitive global position of a very globally-oriented economy.

One way of limiting the damage of a global recession or depression would be to take a decision to more fully integrate the British economy into the wider European economy. With a declining global demand for financial services the EU would at the very least provide a hinterland for the City of London (in much the same way as New York is able to service the internal American market). Once the broad strategic move – away from Wall Street dominated economics and towards Europe – has been made, then whether Britain should go for a quick entry into the eurozone would become a technical matter.

However, this radical change in the geopolitical course will be very difficult to engineer; it will run right up against the British attachment to 'sovereignty', to its history as an imperial and independent power, and to its rigid constitution based upon

331

ancient 'sovereignties' including the monarchy and the culture of 'Queen and country'. In this sense the traditional political culture of Britain's elites directly damages the future economic health of its people.

ENGLAND'S IDENTITY CRISIS

Yet, even if we can downsize our thinking, and see ourselves as we really are, then the great question remains: in the emerging multipolar world of trade blocs where do we British fit in? Is it within the 'American empire' or in the 'European home'? Or, can we continue to avoid this choice and become a smallish 'Little England' offshore island scratching a living in what remains of the globalised economy (and maybe acting as a European base for rising China?)

For a time, during the decade-long premiership of Tony Blair the country was as enmeshed in the American empire as it had ever been. Indeed, when Blair left office British troops were still in American-occupied Iraq, and Britain had intensified her status as Washington's chief European outpost. The country was geopolitically tied to Washington, economically under the sway of the neoliberal American model, and culturally, through television and the tabloidisation of the mass media, increasingly Americanised.

This 'American option' for Britain – of tying the country more and more to America's political and economic coat-tails – was, though, to be dealt a real blow following the failure of the American occupation of Iraq, and then again in 2008 when the great crash on Wall Street severely dented the allure of the American economic model. More important than Britain's view of the US was the changing US view of Britain. Whereas George W. Bush had found Britain useful as political cover for his forward strategy in the Middle East, the election of

Barack Obama in 2009 ushered in a new approach, for the new president had little attachment to Britain (his father had been born in colonial Kenya), and, anyway, was slowly re-orienting American foreign policy away from its historic concentration on Europe and towards a more Asia-centred perspective.

On the face of it the comparative decline of the USA should have improved the chances of Britain adopting the European option. Yet, at the time of the 2010 election, the Conservative party was still divided between those who were hostile to further integration and those who wanted to pull out of the EU altogether while New Labour under Gordon Brown, under the influence of the City, were still tied to an off-shore, 'competitiveness' agenda. In reality Britain's political leadership were not yet willing to make a choice between America and Europe – Blair even argued publicly the case that 'to choose between America and Europe is a false choice'. He simply did not see the need to choose. 'It would be insane – yes, I would put it as strongly as that – for us to give up either relationship.'[15] After the crash Gordon Brown started edging ever more closely towards the European option, but, as the global financial crisis hit the eurozone and the deficits and debt of Greece and other Club Med countries caused strains with Germany, questions were raised about the long-term viability of the eurozone and 'the European option'.

The 'Little England' Option

All in all, the fallout from the great crash could not have come at a worse time for Britain. With the US special relationship in decline and the country still outside the eurozone, Britain had to engineer the bailout of its banks alone. This bailout – which stretched Britain's public debt to almost impossible limits – allowed the illusory 'go it alone' mentality to flourish. A US

State Department official, Dr. Kendall Myers, an Anglophile with a good understanding of contemporary Britain, summed up Britain's 'stand-alone' mentality' rather well. He said 'I think and fear that Britain will draw back from the US without moving closer to Europe. In that sense London bridge is falling down'[16]

A body of opinion in the City, and in the new coalition government formed in 2010, saw Britain's future in these isolationist terms. Some even believed that the future lay in standing offshore from Europe as a global financial centre and host to hedge funds and low tax operations. This finance industry-led strategy would, though, only be sensible if Britain could also remain in the EU single market. And Tony Blair himself had hinted at this as a viable option. 'Of course Britain could survive outside the EU' he had argued in 2000, and 'we could possibly get access to the single market as Norway and Switzerland do'.[17]

Even Eurosceptics were anxious to seek arrangements with the EU which would allow Britain continued access to the single market. Some hoped that Britain could come up with an ingenious scheme to stay in the single market through rejoining EFTA (the European Free Trade Association) and through EFTA join Norway in the AEA (Associated Economic Area). Yet, the idea that after the controversy, rupture and pain of withdrawing from the EU, the union would then grant Britain special continuing access to its single market remains highly fanciful. And even should Britain get the same deal as Norway it will then become a so-called 'Euro fax' country – subject to the rules of the single market – sent to them by fax – but having no say in drawing them up. A British withdrawal would thus likely be exactly what it says – a full withdrawal. It would amount to a 'go it alone' strategy – and face the country with the urgent need to make a living outside of the trade bloc. It would be a dramatic, bold, and risky, move. Yet, during the 1990s some British opinion-formers becoming more and more confident in the viability of this 'go it alone' strategy.

It is a high-risk strategy in which 'Little England', facing the global economy alone, would prosper by remaining highly competitive and entrepreneurial. It would amount to a future role for the country that its supporters – like the novelist Frederick Forsyth – describe as creating 'an independent, global Britain'. Thus 'Little England' would, in effect, become a 'Tiger Economy' – an option named after the 'Tiger economies' of South Asia, the small countries that prospered in the late 1980s and early 1990s through achieving a competitive edge in a rapidly globalising world.

But the big question remains: can Britain, on the other side of the world and offshore of Europe, become a European version of an 'Asian Tiger'? Supporters of the option assume that once outside the EU and its single market, relations with the EU will, maybe after an initial hiccup, remain amicable. In reality there is no such guarantee. After all, Britain would have left in order to seek a competitive advantage (lower costs and taxes) and in such a competitive environment the EU could easily erect trade barriers against British goods and services for many of the same reasons that are deployed against China. In a trade war, trying to live outside a trading bloc could become very uncomfortable.

These isolationist instincts – renewed by xenophobic Englishness – run directly counter to the realities of the real world in which the English people actually live. For instance, in this real world seriously urgent problems were lapping at the shores – problems like carbon emissions, mass immigration, terrorism, and the social and economic effects of globalisation, let alone support against speculation and manic market forces. Not one of these problems can be solved by national solutions alone. But national solutions, based upon 'national sovereignty' and an old ideology of national separateness, was, in 2010, all that was on offer from Britain's established elites.

What Kind of People?

This geopolitical identity crisis was – is – a symptom of something deeper. For, certainly at the turn of the century, there was no certainty about how to answer a crucial question: what kind of people are the British? Are we an 'Anglo' nation ruled by an elite whose political language will forever tie us to Washington? And what are the geopolitical implications of the growth of English nationalism? Will Scotland and Wales gravitate to a European future should England stay out? What are the implications of a multicultural society, and sizeable Islamic populations, for foreign policy? And what of vast, cosmopolitan London? Will London and its environs lead the way into Europe whilst much of the rest of England resists? And, will the British elite's love affair with the US neoliberal economic model propel the country away Europe's 'social model' and towards increasing inequality – with a protected class of super-rich side by side with a sinking and impoverished middle class?

A lot will turn on how the English define themselves over the coming years. It could go either way. England, and 'Englishness', may well be defined by its worst angels, by that narrow xenophobia that still lurks and can be so easily aroused by media moguls and ultra-conservative politicians. In a declining economy and conflicted society this kind of visceral 'Little England' impulse could turn the English in on themselves – leading not just to the breakup of the union but also to the politics of authoritarianism – to what could become a 'very English' form of mild 'gentleman fascism'. And it might not be so mild.

Alternatively, England and Englishness could yet be defined by its better angels – that is by those, informed by the country's historical tradition of liberty, democratic reform and relative openness. But mass prosperity is needed if these better angels are to negotiate the shoals without losing their balance.

A lot more, though, will turn on what happens in the wider west. In facing the global economic crisis and the coming multipolar world (particularly the rise of Asia) will there be one west or two? And if two, then will Britain's elites, their minds and culture strangely still likely imbued with the imperial hangover, ever be capable of joining with others in helping to secure the European future?

If we are going to enter a protracted period of lower living standards – with an all but certain associated increase in class and ethnic tensions – then the one thing that Britain has going for it is its tradition of welfare social democracy, with all the protections this affords to the majority of the people. Indeed, a real shift towards social democracy – or something resembling it – is now the country's last best hope. It is no exaggeration to assert that without it we could lose our liberal democracy and could lapse into becoming something akin to a Latin-American style military slum state governed by a Latin-American style super-rich elite. And all in the name of an ideology that has spectacularly failed. It must not happen.

THERE IS ANOTHER WAY: AN ALTERNATIVE STRATEGY

During the summer of 2010 European governments decided to cut their projected budget deficits, primarily by large public expenditure cuts, in order to secure borrowing. These cuts are likely, in the very probable absence of a private sector boom in lending, to lead to lower growth, further cuts and an economic self-lacerating downward spiral. As set out below:

THE PRESENT COURSE: 'OBEY THE MARKETS'
PHASE ONE: PUBLIC SECTOR CUTS

Result 1: Private sector growth stagnant (because of continuing global credit deleveraging) and public sector growth falling. Therefore Less Growth, Fewer Tax Receipts. Bigger Deficits.

Further Result: Another borrowing crisis. 'Markets' demand deficit cuts.

PHASE TWO: MORE PUBLIC SECTOR CUTS

Result 1: Even Less Growth. Even Bigger Deficits.

Further Result: Crisis. 'Markets' Demand Even More Cuts.

PHASE THREE: EVEN MORE CUTS

Result: Mass Unemployment, Widespread and Deep Economic Insecurity.

Further Result: Serious social instability (including, in the UK, threats to the political unity of the union).

PHASE FOUR: POLITICAL CHANGE: AN AUTHORITARIAN REGIME

AN ALTERNATIVE STRATEGY FOR A BIG SUPERPOWER

Any alternative strategy for a country like Britain will be somewhat different than that for a superpower. Big nations can stand up to 'markets' more easily whereas medium-sized countries (like the UK) will find it more difficult but not impossible.

This 'alternative strategy' will best work for big nation-states, like the USA or potentially the EU or the eurozone (as long, that is, as Europe can co-ordinate policy through a single economic government). Britain, Germany and France are not big enough to complete this challenge to the global markets, but each are powerful enough to start the process – Germany and France because they are in the eurozone, Britain because of the global role of its banks.

This alternative strategy does not involve a revolution or even an upheaval – only a revolution in thinking, Indeed it can be implemented simply by a realisation that national leaders, representing their peoples, do not have to follow the old rules – and always bow before markets.

This Alternative Strategy simply involves refusing to change policy at the behest of 'markets'. Growth and jobs are a greater priority than cutting deficits and balancing books.

THE LIKELY SCENARIO

The Background: It is vital to understand that the crisis we are in is a banking and credit crisis, not a public sector spending crisis. The crash of 2008 – with the default of Lehman Brothers and the bailout of other banks – was the starting-point for a great credit and bank deleveraging that will run for many years. Its latest manifestation (in the summer of 2010) is the banking crisis in Europe, brought on by the potential sovereign defaults of European governments caused in turn by the recession that followed the crash. This therefore is best looked at as the second leg of the global banking crisis – with fears that European governments, now in the role of Lehman Brothers, might default and trigger another round of bank collapses. The Bank For International Settlements made this abundantly clear when it revealed in the summer of 2010 that western banks – primarily French and German banks – had exposure of well over $1,000 billion in Europe and the *Financial Times* in an editorial on 15th June 2010, argued that this 'paralleled' the situation before the great credit freeze and crash of 2007.

1. The USA, or the Euro finds itself with a serious run on its currency following a loss of confidence in the markets. The run has been caused by a fear of sovereign default. 'Markets' demand cuts and deflation.

2. But the USA and Europe are big enough to withstand these pressures. They simply take no notice of the markets and do not change policy. They determine to keep growth and employment as the top priority, refuse to cut the public sector and deflate the economy.

3. Once it is clear that the USA or the EU or the eurozone will not have its policy dictated by markets, and there is no money to be made from speculation – then the crisis will be over. Other big changes will certainly occur – in the global economic and financial structures – but the immediate crisis will be over and deflation in the West will have been avoided.

4. **If it is the USA** that ignores the markets first, then the dollar falls.

   If the run on the currency is dramatic enough the potential default of the USA or EU will threaten the whole international banking system, and 'civilisation as we know it'. The USA will do what it did last time and support the banking and credit system. So will the EU. This will involve increasing, rather than decreasing the government deficit.

The run will continue. The lower dollar will mean that China loses its money in the US Treasury. The resultant lower export prices will cause other trade blocs real problems and could lead to retaliation, and the emergence of protectionist trade blocs, a development the large EU single market can also handle. Global imbalances are dealt with. Balance restored.

The run on the dollar also causes import prices to rise. The USA does not have a large trade exposure (about 12 per cent of GDP) so over time this can be dealt with – primarily by import substitution. Family budgets will be affected, but can be bolstered by higher wages, higher public expenditure or tax cuts – deficits will no longer have to be brought down sharply, they no longer matter so much.

5. **If it is the EU** that ignores the markets first, by, say, allowing a higher 'Stability Pact' deficit level – beyond the 3 per cent of the Maastricht criteria, and up, say, to 10 per cent. – for countries like Italy, Spain, France and Britain – then the run on the euro will continue.

Import prices will rise. Export prices will fall. Rising import price rises will cause difficulties but, over time, can be handled by import substitution (the EU has only about a 11 per cent trade exposure) and a higher wage economy; and in the key area of food Europe is relatively self-sufficient. Export price falls will lead to an immediate crisis in relations with China (possibly too with the USA). China may well retaliate. In any event the upshot will be the emergence of trade blocs. The so-called 'Free Trade' system will wither to be replaced by 'Managed Trade' or 'Strategic Trade' between the regions or blocs.

The real global economy is re-ordered. Trade blocs negotiate with each other. Multinational corporations can no longer play each country off against each other in a race to the bottom. The global financial system is similarly re-ordered. capital globalisation is weakened. Capital flows are increasingly within blocs not global. Above all, European and US economies no longer lose jobs and wealth to low-cost centres.

This new regime involves a cut in the standard of living of Europeans and Americans; but nothing nearly as horrendous as the budget cutting regime this new system will replace.

AN ALTERNATIVE STRATEGY FOR A MEDIUM-SIZED EUROPEAN COUNTRY (THAT'S US IN THE UK)

1. Work flat out – by making major concessions on 'sovereignty' – to help build a serious country out of Europe through an economic government for the EU.

2. But in the Interim: should Europe not get its act together, then the medium-sized country could still try to give top priority to jobs and growth by cutting the deficit by tax rises – by perhaps taxing top people, financial transactions and financial institutions to the extent possible without cutting aggregate demand.

3. If 'markets' continue to lose confidence, causing a further run on the currency, then cut the deficit by public sector cuts that protect front-line services.

4. When these cuts lead to lower growth and higher deficits, then 'the markets' will be back again demanding another round of deficit cutting. At this point refuse these further cuts – as these could lead, in the UK, to political and social consequences – such as the breakup of the union and social instability or worse. Refusal to cut though would lead to a run on sterling and raise the issue of a potential UK national default. Because Britain's banks are so intertwined around the world this will threaten the world's banking system and 'civilisation as we know it'.

5. Global politicians will move to stabilise the situation. An EU solution to the

British problem is the only way out. The EU could:

a) Break up under the pressure, leading to Balkanisation of Europe with each country cutting competitively to disaster

b) Offer some kind of bailout in return for further cuts by Britain or France or Italy, and see authoritarian governments in the heart of Europe. Or

c) It can co-ordinate a Europe-wide reflation, and a 'Fortress Europe' protectionist trade policy. In other words, lead the way towards a new global economic and financial order – a de-globalised world economy based upon regulated markets, regionalisation (USA, EU, Asia), trading blocs, and negotiated, 'strategic' trade'.

THE UNDERLYING PRINCIPLES OF A NEW SOCIAL DEMOCRATIC ECONOMY

- Maintain jobs and growth at all costs – as the overriding priority. Growth and jobs should take precedence over the 'markets' and deficit cutting. Government deficits are not the central problem, they are simply the government's necessary response to the global banking failure.

- Growth needs credit, and if private credit is no longer available, public credit must take over. Much easier if banking system and credit system is publicly-owned.

- As the main financial institutions of the West – the banks, investment houses – have failed the democracies they are supposed to serve, and are existing on the state's life-support system, the banks and investment houses should now be taken into full public ownership.

- Redistribution of income, wealth and power is absolutely essential in the coming downturm. Removing the glaring inequalities of the global market age is not just a moral issue of social justice. but also a prudential issue of social stability. Taxes need to rise on the top 10 per cent of the West's population. Taxes on the globalised mega and super-rich through rises in top end of inheritance, capital gains and income tax, and closing of tax havens. And if not nationalised then the financial and banking industry should be taxed – on financial transactions through a 'Tobin Tax' – which could bring in billions of pounds. – saving the need for massive cuts in the public sector.

- Learn to live with a greater state sector – to balance the business and private sectors, to regulate excesses, keep credit flowing and to provide opportunities for the bottom 75 per cent of society.

- But any larger state must go hand in hand with the democratisation of the state – separating and devolving power – something Britain's elites have always resisted. Britain particularly needs a democratic overhaul at all levels: at the top with the Monarchy, Lords and the voting system for the Commons, and at the bottom, through proper federally entrenched national/regional and local government.

Endnotes

PREFACE

1   *Financial Times*, 14th June 2010

INTRODUCTION

1   See: Andrew G. Haldane: 'Banking on the State' paper at Federal Reserve of Chicago, Chicago, 25th September 2009. For figures and analysis of these statistics, see: Will Hutton, *The Observer*, 6th December 2009

2   Ibid.

3   Gillian Tett, *Fool's Gold*, London, 2009, p. 264

4   Robert Skidelsky, 'The Paradox of Thrift' in *The New Statesman*, 17th May 2010

5   Inflation figures for the 1970s from Abstract of Annual Statistics, ONS, 2001 edition

6   See my own book *The Death of British Democracy*, London, 1976 which added to the gaiety of the times

7   Speech to the Conservative Party conference, 12th October 1990

8   Philip Bobbitt, *The Shield of Achilles: War, Peace and The Course of History*, London, 2002

9   John Redwood, *Stars and Stripes*, London, 2001

10 See: Hank Paulson, *On The Brink, Inside The Race To Stop The Collapse of the Global Financial System*, New York, 2010

11 IMF figures here quoted in 'An Alternative Report on UK Banking Reform' authored by a working group at the ESRC Centre For Research on Socio-Cultural Change at The University of Manchester, 2009

12 Quoted in Tett, p. 286

13 The details of this selling of a state unit to private owners is set out in 'The Qinetiq Scandal' in *The Independent*, 17th January 2006

14 For some analysis on this Asia bubble see various commentaries on the website of RGE [Roubini Global Economics, specifically for 25th January and 11th December 2009]

15 From: Tony Judt 'What Is Living in Social Democracy?' The New York Review of Books, 17th December 2009 – 13th January 2010, p. 86

16 For an informative analysis of Chinese elite attitudes See: Mark Leonard, *What Does China Think?*, London, 2005

17 *The Observer*, 28th March 2010

18 *The New York Times*, 14th March 2010

19 Reported in Hywel Williams, *Britain's Power Elites: The Rebirth of a Ruling Class*, London, 2006, p. 163

20 'An Alternative Report on UK Banking Reform' authored by a working group at the ESRC Centre for Research on Socio-Cultural Change, University of Manchester, 2009

21 Bank of England, *Financial Stability Report*, December 2009, issue no. 26

22 Ambrose Evans-Pritchard, *The Daily Telegraph*, 21st March 2010

23 See: 'In Place of Cuts: Tax Reform To Build a Fairer Society, Compass, 2009, available online at compassonline.org.uk

24 On a mandate from the European Commission Jacques de Larosiere chaired a 'High Level Group on Financial Supervision in the EU'. Report published in 2010

25 Cited in Ralph Miliband, *The State in Capitalist Society: An Analysis of The Western System of Power*, London, 1973, p. 132

26 Joe Rogaly, *The Financial Times*, 8th November 1997

27 See. Will Hutton, *The State We're In*, London, 1995, Chapter 12

CHAPTER ONE

1   Dr. Rodrigue Tremblay, in www.globalresearch.ca

2   See Telegraph website for articles by Ambrose Evans-Pritchard, 2007, 2008

3   See: Susan Strange, *Casino Capitalism*, reprinted (from 1986), Manchester, 1997. Quote from Susan Strange, *Mad Money*, Manchester, 1998, p. 1

4   See; Roubin's RGE Monitor, 22nd December 2007

5   Newsnight interview, general election campaign 2001

6   'An Alternative Report on UK Banking Reform, CRESCC, University of Manchester, 2009

7   Thomas J. Stanley and William D. Danko, *The Millionaire Next Door* (Atlanta, GA: 1997). Some scholars have suggested defining 'the rich' not in terms of millions but rather as those with a family income over nine times the poverty line – in US terms about $95,000 a year in 1987. See S. Danziger, P. Gottschalk and E. Smolensky, 'How The Rich Have Fared, 1973-87', *American Economic Review*, vol. 72, no. 2 (May 1989), p. 312

8   See: *World Wealth Report* 2007, from Capgemini/Merrill Lynch 2007. (Report available on web), Stephen J. Rose, *Social Stratification in The United States*, New York, 2007; Ultra HNWI figures from The *World Wealth Report*, Capgemini/Merrill Lynch, New York, 2007, p. 8

9   Dollar billionaire figures from The UN *Human Development Report* (1996) who put the figure at 358, and *Forbes* magazine's 1997 wealth list put the figure at 447, up from 274 in 1991. China figures see: Peter Kwong, 'China's billionaire bubble', *IHT*, 17th November 2007

10 Reported by BBC News, 19th April 2007. Sunday Times figures reported by BBC News Report, 19th April 2007. BBC website, Business Section, 19th April 2007

11 *Newsweek*, 4th August 1997 (source: Forbes, op. cit.)

12 The figures for the Queen were for 1992 (as published in *The Sunday Times'* 'Rich List', 1997), and were subsequently revised downwards following a complaint to the Press Complaints Commission. See also, Phillip Hall, *Royal Fortune: Tax, Money and The Monarchy* (London, 1992) for a systematic account of the mysteries of the royal finances. One fact about the Queen's money remains: since 1993 she has remained above the law as far as taxation is concerned as she is not treated in exactly the same way – with all tax laws applying to her – as every other British person. Also see; Jon Temple, *Living Off The State*, Progress Books, 2008 for a well-researched guide to royal finances

13 Figures on Gates from *Newsweek*, 4th August 1997, reporting Forbes in June 1997. Also see: *Newsweek*, 'The New Rich', 4th August 1997. 'The richest one percent of this country owns half our country's wealth...five trillion dollars. One third of that comes from hard work, two thirds comes from inheritance... interest accumulating to widows and idiot sons'

14 Paul Raymond's wealth described by John Hills, *Income and Wealth*, London, 1995, p. 9. Hills suggests that 'If Britain's richest man, Soho millionaire Paul Raymond, receives a modest 3 per cent net real return on his reported £1.65 billion fortune' his income would be £1 million a week

15 *World Wealth Report*, 2007

16 GDP here measured by 'purchasing power parity' method

17 In: John Gray, 'Bill Rules the World – And I Don't Mean Clinton', *Daily Express*, 11th September 1998

18 For individual wealth assessment see: *Forbes* Rich List and *Sunday Times* Rich List – reported by BBC News, 19th April 2007. Also, see the World Bank GDP tables in World Bank's *World Atlas 2007*

19 Wealth figures from *The Sunday Times'* 1997 'Rich List', op. cit., population figures for 1995 from *World Development Report* (Washington, DC: World Bank, 1997)

20 These figures are for 1998. By 2007 they would be even more in favour of the billionaires

21 See *Sunday Times* Rich List, 2007 and 1997

22 Andrew Lycett, 'Who Really Owns London?', *The Times*, 17th September 1997

23 *The Guardian*, 23rd September 1997

24 Alan Blinder, Former Vice-Chair of the Federal Reserve Board, quoted in *Newsweek*, 23rd June 1997

25 From Stephen J. Rose, *Social Stratification in the United States*, NY, 2007, p. 27

26 The *Forbes World Wealth Reports*, 1996, 2001 and 2006

27 *2007 World Wealth Report*, p. 2. Chinese figures from Professor Peter Kwong, *IHT*, 17th November 2007

28 See: Jon Temple, op. cit.

29 *World Wealth Report*, 2007

30 *World Wealth Report*, 2007

31 In 1980, of the 252 largest US enterprises only 32 were controlled by families (only two through a majority of shares); and amongst the major shareholders in Union Pacific in 1980 were the Harriman family, the Rothschild family, the Kirby family and the Kemper family, yet not one of these families possessed more than 2 per cent of the total shareholdings, a pattern that had hardly changed since 1938. Reported in John Scott, op. cit., p. 65

32 Edward Luttwak, *The Endangered American Dream*, New York, 1993, p. 175

33 M. Soref and M. Zeitlin, 'Finance Capital and the Internal Structure of the Capitalist Class in the United States', in Mizruchi and Schwartz (eds), *Intercorporate Relations: The Structural Analysis of Business*, (New York: 1988)

34 M. Zeitlin, cited in John Scott, op. cit., p. 300

35 *The Economist*, 27th November 2004

36 Stewart Lansley, *Rich Britain: The Rise and Rise of the New Super-Wealthy*, London, 2006, p. 67

37 For the quotes and financial details see; 'Greed of the Highest Order and the Worst Privatisation Since Rail' by George Monbiot, *Guardian*, 14th February 2006. Carlyle's mission statement, size of investments and board

membership are on the group's website: www.carlyle.com

38 Forbes Special Report on CEO Compensation. www.forbes.com/2005/04/20/
    05ceoland.html

39 *Business Week*, 21st April 1997

40 Tom Nicholas, *The Myth of Meritocracy: An Enquiry into the Social Origins
    of Britain's Business Leaders Since 1850*, Mimeograph, LSE, 1999. p. 26

41 Reported in *The Philadelphia Inquirer*, 26th May 1991

42 *Fortune Magazine*, 4th May 1990

43 Kevin Phillips, *Boiling Point: Republicans, Democrats and the Decline of
    Middle Class Prosperity*, NY, 1993, p. 190

44 See: T. J. Stanley and W. D. Danko, op. cit.

45 For discussion of twentieth-century capitalist wealth concentration see: K.
    Renner, *The Institutions of Private Law and their Social Function*, translation of
    1928 revised edition (London: 1949); R. Hilferding, *Finance Capital* (London:
    1981); A. A. Berle and G. C. Means, *Corporations and Private Property* (New
    York: 1947); C. A. R. Crosland, *The Future of Socialism* (London: 1956); and J.
    Scott, *Corporate Business*, op. cit.

46 Scott, *Corporate Business*, op. cit., p. 303

47 Ibid.

48 A. A. Berle, *The American Economic Republic* (London: 1963). See also J.
    Burnham, *The Managerial Revolution* (Harmondsworth: 1945); C. A. R.
    Crosland, *The Future of Socialism* (London: 1956); A. A. Berle and G. C.
    Means, *The Modern Corporation and Private Property* (New York: 1947,
    1st edn 1932); A. A. Berle, *The Twentieth Century Capitalist Revolution*
    (London: 1955)

49 Estimates from C. Parkes, 'The Birth of Enclave Man', *Financial Times*, 20th-
    21st September 1997

50 Thomas I Friedman, *IHT*, 24th June 1997

51 *NYT*, 18th April 1997

52 Paul Krugman, 'From Hype To Fear', *NYT*, 8th January 2008

53 *Guardian*, 7th June 1997

54 Martin Wolf 'Leona Helmsley Is Alive in Britain', *FT*, 7th March 2008

55 IMF and Gibraltar figures in Hans-Peter Martin and Harald Schumann, *The Global Trap: Globalization and the Assault on Prosperity and Democracy* (London and New York: 1997), p. 63.

CHAPTER TWO

1   See Chapter One on HNWIs

2   The % of net worth of Americans held in stocks and bonds rose from 11 per cent to 18 per cent between 1989 and 1995, and amongst the super-rich top half a million it rose from 17 per cent to 24 per cent. In Britain the rise was just as pronounced. US figures from Arthur B. Kennickell and R. Louise Woodburn, 'Consistent Weight Design For the 1989, 1992 and 1995 SCF's and the Distribution of Wealth', revised July 1997, for Board of Governors the US Federal Reserve System, unpublished. British figures for this period can be found in John Hills, *Income and Wealth* (Joseph Rowntree Foundation, February 1995), p. 94

3   Exact $ figures for 2006 are: USA 44,710, UK 40,560, Germany 36,810, France 36,580 and China 2,000. GNP per capita figures for 1992 were ($): China 470, USA 23,240, UK 17,790, Japan 28,190, Germany 23,030, France 22,260. In the US the average hourly earnings of production and non-supervisory workers on private non-farm payrolls was $11.82 per hour for 34.4 hours per week in 1996. All figures from *World Bank Atlas*, The World Bank, Washington, DC

4   James Goldsmith, *The Trap*, London, 1994, p. 18

5   The % figures in the mid-1990s (for 1994) were: Germany 21.6, France 28.5 (1992 figures), Netherlands 22.01, Sweden 27.5, Portugal 20.8 and Britain 12.8. From: Eurostat 1994

6   Figures from UNCTAD *Annual Survey of Global Investment Trends*

7   *FT*, 12th January 2008

8   Hans-Peter Martin and Harald Schuman, *The Global Trap: Globalisation and the Assault Prosperity and Democracy*, London and New York, 1997, p. 68-9

9   *Newsweek*, 3rd October 1994

10 *Fortune* magazine provides an annual ranking of the 500 largest global corporations

11 For an early 1970s assessment of the power of corporations see Ralph Miliband, *The State in Capitalist Society: An Analysis of the Western System Of Power*, London, 1973

12 These estimates, based upon a Conference Board of New York report, are cited in Mathew Horsman, *After The Nation-State: Citizens, Tribalism and the New World Disorder* (London: 1994), p. 201

13 Analysis in report by Sarah Anderson and John Kavanagh, *IHT*, 23rd October 1996

14 Robert Reich, *The Work Of Nations*, New York, 1991, p. 110

15 Reich, op. cit., p. 110

16 See: Roger Lowenstein, *Origins of The Crash*, 2004

17 David Hale, 'How the Rise of Global Pension Funds Will Change the Global Economy in the 21st Century', prepared for the 1997 Bank Credit Analyst Bermuda Conference, May 1997, unpublished, p. 10

18 John Scott, *Corporate Business and Capitalist Classes* (Oxford: 1997), p. 86

19 Hale, op. cit.

20 Peter Gowan, 'The Dollar Wall Street Regime and the Crisis in Its Heartland', unpublished, 2008

21 Quoted in Sarah Anderson and John Cavanagh, *Field Guide To The Global Economy*, New York, 2005, p. 42. Blair's messianic approach outlined in speech on 'globalisation and faith', 3rd April 2008 in Westminster Cathedral

22 Ravi Batra, *The Myth of Free Trade: The Pooring Of America*, New York, 1993, p. 1

23 John Gray, 'Bill Rules The World – And I Don't Mean Clinton', *Daily Express*, 11th September 1998

24 *The Global Trap*, op. cit., p. 111

25 James Goldsmith, *The Response*, London, 1995, p. 177

26 Luttwak, *Turbo Capitalism*, New York, 1998, p. 182

27 It has been argued that the US employment telephone surveys were not particularly useful. See: Gabor Steingart, *The War for Wealth*, New York, 2008

28 Robert Z. Lawrence, *Single World: Divided Nations: International Trade and OECD Labour Markets*, Paris, 1996, p. 8

29 Lawrence, op. cit., p. 129

30 See; *FT*, 27th January 1998

31 Gregory Clark, 'For East Asia the Western Myth of Free Trade is a Good Joke', *IHT*, 15th August 1996

32 Michael Lind, *The Next American Nation: The New Nationalism and the Fourth American Revolution*, New York, 1995, p. 203

33 See: Gabor Steingart, op. cit.

34 William Greider, *Who will Tell the People?*, New York, 1993, p. 393

35 Bob Herbert, 'How The Labor Game Is Rigged', *IHT*, 21st November 1997

36 Roger Bootle, *The Death Of Inflation*, 1996

37 See: George Akerlof and William Dickens. 'The Macro-economics of Low Inflation', Brookings Papers on Economic activity 1. D.C. 1996

38 'Leisurely Steps Towards EMU', Letters by Joel Barnett and another in *FT*, 8th-9th November 1997

CHAPTER THREE

1   Quoted in *The Independent*, Thursday, 24th February 2000

2   29th January 2002 speech at UC Berkeley

3   Westminster Cathedral Lecture, 3rd April 2008

4   See www.edge.org 'The Second Globalisation Debate'. A Talk with Anthony Giddens, 30th January 2001

5   Quoted in John Ralston Saul, *The Collapse of Globalism*, London, p. 20

6   Joseph Stiglitz, *The Roaring Nineties*, London, 2003, p. 231

7   W. Easterly, T*he White Man's Burden: Why The West's Efforts To Aid The Rest Have Done So Much Ill and So Little Good*, New York, 2006. p. 10

8   See D. Nielson, 2003 'Delegation To International Organisations: Agency Theory and World Bank Reform' in *International Organisation*, vol. 57, 2003

9   Quoted in Ralston Saul, p. 34

10 Ralston Saul, p. 164

11 Speech at World Economic Forum, Davos, Switzerland, 1999

12 George Soros, 'The Crisis of Global Capitalism', extract in *The Times* (of London), 30th November 1998

13 Robert Samuelson, 'Global Capitalism, Once Triumphant, is in Full Retreat', *IHT*, 10th September 1998

14 'America: An Empire in Denial', *The Chronicle of Higher Education*, 28th March 2003

15 William Greider, *One World, Ready Or Not*, New York, 1997, p. 473; Edward Luttwak, *Turbo Capitalism: Winners and Losers in the Global Economy*, London, 1998, p. 187

16 Martin J. Anderson, 'In Defence of Chaos', in Arthur Seldon (ed), *The New Right Enlightenment*, London, 1985

17 Robert Nozick, *Anarchy, State and Utopia*, New York, 1974

18 Arthur Seldon, *The New Right Enlightenment*, op. cit., p. 250

19 See: The Institute For Economic Affairs: www.iea.org.uk

20 Ibid.

21 Quotes and examples from Martin and Schumann., op. cit., p. 201

22 CBI speech, London, 27th November 2006

23 Will Hutton, *The State We're In*, London, 1995, p. 306

24 *IHT*, 20th-21st September 1997

25 Ibid.

26 George Stigler, *The Citizen and the State*, Chicago, 1975

27 Speech by Barack Obama, 26th March 2008; and speech by Henry Paulson, 13th March 2008

28 Full speech by Lindsay Tanner is on the Australian government website – under 'de-regulation', March 2008

29 See: J. W. Burton, *World Society*, Cambridge, 1972; Quote from John Vogler, 'The Structures of Global Politics', in C. Bretherton and G. Ponton (eds), *Global Politics*, Oxford, 1996

30 Francis Fukuyama, *The End of History and The Last Man*, London, 1992

31 See; 'statement of principles': http://www.newamericancentury.org/statementofprinciples.htm

32 Speech to Chicago Economic Club, 22nd April 1999. Full Blair speech on www.pbs.org/?newshour/jan-june/99/blair

33 Labour Party Conference Report, 2001

34 *The Guardian*, 19th September 2005

35 See: Downing Street press briefing on 12th March 2003 for Tony Blair's response to Rumsfeld's remarks. On Downing Street website

36 Reported in *The Guardian*, 17th August 2006

37 This was written in 1951. Quoted in Alex Danchev, *Oliver Franks, Founding Father*, Oxford, 1993. I have used the American spelling of counselor as in this quotation it is appropriate

38 Peter Riddell, *Hug Them Close: Blair, Clinton, Bush and the Special Relationship*, London, 2003. The words 'hug them close' were reportedly those used by a senior Blair advisor

39 Report in *The Independent*, 18th September 2005

40 Article by Tony Blair in *Newsweek*, Series 2006 available in Newsweek 2006 series on msnbc.msn.com

41 Hywell Williams, 'Britain's Ruling Elites Now Exercise Power With A Shameless Rapacity', *The Guardian*, 11th April 2006. See: Hywell Williams, *Britain's Power Elites: The Rebirth of a Ruling Class*, London, 2006

42 Paul Krugman's most recent book is:

43 See Chapter Six for an analysis of Thatcherite economics and inequality

44 See: Chenoworth, p. 247

45 British newspapers broke the story of Ruth Kelly's association with Opus Dei on 22nd December 2004. See *The Times* for that day

46 A conversation recorded in Andrew Neil's memoir, and referred to in 'Rupert Murdoch, Bending With the Wind', Tina Brown, *The Washington Post*, 15th September 2005

47 Chenoweth., op. cit., p. 203

48 Chenoweth, p. 202

49 see: Neil Chenoweth, *Virtual Murdoch: Reality Wars on the Information Highway*, London, 2001 p. 274

50 Chenoweth, p. 277

51 *The Mail on Sunday*, 18th September 2005. Price's exact words were later disputed

52 Reported in *The Guardian*, 31st June or 1st July 0623

53 Hywell Williams, 'Britain's Ruling Elites Now Exercise Power With a Shameless Rapacity.' *The Guardian*, 11th April 2006

54 Jackie Ashley 'Quiet Rise of the King of Downing Street' *The Guardian*, 14th July 2004

55 The MI6 chief, For instance, Richard Dearlove, was reported to have believed that the US 'fixed' the intelligence to create the need to go to war. Reported in *The Sunday Times*, 20th March 2005

CHAPTER FOUR

1 See:Swissinfo.ch, 1st April 2008

2 Film broadcast by Al-Jazeera, 20th April 2007

3 BIS report cited in, and quotes from, 'BIS slams central banks, warns of worse crunch to come', Ambrose Evans Pritchard, *Daily Telegraph* website, 2nd July 2008

4 *NYT*, 16th March 2008

5 Quotations from Willem Buiter: ft.com/maverecon, 20th January 2009

6 N. Roubini and B. Setser, 'The US as a Net Debtor: The Sustainability of External Imbalances', 2004, pp. 4-5. www.stern.nyu/globalmacro/Roubini-Setser-US-External-Imbalances

7 'The US Current Account Deficit and the Global Economy', The Per Jacobsson Lecture, The Per Jacobsson Foundation, October 2004

8 House Budget Committee, 26th June 2007

9 Kevin Phillips. *American Theocracy: The Peril and Politics of Radical Religion, Oil, and Borrowed Money in the 21st Century*, New York, 2006, Figure 9, p. 326. Both quotes from Phillips, p. 296

10 *Daily Telegraph*, 4th April 2008

11 Lawrence Summers, 'Sovereign Wealth Funds', A Global Viewpoint Article adapted from remarks at the Davos World Economic Forum, 2008, reproduced in the *IHT*, 31st January 2008

12 See: Jeffry Frieden, *Global Capital: Its Fall and Rise in the 20th Century*, New York, 2006

13 Both quotes from: David Morgan, 'Could voter anxiety fuel U.S. isolationism?', *IHT*, 9th January 2008

14 Reported in Kenneth F. Sheve and Mathew J. Slaughter, *Globalisation and the Perceptions of American Workers*, Institute for International Economics, 2000.

15 Ralston Saul, p. 163

16 Iwan Morgan, 'The Indebted American Empire: America's Current Account Deficit Problem', *International Politics*, 2008, 45, p. 92-112.

CHAPTER FIVE

1 Debt Statistics compiled by Credit Action. See creditaction.org

2 See: Larry Elliott and Dan Atkinson, *The Age of Insecurity*, London, 1999

3 Figures from CIA World Factbook – drawn from IMF figures – 2009

4 From central bank statistics in *Money Matters: A Monthly Report*, at www.purusaxena.com

5 Figures derived fromThe Labour Force Survey supplied by The Commons Library, and quotations from *News From Labour*, Labour Party Media Office, 29th January 1997

6 See: Kevin Phillips, *American Theocracy: The Perils and Politics of Radical Religion, Oil and Borrowed Money in the 21st Century*, New York, 2006, p. 296. 6. National Statistics, December 2009

7 Office of National Statistics, December 2009

8 For an 'official history' of North Sea Oil see Alex Kemp, *The Official History of North Sea Oil and Gas*, London, 2011

9 Denny Braun, *The Rich Get Richer*, Chicago, 1997, p. 245

10 Bennett Harrison and Barry Bluestone, *The Great U-Turn: Corporate Re-Structuring and the Polarizing of America*, New York, 1998

11 *The New York Times*, 8th August 1997

12 Hutton, *The State We're In*, op. cit., pp. 107-8

13 Bureau of Labor Statistics, Survey Of Contingent Workers, 1995, cited in Braun, op. cit., p. 245

14 *New York Times*, 8th August 1997

15 Harry Shutt, *The Trouble With Capitalism: An Enquiry Into The Causes Of Global Economic Failure*, London, 1998

16 *NYT* report quoted in Martin and Schumann, *The Global Trap*, op. cit., p. 122. The 'con game' employment statistics quote from Steingart, op. cit., p. 86

17 Both quotes from Richard Sennett, 'Work Can Screw You Up', *Financial Times*, 17th October 1998

18 Braun, op. cit., p. 118

19 *Wall Street Journal*, 17th July 1997

20 Paul Ryan, 'Factor Shares and Inequality in the UK', *Oxford Review of Economic Policy*, vol. 12, no. 1, Spring 1996, table 3, p. 117

21 'Poverty and Inequality in Britain: 2005', IFS, 2006

22 Charles Handy, 'The Citizen Corporation', presented at seminar, Birkbeck College, London, 23rd April 1997

23 Figures from James Banks, Andrew Dilnot and Hamish Low, 'Patterns of Financial Wealth Holding in the UK', in Hills, *New Inequalities*, Cambridge, 1996, p. 342

24 Cited in Kevin Phillips, *Boiling Point: Republicans, Democrats and the Decline of Middle Class Prosperity*, New York, 1993, p. 191

25 Phillips, op. cit. [My italics]

26 Reported by William Pfaff, 'The Enron Model of Irresponsible Capitalism', *IHT*, 27th May 2006

27 Monica Castillo, *A Profile of the Working Poor*, Report 896, Bureau of Labour Statistics, Washington, D.C. 1995, p. 1

28 US Census Bureau, 2006, Income Statistics for 2005

29 See; John Hills, op. cit., p. 33

30 Household Below Average Income Survey, DWP, 2008

31 Paul Gregg and Jonathan Wadsworth, 'More Work in Fewer Households', in Hills, *New Inequalities*, op. cit., p. 181. Quote from p. 204

32 See: 'Poverty and Inequality in the UK', 2008, Institute For Fiscal Studies. Also, Harman report quote from: 'An Anatomy of Economic Inequality in the UK', published jointly by The Govt. Equalities Office and The Centre For Analysis of Social Exclusion, LSE, p. 1

33 Paul Krugman, 'America's Oligarchs' *IHT*, 29th February 2006

34 The *Daily Telegraph*, 21st July 2009

35 Harman report, p. 1

36 For OECD figures see: A. Atkinson, L. Rainwater and T. Smeeding, *Income Distribution in OECD Countries*, Paris, OECD, 1995

37 Latest figures from UN can be found at http://en.wikipedia.org/wiki/List_of_countries_by_income_inequality

38 See; Hills, op. cit., p. 45. Figures taken from P. Saunders, *Rising on the Tasman Tide: Income Inequality in Australia and New Zealand in the 1980s*, University of NSW, 1994

39 Braun, op. cit., p. 118

40 Phillips, op. cit., Appendix A

41 Summary Federal Tax Information By Income Group and Family Type, based upon Congressional Budget Office January 1997 forecast

42 Gini co-efficient figures set out in wikipedia.org

43 Cited in Stephen Haseler, *The Super-Rich*, 2001, p. 46. (See footnote 16, Chapter Three)

44 Zhu Xiao Di, *Growing Wealth, Inequality, and Housing in the United States*, Joint Center For Housing Studies, Harvard University, February 2007

45 Charles Feinstein,'The Equalising of Wealth in Britain Since The Second World War', *Oxford Review of Economic Policy*, vol. 12, no. 1 (Spring 1996)

46 John Scott, *Who Rules Britain?*, Cambridge, UK, 1991, p. 83

CHAPTER SIX

1 Reported in The Guardian, 21st October 2009

2 Turner Speech reported in *The Guardian*, 27th August 2009

3 Reported in Reuters, 23rd October 2008

4 Jeff Gates, *The Ownership Solution* (London: 1998), p. 217

5 Arthur Seldon, *Capitalism*, op. cit., p. 278

6 R. H. Tawney, *Religion and the Rise of Capitalism* (London: 1960), Max Weber, *The Protestant Ethic and the Spirit of Capitalism*, trans. Talcott Parsons (New York: 1958); H. Gutman, *Work, Culture and Society in*

Industrialising America (Oxford: 1977)

7   Martin Wolf, 'Caging The Bankers', *Financial Times*, 20th January 1998

8   Edward Luce, 'Age Of Uncertainty', *Prospect*, July 1998, p. 27

9   Reported by Larry Elliott, 'Sending Out an S.O.S.', *The Guardian*, 12th January 1998. See also Larry Elliott and Dan Atkinson, *The Age of Insecurity* (London: 1998). The 'Chapter Eleven' procedure allows a business in trouble to seek protection from its creditors without necessarily closing down

10 Cited in Phillips, *Boiling Point*, op. cit., p. 191

11 Ibid.

12 Thomas J. Stanley and William B. Danko, op. cit.

13 Edward Wolf's projection and the quote are from Phillips, *Boiling Point*, op. cit., p. 192

14 Friedrich von Hayek, *The Constitution Of Liberty*, London, 1960, pp. 90-1

15 *The Spectator*, 17th October 2007

16 Estimated in Stanley and Danko, op. cit., p. 143

17 Ibid., table 5-1, p. 145

18 Ibid., p. 91

19 Ibid., p. 143

20 Phillips, *Boiling Point*, op. cit., p. 190, citing a *Boston Globe* report of 6th October 1991

21 Stanley and Danko, op. cit., p. 153

22 Figures from Stanley and Danko, table 1-1, p. 17

23 Quoted in William Greider, *One World: Ready Or Not: The Manic Logic of Global Capitalism*, New York, 1997, p. 288

24 George Gilder, *Wealth and Poverty*, New York, 1981

25 Quoted in Adam Smith, *The Roaring Eighties*, New York, 1988, p. 209

26 Seldon, *Capitalism*, op. cit., p. 311

27 Braun, op. cit., p. 32

28 Gates, op. cit., p. 217

29 Hayek, op. cit., p. 397

30 Marc-Henri Glendening, 'Thatcherism and Libertarianism' in: Arthur Seldon (ed), *The New Right Enlightenment*, op. cit., p. 127

31 Karl Popper, *The Open Society and its Enemies*, London, 1962. For his views on the Thatcher governments' strategy of social mobility see: Norman Tebbit, *Upwardly Mobile*, London, 1988

32 J. M. Buchanan, *The Economics of Politics*, London, IEA, 1978, p. 18

33 George Soros, 'The Capitalist Threat', *The Atlantic Monthly*, February 1997 (emphasis added). Also see: Soros, *The Crisis of Global Capitalism*, New York, 1998

34 These expenses were released under a request brought under the Freedom of Information Act 2000

35 Seldon, *Capitalism*, op. cit., p. 11

36 On the TV show 'The Des O'Connor Show' Blair agreed to take second place to the singer Elton John (LWT, July 1998)

37 See particularly Julian Le Grand and Robert Goodin, *Not Only The Poor*, London, 1987

CHAPTER SEVEN

1   Speech by Spanish PM at a Progressive Governance Conference in London, 19th February 2010

2   Report in Wall Street Journal: online.wsj.com, 28th January 2010

3   S. Mulhall and A. Swift, *Liberals and Communitarians*, Oxford: 1992, p. 67

4   Alan S. Milward, *The European Rescue of the Nation State*, London: 1992

5   Linda Colley, *Britons: Forging The Nation 1707-1837*, London: 1992, p. 291. She reports that by early eighteenth century standards 'they [the statistics of willingness to serve in the armed forces] confront [both] those who argue on the one hand for widespread loyalty and deference throughout Great Britain...and those who claim on the other hand that the mass of Britons were alienated from their rulers'.[5]

6   See; Maurice Cranston, *Freedom: A New Analysis*, 2nd edition (London, 1955)

7   Kenneth Minogue, *Politics: A Very Short Introduction*, Oxford, 1995

8   Maurice Duverger, *The Study of Politics*, Walton-on-Thames, 1972

9   From Soros, 'Global Meltdown', *The Times*, 30th November 1998, extracted

from Soros, op. cit.

10   Seldon, *Capitalism*, op. cit., p. 98

11   Charles Handy, 'The Citizen Corporation', lecture, op. cit.

12   D. Miller, *Market, State and Community: Theoretical Foundations of Market Socialism*, Oxford, 1989

13   Anthony Giddens, *The Third Way: The Renewal of Social Democracy*, London, 1998, pp. 70-80

14. Seldon, *Capitalism*, op. cit., p. 99

15. Christopher Pierson, 'Democracy, Markets and Capital', in David Held (ed), *Prospects For Democracy*, Oxford, 1992

16   Mathew Josephson, *The Robber Barons*, London, 1962, p. 316

17   Ibid.

18   Alfred D. Chandler, Jr., *The Visible Hand: The Managerial Revolution in American Business*, Cambridge, Mass: 1977, p. 1

19   Werner Sombart, 'Capitalism', in *The Encyclopaedia of the Social Sciences*, New York, 1930

20   John Sheldrake, *Management Theory: From Taylorism to Japanization*, London: International Thomson Business Press, 1996. See also R. Gillespie, *Manufacturing Knowledge: A History of the Hawthorne Experiment*, Cambridge: 1991; David Hounshell, *From The American System To Mass Production 1800-1932: the Development of Manufacturing Technology in the USA*, Baltimore, MD, 1984

21   F. M. L. Thompson, *The Rise of Respectable Society: A Social History of Victorian Britain 1830-1900*, London: 1988

22   See Frederick W. Taylor, *Shop Management*, New York: 1911. The standard biography is Frank B. Copley, *Frederick W. Taylor, Father of Scientific Management*, 2 vols, New York, 1923

23   Josephson, *The Robber Barons*, op. cit., p. 322

24   See: Kim McQuaid, *Uneasy Partners: Big Business in American Politics, 1945-90*, Google Books

25   See particularly Paul Hirst and Grahame Thompson, *Globalisation in Question*, London: 1996

26 Eric Shaw describing the views of British social democrat Anthony Crosland in 'Capitalism's Premature Mourner', *The Times Higher Education Supplement*, 3rd October 1997

27 J. G. Ikenberry, 'Funk de Siecle: Impasses of Western Industrial Society at Century's End', *Millenium*, vol. 24, no. 1 (1995)

28 Quotes from K. McQuaid, *Uneasy Partners: Big Business in American Politics 1945-90*, op. cit., p. 49

29 See: Charles Levinson, *Vodka-Cola*, Horsham, 1980

30 For a discussion of technology transfers by transnational corporations during the Cold War see: Peter Dicken, *Global Shift*, London, 1992, ch. 12

CHAPTER EIGHT

1 Debt figures from Office of National Statistics at www.statistics.gov.uk

2 See: charter2010.co.uk for both statements, 19th February and 25th February

3 See; Robert Skidelsky, 'The Paradox of Thrift', *The New Statesman*, 17th May 2010 and David Marquand, *The Guardian*, 26th May 2010

4 'The New Face of Protectionism' *IHT*, 2nd September 2009

5 Larry Elliott *The Guardian*, 15th March 2010

6 Reported in guardian.co.uk 30th January 2009. See also, 'British Jobs For British Workers Is The Cry Of Our Worst Instincts' by Mary Riddell, *The Daily Telegraph*, 4th February 2009

7 IMF figures for nominal GDP. These rankings depend on exchange-rate fluctuations

8 B.W.E. Alford, *Britain in the World Economy Since 1880*, London, 1996, p. 33

9 See: Hywel Williams, *Britain's Power elites: The Rebirth of a Ruling Class*, London, 2006, p. 163

10. Daniel Dorling and Bethan Thomas, *People and Places: A 2001 Census atlas of the UK*, Bristol, 2004

11 *The Guardian*, 5th July 2004

12 Williams, op. cit., p. 163. See his Chapter Four on 'The Financial and Business Elites; Dividing the Spoils'

13 Reported in, and quoted from, Gideon Rachman, 'How The Square Mile Fell Out Of Love with Brussels', *FT*, 12th December 2006

14 Reported BBC News website news.bbc.co.uk/1/hi/business/4366225.stm

15 Speech at Lord Mayor's Banquet, 13th September 2006

16 Quoted in Haseler, Sidekick, 2006, p. 211

17 Blair speech in Ghent, Belgium, 2000

Index

Lightning Source UK Ltd.
Milton Keynes UK
05 August 2010

157966UK00002B/2/P